THEY SPREAD THEIR WINGS

THEY SPREAD THEIR WINGS

Six Courageous Airmen
in Combat in the
Second World War

Alastair Goodrum

The
History
Press

PREVIOUS BOOKS BY ALASTAIR GOODRUM PUBLISHED BY THE HISTORY PRESS:

Dying to Fly: The Human Cost of Military Flying, East Midlands (2010)
Balloons, Bleriots and Barnstormers: 200 Years of Flying for Fun (2009)

Cover illustrations. Front, clockwise from top left: Flying Officer Jack Cheney, pilot with No 25 Squadron, Church Fenton, 1943 (J. Cheney Collection); Howard Clark tries out a Bf 109 for size, Tunisia, 1943 (Clark Collection); No 6 Squadron Hurricane IIDs, Tunisia, 6 April 1943 (Via Martyn Chorlton). *Back, top to bottom:* Arthur Edgley (Arthur Edgley); Jim Crampton (Ted Crampton); Jack Cheney (Jack Cheney Collection); Kenneth Summerson (John Summerson); Howard Clark (Clark Collection); Walter Dring (Author's Collection).

First published 2013

The History Press
The Mill, Brimscombe Port
Stroud, Gloucestershire, GL5 2QG
www.thehistorypress.co.uk

© Alastair Goodrum, 2013

The right of Alastair Goodrum to be identified
of this work has been asserted in accordance wi
Copyrights, Designs and Patents Act 1988.

British Library Cataloguing in Publication Data.
A catalogue record for this book is available from the British Library.

ISBN 978 0 7524 8758 8

Typesetting and origination by The History Press
Printed and bound in Great Britain by
Marston Book Services Limited, Didcot

CONTENTS

ACKNOWLEDGEMENTS

I wish to thank the following people for their kindness and generosity in permitting me to access and use written and photographic material from their archives and for their personal reminiscences about the airmen in this book:

Paul R. Becker, relating to his father's work on the Second World War Turbinlite project.

Peter Brett, for memories of his time flying the Hawker Typhoon operationally during the Second World War.

Richard Boston, Uppingham School archivist.

Howard Clark, of A.H. Clark (Farms) Ltd, for material relating to his uncle, Fg Off Alfred Howard Mayhew Clark.

Mrs Barbara Crampton and her daughter Rachel, relating to Jim Crampton. Thanks also to Ted Crampton for memories of his brother Jim.

Arthur Edgley, for allowing me to visit and chat about his experiences during his time in the RAF and as a POW; Jonathan Falconer for permission to use material about Arthur from his book *Stirling Wings*; and John Reid for his help with all things Stirling and for photographs relating to Arthur's story.

Mrs Sybil Summerson, widow of Sqn Ldr Alan Summerson, for detailed information about her husband's long career in the RAF; John Summerson for material relating to his brother, Alan; John Evans and the Pembroke Dock Sunderland Trust for particular help relating to Alan Summerson's service in Sunderland Flying Boats; and Peter Gosling for material from his article about Alan, published in *Air Enthusiast* in September/October 2004.

John Rowe and his wife Susan, daughter of Wg Cdr Walter Dring, for detailed information and images relating to her father's distinguished career; and Peter Dring for personal recollections of his cousin Walter.

I would also like to acknowledge the help given by the editor and staff of the *Lincolnshire Free Press* and *Spalding Guardian* for local newspaper archive material; the president and council of Spalding Gentlemen's Society for the use of museum archive material relating to local airmen; Andy Thomas, Peter Green, Ken Ellis and Dale Parker (www.aquatax.ca) for aircraft images from their collections; and finally Amy Rigg with Abigail Wood and the team at The History Press, who have helped me to bring this project to fruition.

INTRODUCTION

What turns an ordinary man into an extraordinary one? Read this collection of the exploits of six airmen caught up in extraordinary personal and operational circumstances during the Second World War and you will soon discover the answer.

These unassuming chaps, people you might rub shoulders with anywhere in the land, were once – a lifetime ago – the backbone of the Royal Air Force and they represent the thousands who volunteered for aircrew during the Second World War. All were young men; most still in their teens when they volunteered. Many cast off school uniform one day and put on Air Force Blue the next, taking a step into the unknown; yes, it was an adventure, but one with a hugely tempting prospect – the opportunity to *fly*.

What follows are the emotional, action-packed journeys of six airmen through flying training in England or Canada, then war in the air campaigns over Europe, the Middle East and the Far East. We meet and accompany each character through his early family life. We relive with him the nervous anticipation of joining up, then going solo in the air for the first time; the patient hours of training; the pride of gaining those coveted 'Wings'; the excitement of that first operational posting and becoming part of a close-knit team. Then we wait impatiently with our men before feeling the adrenaline rush of their first sortie over enemy territory, waiting and wondering what the next 'op' might bring. That is not the end of the story, though; it's only a beginning, as some are shot down in enemy territory and those that survive experience hardship and adventures they could never have imagined.

Without doubt such men would dismiss accolades of 'hero' or 'extraordinary' out of hand and say with a shrug, 'We just did what we had to do.' Viewed from a distance of seventy years, however, these brushes with death, actions under enemy fire, dangers from wounds and injury, perils of escape and evasion in occupied territory, and privations of life in POW camps, will be judged by any measure as hair-raising adventures denied to most of us in modern times. As in any adventure involving armed conflict, it turned adolescents into men, some of whom returned safely while others paid the ultimate price. All are remembered with affection and pride through the stories that follow.

1

FLYING TIN-OPENERS

Flying Officer Alfred Howard Mayhew Clark

Alfred Howard Mayhew Clark – known to his family and friends as Howard – was born in the Lincolnshire village of Moulton Eaugate, near Spalding, on 31 March 1922 into a long-established farming family. He was a farmer's son who wanted to become a racing driver, but due to the turbulent times in which he grew up, he became a fighter pilot instead.

Howard's first taste of the wider world came in 1930 as a boarder at Ashdown House Preparatory School in Sussex, where he soon displayed a competitive spirit both in the classroom and on the sports field. His letters home show how proud he was of his achievements in class and how he was already keen on cricket, football and athletics. Pupils at Ashdown were encouraged to write letters and it is due to the enthusiasm with which Howard took to this task that, by continuing to do so into adult life, such a comprehensive picture of his life has come to light – and indeed it has to be said that his parents and family reciprocated this keenness.

In July 1931, for example, he wrote about Sports Day: 'I am going in for the 100 yards (under ten), four-legged race, sack race, long jump, egg & spoon (under ten), and 200 yards (under ten); so I am going in for quite a lot.' The year 1934 saw Howard moving on to The Knoll, a boarding school in Woburn Sands, Bedfordshire. Here he developed an interest in hockey and earned himself a place in the school team. In February 1935 his competitive spirit was much in evidence when he wrote home: 'We have had some good games of hockey this last week. On Monday I shoot one goal, Friday: three and Saturday: one.' In June that year he was in the cricket team and wrote anxiously to ensure his parents visited when he was playing a match.

Alfred Howard Mayhew Clark, as a schoolboy wearing his hockey colours at Uppingham School, May 1940. (Clark Collection)

Aged 14 now, in September 1936 Howard went to Uppingham Public School where he joined West Deyne boarding house, the house in which his father, Capt A.H. Clark, had been taught back in 1907. Howard's younger brother, Bertram, also joined the same house a few years later and his nephew, Howard, continued the family tradition in 1969. Sport still featured much in Howard's letters home; in 1936 he was playing rugby – and scoring tries – and by 1940 it was clear he was a good all-round athlete and team sport player. In June of that year he was runner-up in the school sports championship – winning the Guthridge Cup for the quarter-mile – and was awarded his hockey colours. His letters also show his resolve to do well in his School Certificate exams and an awareness of the current war situation, not least due to air raids in the local area and economy measures imposed at the school: 'We don't have to wear straw hats any longer because they can't get any more straw to make new ones from, and we only get five ounces of sugar a week and it doesn't last long,' he wrote.

In an undated letter, written to his parents during May 1940, comes the first indication of Howard's interest in joining the armed forces: 'I enclose a cutting from yesterday's *Times* about the RAF. They want people from 18 to 28, as you will see, for pilots.' It seems that in his characteristically decisive way Howard had made up his mind what he should do and got on with it, for in his next letter he wrote:

I passed my interview into the Air Force last Monday. The bloke (a Flight Lieutenant) recommended me for a pilot or an observer, which are the two best things that you can get, because to be either of these you are an officer. He asked lots of questions and filled in lots of forms … and I have a thing signed by him exempting me from any selection boards and things … all I have to do now is pass the medical examination. Well, I hope that School Cert isn't too difficult. It doesn't matter about having it for the RAF but

they like you to have passed in maths with a credit if possible, which I think
I can do.

Thus Howard Clark, his exams behind him, left Uppingham School during
that summer of 1940 to join the RAF with an ambition to fly fighters. There
is a gap in his letters between June and December 1940 but this is most likely
due to him killing time at the family home awaiting, like thousands of his
contemporaries, the call to report for duty. That call came in December
1940, when Howard was ordered to report to No 3 Recruit Centre at RAF
Padgate – through whose notorious portals many were to enter and have their
rough edges rubbed off! Howard emerged from Padgate as No 1125783 AC2
A.H.M. Clark and began the long and tortuous journey along the path to
becoming a fighter pilot. His first few months' service, rubbing shoulders with
every type of the nation's youth and every type of RAF drill instructor, came
as something of a shake-up to him, but no doubt this would have resonated
with all those who went before him and those afterwards.

His first move after Padgate was to No 9 Receiving Wing (RW) at Stratford-
upon-Avon. The main purpose of RWs was to provide a pool of manpower
with which to feed the Initial Training Wings (ITW), which were the starting
points for aircrew training. Here he was allocated to No 3 Flight, No 2 Section
and by 22 December was housed in the appropriately named Shakespeare
Hotel. He wrote home:

It is a pretty awful place and hundreds of folks are here, not many of them
stay here. I expect that it will get better as we move on. I don't look like
having a very good Christmas! The food is better than at Padgate but the
worst of it is that you have to queue up for it for so long before you get it.

Later, he wrote again:

Yesterday I was vaccinated, inoculated for typhoid and tetanus and had a
whole lot of blood taken to find my group. All this took precisely five minutes! Now we have got such stiff arms we can hardly get dressed. I have got
a uniform but as no single part fitted, it has gone to be altered so I am back
in ordinary clothes again. We are only issued with two pairs of socks so if
you want to start knitting you can start with socks. Apparently, although they
tell you that you only stay here for a few days it is most likely you stay for a
month. I will probably leave on January 18 … possibly to go to Scarborough
… a new training place. The beds are frightfully hard. We are up at 06.30,
breakfast at 07.15, lunch at 12.30, tea at 16.30. The food is not too bad but

I go out every night and get some sort of a meal because the only dinner provided is a mug of soup and dry bread. The canteen is very bad and miles away from here, so we don't go to it.

There was little respite when his posting came to No 10 ITW at Scarborough, where he arrived on 5 January 1941 in 4in of snow and freezing weather. Howard was placed in No 1 Flight of No 3 Squadron and accommodated in the Crown Hotel. By the end of that month he was coping with the theoretical instructional courses and doing well in maths ('passed maths with 87%; … morse code 94%') and navigation. The food was still lousy and he and his compatriots took extra meals at a nearby hotel. His spirits were raised, however, when he was issued with a white band to put round his forage cap, which signified an airman under aircrew training. 'This makes us a bit different from the ordinary AC2s,' he wrote.

As a growing, energetic lad the subject of food always loomed large and on 24 February 1941 he wrote:

The food does not improve and you can't buy any fruit in Scarborough for love nor money. The pork pie was jolly good thanks and so were the sweets. As we don't get off 'till 19.00 it's very difficult to get anything because the shops are shut. Everyone has to go out at night and get some more food from somewhere. The best canteen is the Salvation Army, it's better than the YMCA and the ordinary canteens. The socks are lovely. They have got some heat on in this place now … and the mattresses arrived on Thursday so we can sleep at nights now.

During February, Howard spoke of the next stages of training, telling his parents:

I think we are almost sure to get sent abroad for flying training, as they are now needing more and more aerodromes in England for active service aerodromes as the number of aircraft in the country is increasing so rapidly. Actually, the squadrons who are a week in front of us in this course, have already been asked to volunteer for training either in Canada or South Africa. I think I shall volunteer for Canada if I get the chance.

In the event, Howard was stuck in Scarborough until the end of April, the reason probably due to delays in the Elementary Flying Training School (EFTS) training programme caused by lots of bad weather earlier in the year. A letter dated 6 May 1941 locates him in Wilmslow at a despatch centre waiting to be posted abroad. He travelled that night to Scotland for embarkation but due to enemy air raids had to spend three nights in Kilmarnock, sleeping on the floor of the Town Hall, before he could board ship and sail from the Clyde on 10 May 1941. The next time the family heard from him was via a cablegram dated 22 May, saying he had arrived safely in Canada.

True to form, it was not long before a letter arrived at the family home. On 25 May Howard brought the family up to date:

It was good food on the ship. Masses of cigarettes at 1/6 [one shilling and sixpence] for sixty – they are duty free you see. I arrived in Toronto on 24 May and it was a thirty hour train journey from Halifax [in Nova Scotia], via Montreal. We expect to stay ten to fourteen days here. Billeted in the Exhibition Grounds, waiting to be posted to an Elementary Flying Training School near here. You've no idea what it is like out here – no blackout or rationing or anything, it's really marvellous to see all the lights again. The Canadians are awfully good to us; treat us like guests, make us feel very welcome. Everybody out here almost lives on Coca Cola and ice cream sodas and various milk shake concoctions. All these are iced and are jolly good. Everything out here is iced! I have gone halves with another fellow who came out with me and we have bought a car for the equivalent of about £10. There is a big fun fair by the lake – like Blackpool – and Niagara Falls is only eighty miles from here. I am looking forward to starting flying very much indeed.

Howard had reached No 1 Manning Pool/Depot RCAF, located in the Coliseum part of the impressive Toronto Exhibition Grounds. Here he would become just one more anonymous airman among the thousands of trainees being split up and despatched to the plethora of flying training stations throughout Canada.

Events now moved apace. Howard left Toronto on 27 May and arrived at No 1 EFTS at a place called Malton, Ontario, and he told his parents he was now a Leading Aircraftman (LAC) and learning to fly the de Havilland Tiger Moth. Less than two weeks later he wrote again, telling them proudly: 'I have been doing quite a lot of flying and I went solo yesterday [5 June 1941] for the first time.' And a week later: 'I have been going solo quite a lot since my first one. Have done about 750 miles in the car – no gas [petrol] rationing.'

At the end of June he wrote:

I am getting along OK with flying. I've got forty hours in now, twenty of them solo. This course finishes in a fortnight. It's still hot here and I fly in my

Pilot under training Howard Clark with his car, at No 1 EFTS in Malton, Canada, May 1941. (Clark Collection)

shirt sleeves and you have to go up to 7,000 or 8,000 feet to keep cool even in an open cockpit.

Howard was coming to a crucial period. The end of the course was looming and on 7 July the time for exams arrived. He was confident he would do well and expected to leave Malton mid-month for his next posting, a Service Flying Training School (SFTS) where he would fly the twin-engine Avro Anson. After a forty-eight-hour pass he reported for duty at No 5 SFTS at Brantford aerodrome, about 45 miles from Toronto. He said: 'I'm flying Ansons now. They are really rather nice. I thought I would not like them much after the Tiger Moth but I have changed my mind, although they seem rather like driving an old ten-ton lorry after a sports car.' By the end of August Howard moved on to the senior course. Having completed all his night and cross-country flying exercises, and with eighty-five hours in Ansons and sixty-five in Tiger Moths, he was about to be awarded the coveted 'Wings'. That eagerly awaited event arrived in the form of a parade at Brantford on 22 September 1941 and on 4 October he cabled his parents to tell them he had been commissioned and was now 109112 Pilot Officer Howard Clark.

At this juncture there is a break in correspondence, but the next letter shows that much had taken place in the meantime; he wrote it on 8 December 1941 from the officers' mess of No 52 Operational Training Unit (52 OTU) RAF Aston Down, near Cirencester in Gloucestershire – a Spitfire OTU. He was back in England and had at last achieved his dream of becoming a fighter pilot.

By building up his hours on the Spitfire during the month, Howard seems to have gained experience and confidence to such an extent that in January 1942 he was asked to remain as an instructor for two more months. While disappointed not to be going to a squadron, he nevertheless relished the prospect of putting in more hours in the Spitfire and felt it should give him a better chance of being posted into action with a 'crack' fighter squadron. After a few days' leave this chance seemed to materialise when, on 15 March 1942, he wrote to his parents from RAF Blackpool, No 4 Personnel Despatch Centre, where he was waiting to go overseas, to say he had been posted to the 'Middle East Pool' in Egypt. He was destined to twiddle his thumbs – a situation he described as 'stooging' – in Blackpool until 21 March:

Sat 21/3 Left Blackpool at 8.30pm for Greenock – all night travelling. Bloody awful. Very cold, bloody draughty carriage. Soon ate all the food provided. 1/6-worth of bully beef sandwiches. Sun 22/3 Arrived Gourock 9am. Wrong place. Eventually arrived Greenock at 10.30am. Embarked on SS *Alcantara* [22,000 tons]. Pretty bloody boat. B-awful cabins.

This former cruise-ship-turned-trooper sailed at midnight on 23 March to join a convoy off Ireland for the run down to Freetown, capital and principal port of Sierra Leone in West Africa. Their southerly progress was most visibly marked by the gradual increase in temperature and Howard was in shirt and shorts and complaining about the heat by the time the ship tied up in Freetown on 6 April. His patience was tested still further when, the next day, he and his travelling companions left the *Alcantara* to embark on the SS *New Northland* (3,400 tons) – a tramp steamer that would make the *Alcantara* seem positively luxurious:

> Loading cargo and taking on native troops. The boat is B----- awful, we are all very, very browned off, still on this B----- *Altmark* [a pointed reference to the captured German prison ship] it is full of cockroaches and beetles, water supply only on for one hour a day. Found a mosquito in my porridge at breakfast. We keep being told we are sailing tomorrow, always tomorrow.

His feelings were summed up in a note, written on the back cover of his diary: 'FREETOWN IS THE A★★★HOLE OF THE WORLD.' The ship sailed on 15 April for the port of Takoradi in the Gold Coast (now Ghana), escorted by

Howard Clark's course at No 5 SFTS Brantford, July to September 1941. Howard is seventh from the left on the front row. (Clark Collection)

Newly qualified pilot Howard
Clark with an Avro Anson
after his 'Wings' parade, No 5
SFTS Brantford, Canada. (Clark
Collection)

Plt Off Howard Clark at No 52
OTU Aston Down, England,
December 1941. (Clark
Collection)

one corvette. By the 19th it was even hotter and the bar had run dry. The *New Northland* docked in Takoradi on 19 April and Howard was able to slake his thirst for a beer during a run ashore. Upon his return he discovered that his party was to remain on board and sail the next day to Lagos in Nigeria, which was reached a day later. Their arrival being unexpected, they were ordered to sleep on board. 'God, what organisation,' wrote an exasperated Howard. However, things perked up when they vacated the *New Northland* on 23 April and were taken to the Royal Hotel and 'had a wizard dinner'. Howard was accommodated in a villa annexe of the hotel, cooled by a breeze off the sea, with excellent food, swimming and a number of sporting clubs (such as the Apapa and Tkoya) to break the monotony of waiting for the flight to Cairo. There were 300 airmen waiting with him for a flight, but his turn came at 11.35 on 29 April and he winged his way across Africa in an American C–47 (DC–3 or Dakota).

After leaving Lagos, the first stop, of one hour at 15.10, was at Kano in the north of Nigeria; 'an incredible place,' wrote Howard, 'fed on goat meat. One whole goat costs two shillings, a chicken costs one penny and a dozen eggs cost half a penny.' The next leg was from Kano to Maiduguri in the east of the country, where they arrived at 18.10. 'We are stopping at the Pan American Airways place. Wizard food in darkest Africa.'

After an overnight stop the aircraft left Maiduguri at 05.45 bound for El Geneina, which Howard described as 'hot and miles from anywhere'. It was 950 miles east of Kano in Anglo-Egyptian Sudan close to the border with what is now Chad. They touched down at 09.45 for an hour before pressing on to El Fasher, another 200 miles east – 'hotter still' – arriving at 11.55. They departed half an hour later for Khartoum, 500 miles to the north, where they landed at 16.35 on 30 April. With another overnight rest, Howard was on his way again at 08.00 the next morning, heading for Cairo. The DC–3 flew via Wadi Halfa, landing at Heliopolis airport, Cairo, at 14.30 on 1 May. Howard stayed at the Metropolitan Hotel where, once again, he found he had to kick his heels for a while. In one of his letters home, on 4 May, he said: 'I have been in Cairo now for about three days. A pretty good spot but frightfully expensive. I expect to go out into the desert any day now.' His optimism was, however, misplaced since he was ordered to go to the Almaza Transit Camp (No 22 Personnel Transit Centre), located on an airfield on the outskirts of Cairo, where he was billeted to await his next posting. There followed another period of waiting, while the powers that be decided what to do with him. He wrote in his diary: 'bags of pilots out here and no planes for them to fly', and this situation would only change when the desert campaign hotted up and aircrew casualties began to rise. While he was 'stooging', Howard made the best of it and

A refreshing cuppa for Howard Clark at the Gezira Sporting Club, Cairo, 1942. (Clark Collection)

spent his time 'meeting Old Uppingham types', sightseeing (Pyramids and Sphinx), cinema-going or playing golf, tennis, cricket and swimming at the Gezira Sporting Club, a huge social facility on a large island in the Nile in central Cairo used by officers and European civilians. After three weeks, this way of life began to pall somewhat and he complained: 'Still no news [of posting], horribly browned off. Hope to god I leave here soon; want to fly.' To relieve the monotony of the transit camp he spent a week's leave at the New Hotel in Cairo, but returned to Almaza when that finished because his foot had been causing him trouble since 24 May (no explanation given) to the extent that he needed to see the medical officer (MO). He was told to rest it for four or five days, which he did willingly because he was anxious for it not to affect his posting. Although it was still playing him up on 13 June, by the 16th he noted it was 'almost better now'.

By 18 June 1942 the Allied situation in the desert war had deteriorated and everyone was retreating eastwards towards the Alamein Line. A few days later Tobruk fell to the Germans; things were looking grim and for Howard his time had come. On Sunday 21 June he was interviewed by Sqn Ldr Kettlewell and told he was posted to No 6 Squadron to fly the Hawker Hurricane. He was to report to the squadron at Shandur, an airfield close to the Little Bitter Lake on the Suez Canal, on Tuesday 23 June 1942. It was two months since he had arrived in Cairo and eighteen months since he had joined the RAF.

★ ★ ★

No 6 Squadron, after months of relative inactivity, had moved to Shandur on 10 May to convert to the Hurricane IID anti-tank aircraft. The squadron then moved out with nine Hurricane IIDs to Gambut in Libya on 4 June, operating as part of No 239 Wing of the Desert Air Force: No 6 Squadron with Hurricane IID; Nos 112 and 3 Squadrons (RAAF) with Curtiss P-40 Kittyhawk fighter-bombers; Nos 250 and 450 Squadrons (RAAF) with Kittyhawk fighters. Here the squadron began ground attack operations in support of Free French forces in the critical battles in the 'Cauldron' around Bir Hacheim. The Hurricane IIDs of No 6 Squadron made their operational debut on 7 June, west of Bir Hacheim, although the enemy was not engaged on that occasion. By 18 June, however, the squadron had been pulled back and was operating from Landing Ground (LG) 102, Sidi Haneish airfield, having vacated Gambut in a hurry to keep ahead of the advancing Germans.

Like the Eighth Army, the Desert Air Force was being built up with men and materials in preparation for a big counter-offensive and Plt Off Howard Clark was just one small pawn in that grand strategy. Thus, along with another nine fresh-faced English, Australian, New Zealand and American pilots, Howard proceeded to Shandur airfield. Here they became part of the Western Desert Air Force (usually abbreviated to Desert Air Force) and underwent intensive training on the Hawker Hurricane IID with No 6 Squadron's training flight.

The Hurricane IID, the aeroplane that Howard would fly, was the outcome of experiments to determine if existing 40mm armour-piercing (AP) cannon shells could be used effectively by aeroplanes against tanks and other armoured fighting vehicles. The 40mm cannon was a weapon of relatively light weight and Hawker found it was entirely practicable to install one beneath each wing of a Hurricane; thus, the Mk IID version came into being. A standard Hurricane Mk II was adapted to become a pure ground attack machine by removing all but two of the wing-mounted .303in machine guns; these two were retained to fire tracer ammunition as an aid for sighting the two 40mm cannon mounted in pods, attached one on each side to the specially strengthened under-wing hard points. Two designs of 40mm cannon were originally considered for this project: a Vickers 'S' and a Rolls-Royce 'BF' model. Ammunition to feed the former was contained in a spring-loaded drum magazine, while the latter was belt-fed. The drum-feed became the preferred option as it was more reliable and the 'S' drum held fifteen rounds per gun compared to twelve in the 'BF' version. Although about 200 of the RR/BF version were built, after several mishaps due to breech explosions it was discarded for the Hurricane IID in favour of the Vickers 'S' gun. Almost all of the IIDs produced were sent to overseas squadrons and during May 1942, No 6 Squadron – at that time under the command of Wg Cdr Roger Porteous in Egypt – was the first to receive the aircraft for combat operations.

The batch of new pilots began their training at Shandur airfield under the watchful eye of Wg Cdr Stephen Dru Drury, who had been in charge of this particular weapons project since its inception. Now he was helping to bring it into service as soon as possible. Under his guidance, pilots learned how to handle the tricky tendency of the Hurricane's nose to drop, resulting from the recoil of the 40mm guns when fired. It was necessary to take minor corrective action to 'catch' and correct this tendency before the next salvo (one pair of shells) could be lined up and fired because flying at about 50ft above the ground left little room for error. The 40mm guns were aimed using the usual Mk II reflector sight and tracer rounds from the simultaneous firing of the machine guns gave a good indication of the impact point. Although the gun's range was quoted as over 2,000 yards, the range at which the 40mm gun became most effective was about 1,000 yards and with practice, it soon became clear that it was possible to get two salvos off before overrunning a target. During training it was even found that a third salvo could be fired on some occasions. With solid, tungsten-tipped AP shells as standard, it was possible to penetrate 55mm armour plate. A downside to this lethal weapon system was that when the guns and an engine sand filter were installed on a Hurricane IID, its speed was reduced by about 40mph.

Tank-buster Hawker Hurricane IID armed with two 40mm cannon, the type flown by Howard Clark with No 6 Squadron in the Western Desert. (J. Cheney Collection)

At the beginning of January 1942 the squadron went to Helwan in preparation for a move to Iraq, by which time it had reached an all-time low point with just one lone Hurricane Mk I left on its inventory. However, all was not lost because in the end the squadron did not go to Iraq, but remained in Egypt instead. It took up residence on LG 224, also known as LG Kilo 26 and later as Cairo-West, to await re-equipment with the Hurricane IID. The airfield was located near the Cairo to Alexandria road, about 16 miles west of Cairo itself. Once all the air and ground personnel and the first batch of the long-awaited new aircraft had been brought together at this location, on 20 April 1942 it moved out as a squadron to its initial operating base at Shandur to begin training with the new Hurricane IID.

With five weeks' training under its belt, No 6 Squadron was declared ready for battle and in mid-May was sent forward to Gambut airfield near the coast – about 30 miles south-east of Tobruk and 400 miles west of Alexandria – to begin operations against the enemy once again. However, in the fluid situation then existing in the desert war, the squadron was under constant orders to move – forward or backward(!) – at two hours' notice. In common with many of these desert landing grounds, Gambut had several 'satellite' airstrips and it acquired a dubious reputation as 'the worst 'drome for dust in the desert'.

The Hurricane IID had its baptism of fire with No 6 Squadron on 8 June 1942 when several tanks and vehicles were destroyed with the new weapon. While extremely effective, the very nature of the type of attack profile carried out by the Hurricane IID left it exposed to enemy air opposition. Major Hugh Rice, a former army air liaison officer (ALO) with No 6 Squadron, recalled:

> The Hurricane IIDs were few in number and vulnerable and were therefore never sent out without medium or top cover. As a result, the planning of a strike was a relatively complicated job, particularly as the covering squadrons were themselves pretty busy on routine work. Only targets that were certain to be identifiable at low level, which were not in the thick of the heaviest flak and whose existence and location were absolutely certain, were attacked. This policy resulted in a very high percentage of successful operations, with great damage to enemy armour and with low casualty rates.
>
> As the battle moved forward, the IIDs were sent out unescorted [due] to the reduction in enemy air resistance and the difficulty of getting escort from different airfields when the whole air force was moving forward daily. By the time the Tunisian show was over, casualties had reached a worrying level and the IID was clearly past its prime.

In that short period the Hurricane IID was extremely effective – particularly when its pilots were given timely information, accurate directions and had top cover – at unblocking localised enemy armoured obstructions encountered by the Eighth Army.

During June 1942 this initial contingent of pilots, ground crew and aircraft, effectively comprising 'A' Flight No 6 Squadron, gradually retreated eastwards to LG 102 Sidi Haneish, located adjacent to the main Libyan coastal highway, 20 miles east of Mersa Matruh and 240 miles west of Cairo. The squadron's base organisation was sent to No 239 Wing HQ sharing LG 91 Amriya (or Amiriya), an airfield on the Alexandria–Cairo road, 15 miles west of Alexandria. On 24 June, Desert Air Force HQ ordered 'B' Flight to take its batch of new pilots and aircraft from Shandur forward to join 'A' Flight at Sidi Haneish. Once again, though, in the fluid situation and with Sidi Haneish now under regular air attack, this signal was countermanded on the 25th and 'B' Flight moved to LG 91 Amriya instead. This was now the base for No 7 (South African) Wing which was composed of Nos 6 (Hurri IID), 127 (IIB) and 274 (IIB) RAF Squadrons and No 7 SAAF (Hurri IIB) Squadron.

Next day, while 'B' Flight moved west to join 'A' Flight at Amriya, Howard had his first thirty-five-minute Hurricane sortie in 'a rather ropey Mark I' with the training flight back at Shandur. All the 'new boys' received lectures in tank recognition. Meanwhile, 'A' Flight was in action searching for a squadron of enemy tanks reported to the west of Mersa Matruh. None were found but a convoy of lorries, armoured cars, guns and troop carriers was attacked with some success by Wg Cdr Porteous and four other pilots. In the evening of the 26th, No 211 Group HQ ordered all aircraft to pull back immediately to landing ground LG 106 at El Daba near Ghazal, 50 miles east of Sidi Haneish. The ground personnel were to follow at first light the next morning. With a stop at Fuka landing strip (LG 17) en route – the ground party scrounging rations, equipment and tents as they went – the air and ground echelons were safely installed at Ghazal by evening on the 27th, just in time to be bombed again, fortunately without damage to life or equipment.

Despite hopping from one airstrip to another at extremely short notice, during June 1942 No 6 Squadron claimed twenty-six tanks, thirty-one armoured troop carriers and large numbers of other vehicles destroyed. Field Marshal Erwin Rommel was pushing hard in his drive eastwards and that thorn in his side, Tobruk – now without fighter and ground attack cover because those units had had to pull so far back – fell to Axis forces on 21 June. There were periods of several days or even a week when No 6 Squadron did not mount anti-tank operations. This is perhaps not so surprising in view of the need for care in mounting their type of sorties, which required the co-operation of one or more other squadrons as escort, and the extreme fluidity of the ground war at this time. The Hurricane fighter squadrons and Hurri-bombers were still in the thick of it and wrested air supremacy – or at least air superiority – from the Luftwaffe. However, the Afrika Korps was thrusting towards Alexandria and rolling the Eighth Army back day after day. But Rommel's lines of communication and supply were stretched thinly and in August 1942, the Eighth Army acquired a new commander: Lt Gen Bernard Montgomery. As the opposing forces reached a natural 'funnel' that squeezed the effective fighting front into a narrow gap between the sea in the north and the 'depressions' region to the south, El Alamein would become Montgomery's 'line in the sand'. This was where he would make his stand.

While all this action and retreating was going on, Howard was still at Shandur trying to put in some flying hours, but there was little chance due to a shortage of aircraft and a large number of new pilots trying to fly, so he filled in time playing cricket. On 27 June three of the new boys each flew a Hurricane IID to the squadron at LG 106, but within another twenty-four hours 'A' Flight was ordered all the way back to join 'B' Flight at LG 91 Amriya. Still waiting to go into action, Howard took the opportunity to go sightseeing in Suez town, which he described as 'pretty horrible, although the French Club was OK'.

The ground fighting situation was now so grave that on 30 June Air HQ Egypt sent a 'Most Immediate' signal to all squadrons to the effect that: 'Every available aircraft is immediately to be made serviceable, to be armed and where applicable be made ready to carry bombs. Major inspections may be ignored during the present crisis.' The following day, 'B' Flight of No 6 Squadron began its withdrawal from LG 91 back to Shandur and a couple of days later, on 3 July, Howard managed to get airborne for thirty minutes in a Hurricane I, to practise low flying. He was putting in more hours swimming in the Suez Canal than he was in a Hurricane! On 4 June he had another forty minutes of low flying; on the 6th fifty-five minutes formation flying and then on the 7th, wonder upon wonders, he finally got to fly in a Hurricane IID: first forty minutes familiarisation in BD136, then thirty minutes in BD979 during which he fired the machine guns. To round off what must have felt like his best day so far, he carried out a one-hour, twenty-minute operational patrol in Hurricane Mk I, Z4350, over the Alexandria port area. Next day Howard had forty-five minutes formation flying in IID, BD979, and on 10 July he was let loose in IID, BD136, to fire its 40mm cannon on the range for thirty minutes – he was delighted with his performance, too. The main part of the squadron was still mounting operational sorties from LG 91 Amriya as part of No 239 Wing, where the squadron war diarist noted: 'so far all is well and we are holding the Alamein Line all right. Every day we are here means we are getting safer as our defences are getting reinforcements from the 9th Army and the Australians.' Everyone was optimistic that the Germans could be held then thrown back. Even Howard wrote: 'the general opinion out here is that we shall be in Tripoli in six months.' He had another sortie over the range firing the 40mm cannon in IID, BD979, on 11 July.

With the ground situation still fluid, on 28 July the squadron was ordered to LG 89, but this strip was still in the Amriya area – one of a number of LGs in this general vicinity – and described as 'just across the road' from LG 91. Here the squadron, under the control of No 244 Wing, occupied the LG alongside No 7 Squadron, South African Air Force (7 SAAF), who operated Hurricane Mk Is with bombs, and it was intended that the two squadrons should co-operate in due course.

In a letter to his parents dated 1 August, Howard told them of his couple of days' leave in Alexandria and how it had been 'damn nice to have a bath'. He also mentioned that the two ground crew of his aircraft came from Boston, Lincolnshire, and since Howard flew his first operational sortie in a Hurricane IID on 6 August, it seems likely he would have moved out into the desert a few days earlier. The squadron war diarist recorded that first sortie as follows:

6.8.42. At about 08.30 this morning, Wg Cdr Porteous [squadron CO], Sqn Ldr Weston-Burt, Flt Lt 'Pinky' Bluett, Carswell and Sgts Robey and Wilcox, carried out an anti-tank sweep over the southern sector of the German front but located no target. It was the initiation run for the last two named and here's hoping they all have better luck next time. A similar 'nursery' sweep was made at 12.17 hours with same result and the participants were Fg Off Julian Walford, Plt Offs MacDonald, Jones, Freeland, Clark and Sgt Hastings.

In his next letter home, dated 7 August, Howard only remarked that he was very fit and losing some weight, he thought; he would not have been able to get any comments on operational matters past the censor anyway. On the 11th, however, he wrote to say his flight had returned to base – believed to mean Shandur – for a week's 'rest'. The squadron diary stated that on 9 August, 'C' Flight had moved to Shandur for a week's refresher training, so it can be construed by this that Howard was in 'C' Flight.

A training incident on the firing range at this time illustrates just how 'hairy' one of these 40mm firing runs could be. On 14 August it was noted in the squadron diary:

Plt Off Petersen crashed Hurricane IID at 11.00 hours while firing at a screen target. He was slightly injured and the accident attributed to failing to pull up in time after firing. The attack was being carried out at ten feet and the starboard wing root and airscrew struck one of the railway lines [an upright] supporting the target. Landing was made wheels up and the aircraft was Cat B.

'C' Flight returned to LG 89 on 16 August and, interestingly, on that date it was also mentioned that signal exercises had been carried out between Wadi Natrum and the Delta, to discover if it was possible to vector aircraft (IIDs) on to ground targets by using a Forward Fighter Control unit. In another organisational change, as from 19 August 1942, No 7 South African (SA) Wing was formed and from that date No 6 Squadron came under its administrative as well as operational control. The squadron's holding of aircraft was increased to twenty (IID); two Hurricane Is were to be allocated for training and one flight was to be retained at Shandur for training. This latter would be designated 'D' Flight.

Howard's real baptism of fire came at the close of the Battle of Alam el Halfa in which Erwin Rommel mounted what became his last major offensive against the Eighth Army. This battle was the result of a German effort to surround British forces gathered in the area of El Alamein. The Battle of Alam el Halfa began on 30 August 1942 and lasted until 6 September when Rommel's attack was repulsed. Rather than chase his enemy, Montgomery took this opportunity to hold this line of defence in order to consolidate and train his forces and assimilate intelligence presented to him by the top secret 'Ultra' system, so that he could make an all-out attack on Rommel at a time of his own choosing.

On 31 August all squadrons received a personal signal from the air officer commanding (AOC-in-C) that, 'Everyone must do his utmost and more than his utmost. The enemy this time can and must be finally crushed.' However, things had quietened down somewhat for No 6 Squadron at LG 89 – to the extent that in a letter dated 1 September, Howard wrote: 'It is still pretty hot here and … a lot of dust storms. We don't do much out here except read and play cards and we do a lot of both these.' Things changed later that day: the commanding officer (CO) led an attack by three IIDs against three tanks and thirty mechanised transport vehicles, but with little visible result. A similar operation was mounted the next day but once again the tanks could not be found, although two of the three pilots hit an armoured car and machine-gunned some troop transports.

As the German forces began to fall back, on 3 September No 6 had a good day when six IIDs attacked eight enemy tanks and other armoured vehicles, claiming hits on five tanks, one armoured car and a lorry. Howard was not on that particular op, but his chance came on 5 September, when six IIDs set out to engage a formation of enemy tanks. Flying Hurricane IID, BP 168,

Plt Off Clark was one of six aircraft led by Wg Cdr Porteous that took off from LG 89 at 10.12 to attack a group of nine enemy tanks located north of Lake Maghra. Fifteen minutes later, ground control instructed Porteous to orbit the target area and change altitude due to a formation of enemy fighters in the vicinity. No 127 Squadron provided top cover with its Hurricane IIBs and engaged twenty-five Bf 109s and Macchi MC202s. This was a potentially dangerous situation for the IIDs of No 6, so the controller ordered them and their close escort squadron to return to base where they all landed safely at 11.12, without having engaged the tanks.

By this time the German thrust had run out of steam, Montgomery sent a signal thanking the RAF for its splendid co-operation during the operations that began on 31 August and No 6 was back twiddling its thumbs – while Montgomery made ready for the next, key battle. This hiatus brought yet another reorganisation when, on 8 September, No 7 (SA) Wing and its squadrons, including No 6 Squadron, were 'rested', its squadrons – with the exception of No 6 – moved away to Kilo 8, Heliopolis. No 6 Squadron, probably because it had only been back in 'the line' for a couple of months, was ordered to remain at LG 89 under the temporary control of No 243 Wing. For the next three weeks it was to maintain one flight at operational readiness; one flight on refresher training at Shandur; and one flight on seven days' leave. 'D' Flight still functioned as the 'training flight' at Shandur. As a result of all this, Howard spent his leave in Cairo, 'having a marvellous time, playing squash quite a lot at the Gezira Club and spending no end of money'.

At the beginning of October 1942 it was back to the serious business. The Alamein Line had stabilised but German armour was still probing Allied defences, so Howard Clark went back into action on 5 October. Escorted by twelve Hurricanes of No 238 Squadron, he and two other IIDs took off at 09.00 to attack three enemy armoured cars somewhere in the southern sector. No 1 (SAAF) Squadron provided top cover and it took on several Bf 109s that tried to intercept the ground attack formation. The armoured cars proved impossible to locate but various other vehicles were hit before the three IIDs returned to base.

With the general lack of activity, Howard started to grow a moustache 'for something to do'. There was even some rain to cool things down a bit: 'it is the first [rain] I have seen since I left West Africa in April. It makes everything a terrible mess in the desert and runs into our tents and dugouts.' A sign that things were beginning to hot up again came on 9 October when No 274 Squadron arrived at LG 89 and set up camp on the north-west corner of the airfield. Next day, No 127 Squadron flew in to LG 89 and occupied the south-east corner. Both these squadrons operated the Hurri-bomber.

No 6's CO, Wg Cdr Porteous, had spent much time recently in Cairo, discussing yet more reorganisation with senior officers at HQ. He returned to LG 89 on 11 October with the news that No 6 Squadron was to reduce to two-flight status. Confirmation came in a signal on 13 October ordering No 6 Squadron and No 7 (SAAF) Squadron (both IID) to sever connections with No 7 (SA) Wing and operate as an independent, purely anti-tank wing, with operational control being exercised by Wg Cdr Porteous, who would report to HQ 211 Group. No 7 (SAAF) Squadron duly took up residence at LG 89 on 19 October. Coinciding with this latest shuffle was another exercise, lasting several days, involving the squadron in the Wadi Natrum area with the aim of trying out methods of ground control, this time including the use of AMES (radar) equipment, for its ground attack operations.

At midnight on 20 October, all leave was stopped. Then, at 14.30 on 23 October, Wg Cdr Porteous called all squadron pilots and officers together in the mess for a briefing about the forthcoming offensive and he read out the following message from the AOC-in-C:

> For the defence of Egypt I called for a supreme effort. You gave and gave magnificently. We now pass to the offensive. Once again it is for each one of us wherever our duty calls us, to do our utmost and more. Our duty is clear, to help our comrades in the Army in their battle and relentlessly to smash the enemy in the air, on land and at sea. With the inspiration of a great cause and cold determination to destroy an evil power, we now have our great opportunity to strike a decisive blow to end this war. On with the job.

At 22.00 that same night, Montgomery's offensive to drive Rommel's forces out of North Africa began with the opening barrage of the Battle of El Alamein (sometimes referred to as the Second Battle of El Alamein). Fifteen Hurricane squadrons were involved, in addition to many other bomber and fighter types, providing day- and night-fighter cover, ground strafing and dive-bombing. However, the most effective ground attack aircraft was the Hurricane IID, as flown by No 6 Squadron and No 7 (SAAF) Squadron – the latter having re-equipped from No 6 Squadron's holdings. Although Howard did not participate in operations during the next few days, both squadrons were soon in the thick of battle on the 24th, No 6 Squadron claiming at least sixteen enemy tanks. On the 26th it claimed five tanks, five armoured cars, a half-track and a lorry; on the 28th they scored two tanks, two half-tracks, seven lorries and a wireless truck; and on the 29th three lorries and a half-track. Flak was intense on all these ops but only two aircraft were lost with both pilots escaping safely. On the 28th the squadron was ordered to detach six IIDs to

LG 37 to give support to the 9th Australian Division. 'A' Flight's seven aircraft were sent to fulfil this mission but returned a day later without having been called into action.

On 2 November 1942 a general signal was received by the squadron:

Eighth Army broke through enemy positions this morning. All units to check mobility.

When the Allied breakout from El Alamein came on 2 November, the enemy retreated in earnest. The coast road became packed with every type of transport heading west and every RAF fighter was immediately put to work strafing the road. On the 3rd, No 6 was refused permission to join in but was allowed to go free-hunting for anything that moved in the southern sector. No air escorts were needed now as there were no enemy aircraft about and, operating in twos, threes and sixes, the squadron claimed twelve lorries, three semi-tracked vehicles and a tank transporter. Another sortie later that day accounted for six tanks, one armoured car and seventeen lorries. The lethal effectiveness of the Hurricane IID's 40mm cannon was confirmed by a German prisoner who, during interrogation, described how his company of twelve tanks was decimated in a surprise attack by aircraft firing AP shells. He said six tanks were knocked out and left in flames, while the other six, though hit several times, were able to retreat to their lines. One of these tanks was hit by six cannon shells and the turret of another had a hole punched right through it by an AP shell. The prisoner said the appearance of British tank-busters came as a great surprise and they caused panic wherever they materialised.

By 5 November 1942 the enemy was in full retreat westwards. With the success of the Allied seaborne landings in Operation Torch, German forces were now squeezed from both east and west into a pocket in Tunisia where they would eventually capitulate. During November No 6 Squadron moved 'A' Flight with six aircraft and ground staff forward to landing ground LG 172. This was located near Hammam close to the Egyptian coast, still 30 miles east of El Alamein but 25 miles west of Amriya. The detachment was kept at instant readiness to move further forward, but the call never came. Howard and a number of other pilots in the squadron had seen no air action during the Battle of El Alamein and it was becoming ever clearer, to the aircrew at least, that the day of the tank-buster was temporarily suspended.

Much of this enforced period of inactivity was taken up with sorties by lorry all over the recent battlefields around Alamein to find and examine knocked-out enemy tanks and other armour so that the pilots could see the effects of their 40mm cannon up close. The CO and his deputy, Sqn Ldr Donald

Weston-Burt, also spent a great deal of time and effort producing detailed reports, such as: (1) 'Operations of No 6 Squadron RAF – Hurricane IID aircraft'; (2) 'Training of Pilots since July 1942'; (3) 'Individual claims of direct hits'; and (4) 'Handling notes – Hurricane IID aircraft' – all of which were sent to Air HQ (AHQ) Western Desert in the hope of stimulating the higher authority's view of the value of IID operations.

The squadron did not take kindly to being left out of the action against Rommel and his tanks, particularly when, on 6 December, the following signal was received from HQ Middle East:

Two Flights of No 6 Squadron to rearm with Hurricane IICs and to be transferred to the operational control of AHQ Egypt for shipping protection and fighter operations duties. Third Flight is to remain at Shandur as a Hurricane IID Training Flight.

The CO, Wg Cdr Porteous, was not amused and on 6 December sent a letter to AHQ Egypt:

A considerable number of tanks appear to be in Tunisia and it is suggested that if this unit could be sent to Tunisia to fill the role of an anti-tank squadron with Hurricane IIDs, we might be of value to our own forces. The Squadron at the present time is very well trained in the above tactics and operations, both in air and ground crews, and it would appear to be rather a waste of effort if this training could not be utilised to some good purpose. It is understood there would be considerable difficulties in transporting the unit from the Middle East to Tunisia, but possibly this could be overcome.

The same day, the CO was instructed to fly to Edku (or Idku) airfield 'to confer with the station commander concerning the move of the squadron [from LG 172 to Edku]'. The order stood but everyone was disappointed with the change of role, prompting several pilots to apply for posting to squadrons 'where they could take a more aggressive part against the enemy'. These applications were deferred mainly on the grounds that, since No 6 would now work to 'normal' fighter squadron establishment, there would need to be a reduction in flying personnel anyway. The change of role took effect on 1 January 1943, when No 6's 'D' Flight at Shandur was also disbanded and its personnel dispersed. The Hurricane IIDs were to be handed over to No 109 Maintenance Unit at Abu Seuir to be given a thorough servicing. Howard Clark was one of the pilots staying with No 6 and received further good news on 23 December 1942 when he was promoted to the war substantive rank of flying officer, backdated to 25 September. In a letter home, Howard commented: 'they should pay into my bank account £6 more now and there should be a lump sum for the back-pay.' Christmas 1942 was celebrated by the squadron in fine – and wet – style, but the next day, 26 December, saw the first convoy patrol flown by Flt Lt Bluett and Fg Off Carswell.

Even when AHQ WD had ordered the transition and the squadron had actually moved to Edku, Wg Cdr Porteous still did not give up trying to have the squadron deployed as a IID tank-buster unit, bombarding AHQ with signals trying to get them to change their mind – but without success. Thus, on 9 December No 6 Squadron joined No 219 Group at Edku, which was on the coast about 20 miles east of Alexandria, where it was to be equipped with Hurricane IICs, each armed with four 20mm cannon. These Hurricane IICs had previously been fitted with just two 20mm cannon in an effort to improve their combat performance, but now AHQ decreed that since there were few to no enemy fighters to contend with and targets would be mostly enemy bombers, the aircraft were to be returned to four-cannon configuration. What actually took place was that a new signal from AHQ WD required No 6 Squadron to adopt a two-flight status in which one flight would be equipped with Hurricane IICs and the second flight would retain some of the original Hurricane IIDs. The training flight at Shandur was disbanded, its aircraft sent to Helwan and its personnel to Edku, where the overall squadron strength was to be reduced to twenty-six pilots and the remainder posted away. Another signal on 25 January would order the complete removal of IIDs to No 2 Aircraft Repair Unit at Helwan and replacement with IICs.

Whether or not Wg Cdr Porteous had rubbed someone at AHQ the wrong way by his persistent lobbying for action, on 1 January 1943 he was posted to No 74 Operational Training Unit and Sqn Ldr Donald Weston-Burt assumed command of No 6 Squadron. No 74 OTU was a training unit for tactical desert reconnaissance based at Aqir, north-east of Jerusalem in Palestine, but this pill was sweetened by the well-deserved award of a DSO for 'courage, determination and devotion to duty during his tenure in command of No 6 Squadron'.

Edku airfield itself was located on a narrow strip of land 2 miles wide, bordered to the south by Lake Edku and to the north by the Mediterranean Sea. Much of December was taken up with practising air combat manoeuvres, aerobatics, cloud-flying and formation exercises, and it was from Edku that on 3 January, then on the 8th and again on the 10th, Fg Off Clark flew operational convoy patrols. These were usually around the Alexandria coastal area, for example picking up an inbound convoy off the coast north-east of Hammam and covering it until safely in Alexandria harbour. For a change, on some days he flew practice 'scrambles' and interceptions against Boston light bombers – but saw nothing by way of combat action.

Back on the ground there was plenty of time for recreation, such as hockey, rugby and football matches against neighbouring army and air force units, plus gramophone recitals and dances – one of the latter said to be 'for the entertainment of Sisters and VAs from an Australian hospital and WRNS from Alexandria' – and trying to avoid an outbreak of jaundice running through the squadron. As if this was not enough, there was continual trouble with thieving by the 'natives' who nicked *anything* that was not tied down or guarded – even from inside pilots' tents!

There now began a programme of training to accustom pilots to a 'fighter squadron' way of life. This included pre-dawn sorties on alternate days by alternate flights and night flying practice on a similar basis on favourable nights. Howard still found time to write home frequently, but there was little he was allowed to say about the squadron activities.

Next day (19 January), Howard led a practice scramble with Sgt F. Harris and the squadron mounted convoy patrols of two or three aircraft during most days. After three or four weeks of this routine convoy work, things were beginning to hot up again out in the desert. Although in retreat, the Germans were proving hard to prise out of the area around Tunis and even resupply operations were being mounted by the enemy to try to kick-start a new offensive. On 21 January Sqn Ldr Weston-Burt flew to Cairo for a conference on the subject of equipping the squadron for a projected move to a different sector. On 23 January Fg Off Howard Clark returned from leading another section scramble with Plt Off F. Robey, this time an attempt to intercept a hostile aircraft, but they returned without finding any target. Always keen to get to grips with the enemy, he wrote in his next letter: 'I am still flying the same Hurris, I wish we could get Spits out here; there are not many out here and they are really needed more out here than in England.' Upon landing, however, he found that the squadron had received orders to come to a mobile state in preparation for a move to Sidi Bu Amud, near the main coastal road some 35 miles west of Tobruk. Were they going to rejoin the shooting war?

The ground echelon set off on the morning of 28 January. After delays due to a severe dust storm, the squadron's twenty-one aircraft – all Hurricane IICs by now – staged via Buqbuq and Mersa Matruh to arrive at Sidi Bu Amud airfield on 2 February 1943. Here, once again, the squadron settled down to convoy escort duty.

The squadron Operational Record Book (ORB) writer clearly felt the need to wax lyrical and on 1 February, upon arrival at Sidi Bu Amud, he was moved to write:

At this season of the year the desert puts on its best garment and the landscape is very pleasing to the eye, with a profusion of wild flowers in the wadis. This squadron knows this part of the desert from previous campaigns and in the dry heat of summer with the *Khamseen* [or *Khamsin*: a dry, hot, dusty wind off the Sahara] blowing it can be one of the least desirable places on Earth. To visit here in spring is a refreshing experience for everyone.

On the matter of 'living in the desert', life for Howard and his colleagues was decidedly rough and ready – with the emphasis on rough. It could hardly be anything else, when one considers the terrain, the distances involved and the need for mobility at short notice. Sleeping in small two-man tents, dug into the ground or with sand piled up around them to give the impression of protection from bomb blast and flying splinters, everything else was done out in the open: messing, briefing, ablutions and suchlike. Food was scarce and usually tinned. Drinking water was like gold; water for washing and shaving was extremely limited. Howard grew a moustache and when he sent a picture home the opinion was that he looked a bit like Clark Gable! To combat the absence of fresh food, vitamin C tablets were issued and if personnel visited any liberated town or official unit, they were ordered to take their own meagre rations with them. In Tripoli, for example, due to extreme food shortage in the city, troops were ordered not to have meals in cafes or hotels, although they were told 'this does not apply to tea or coffee or like beverages …'

In the heat and dust, clothes became dirty, smelly and ragged. Off-duty time was generally boring with occasional football or cricket, until the heat made it

Home sweet home! Howard's tent in the desert. (Clark Collection)

unbearable, or sleeping, reading, writing letters if so inclined – although paper was scarce, too – and trying to keep out of the sun, the dust and the ever-present flies. High winds or sudden sand storms lasting days filled every aperture – human and machine – with sand and dust. Very occasionally it rained, turning everything to mud, seeping into tents and turning slit trenches into swamps until it soaked away or dried up when the sun returned. As they moved through the desert, there were constant reminders from HQ medical staff about the presence of malaria, typhus and dysentery, and the dangers of flies and of not disposing of refuse properly. Apart from these discomforts, the Luftwaffe sought out landing grounds on nightly bombing raids in order to make things even more uncomfortable. After this, a swim in the sea was sheer bliss.

On 4 February the Eighth Army, having secured Libya, rolled into Tunisia, but that wily fox Rommel was not finished yet. Using the former French fortified Mareth Line as his base, and now with relatively short lines of supply, Rommel attacked the Americans in the west and the British in the east.

Fg Off Clark was airborne on patrol on 5 February, when convoy 'Tow' was picked up off Ras Beddad and escorted into Tobruk harbour, and again on 11 February when convoy 'Funnel' was contacted 8 miles north of Ras Beddad and handed on 15 miles north of Sidi Bu Amud. Although enemy subs shelled various convoys, No 6's air patrols still made no contact with the enemy. At dawn on 15 February, in an effort to find some action, the CO launched a squadron sweep with ten Hurricanes, but despite spotting two Italian Savoia 79s late in the operation about 100 miles north of Salum, which were chased towards Crete, they could not be brought to close action. The CO and Plt Off Freeland managed to get within 700 yards and fired a few squirts at the enemy before the Hurricanes had to break off due to low fuel levels. They both landed at base with just 10 gallons of petrol remaining. These interception 'sweeps' were a slight relief from the more mundane convoy patrols and Howard flew his last of this latter type on 18 February when he was part of the continuous air cover flown over convoy 'Roman' between 13.00 and 19.00.

Strange as it may seem, things began to look more promising when a signal arrived declaring the squadron non-operational with effect from 20 February. Orders were to fly twelve Hurricane IICs back to LG 237 (or Kilo 40) Jebal Hamzi, an airfield on the Cairo to Alex road 20 miles west of Cairo. Officialdom seemed to be having a field day again, shuffling Hurricane IICs and IIDs around like a pack of cards. The big news this time was that it was all to happen on 21 February and twelve Hurricane IIDs were to be collected in exchange for the IICs. A further nine IIDs would be collected from LG 237 in due course, giving the squadron a total of twenty-one IID aircraft. At 08.00 that day the overjoyed pilots began flying their IICs back to Cairo and morale rose skywards with anticipation. Fg Off Howard Clark was one of those involved and he duly set off in HL610. However, after thirty minutes in the air the engine failed and he had to force-land in the desert. He was unhurt but the Hurricane suffered Cat B damage to its airscrew, radiator, engine and port wing tip:

I had a high speed supercharger blow up on me in the air the other day and I had to do a forced landing with the wheels up in rather rough country, but I was quite OK, although the aeroplane was knocked about a bit.

He was picked up and returned to Sidi Bu Amud, from whence he took another IIC and set off again, this time successfully. The pilots picked up the IIDs but while they were airborne the weather deteriorated and they were told that back at Bu Amud it had developed into a fierce sandstorm, so some turned back to Heliopolis, while others put down at Alexandria for the night. Howard wrote:

I took my aeroplane down to Alex the other day and got stuck there owing to bad weather, so instead of staying one night I had to stay three, which was quite fun. It is getting a long way back there now, even flying. We are on the move again.

In fact, the sandstorm persisted for two whole days, but by 08.00 on 24 February all twenty-one IIDs had been successfully flown to Sidi Bu Amud.

In the meantime everyone was keen to return the squadron to the fray and were packing furiously so that the ground party and transport could depart on the long journey forward as soon as possible. Having drawn rations from stores in Tobruk for seven days and arranged for three more days' reserve rations to be available at Benina/Benghazi, the ground convoy departed Sidi Bu Amud at 08.00 on the 24th – destined for Castel Benito airfield. Pilots and aircraft ground crew remained at Bu Amud and, while they awaited the arrival of the support convoy like the return of old friends, the Hurricane IIDs were serviced and air tested. Later, armoury personnel checked over and harmonised the 40mm weapons ready for action. On the 27th they tested the Browning guns on knocked-out tanks that littered the former 'Cauldron' battlefield area around Bir Hacheim, then on 3 March pilots tested the 'S' guns against more derelict tanks and assorted vehicles strewn around the old battlefields of Knightsbridge and Acroma.

By 5 March 1943, the ground convoy had completed its long, hot, dusty trek to Castel Benito aerodrome near Tripoli. All Hurricanes were flown in a couple of days earlier and the squadron stayed at the base for a few more days until the rear echelon of ground crew caught up; then it was off again to a new operational airfield located at Sorman, where No 6 Squadron took up residence on 7 March. This former Italian Air Force base was a relatively attractive, palm-fringed aerodrome with two hangars, built on a hard-surfaced salt lake. It was located on the coast, halfway between Tripoli and Zuara, not far from Tunisia's eastern border with Libya. The AOC, AVM Harry Broadhurst, sent a signal to the CO advising him that: 'the Air Ministry desired to discover the effectiveness of the "tank-buster" in modern warfare and it was to be expected that as many targets as possible would be found for the Squadron.'

Under the control of No 244 Wing, operations from Sorman commenced on 9 March with Sqn Ldr Weston-Burt and six pilots flying over the Tunisian border to take up a standby position at an advanced landing ground called An Naffatiyah, located near the main coastal highway halfway between Ben Gardane and Medenine. This turned out to be a disappointment and the detachment returned to Sorman later the same day. Something was in the offing, though, for a telephone call came through from no less a person than AVM Harry Broadhurst ordering Sqn Ldr Weston-Burt to have twelve aircraft at readiness on Hazbub satellite airfield at first light on 10 March. The CO was also briefed about the target to be attacked. Hazbub was also in Tunisia, south of Medenine and some 20 miles north of Tataouine. Howard's view of these parts was: 'we are in rather nice country now, absolutely wizard after the desert. I have been swimming again and the sea is getting warmer every time we go and bathe.' When dawn broke next morning the CO and eleven pilots, including Fg Off Howard Clark, were at readiness on Hazbub as ordered. The background to this new deployment is as follows.

Rommel's Afrika Korps was being squeezed into Tunisia and, in mid-February 1943, was sheltering behind the Mareth Line defences near the border with Tripolitania (Libya). Rommel was receiving supplies and reinforcements through the ports and airfields around Tunis but was in danger of being rolled back to the sea. On 19 February he tried to break out through American lines around the Kasserine Pass in an effort to capture a large Allied supply depot at Tebessa. The attack was initially successful but the advance ground to a halt due to increasing resistance and severe weather. When the bad weather cleared, Hurri-bombers wrought havoc on German vehicles and the Afrika Korps was pushed back to its original position. General von Arnhim then began an offensive in the northern Tunis sector on 26 February, aiming for Beja. This attack was also contained and eventually ground to a halt.

The Eighth Army prepared for an attack on the Mareth Line but on 6 March Rommel tried to disrupt these preparations by launching a thrust

Howard Clark and No 6 Squadron's 'Flying Tin-Openers' badge. (Clark Collection)

against Medenine. This battle took place before No 6 Squadron had reached Sorman. Good intelligence information forewarned Montgomery, however, and his forces withstood the German attack. By good use of artillery, they destroyed a large quantity of German tanks for very little loss on the British side. The German forces were now hemmed in.

Rommel turned his attention to the southern sector around Ksar Ghilane. Here Gen Jacques Leclerc's Free French force, having crossed the Sahara with great difficulty, was now positioned to support Montgomery's flank for the push against the Mareth Line. Attacked on 10 March by a strong Panzer Group, Leclerc's force called in air support and the Hurricane IIDs of No 6 Squadron were on readiness at Hazbub to respond.

At 10.05 on the 10th, Sqn Ldr Weston-Burt led a formation of six IIDs to a target of tanks and mixed armoured and soft-skinned vehicles threatening Free French positions east of Zamlet el Hadid. He led the Hurricanes down and for nearly an hour they made run after run against the enemy until, out of ammunition and low on fuel, they returned to Hazbub, landing at 12.55 without having sustained any casualties.

Airborne at 11.50, Flt Lts Anthony Bluett and A.E. Morrison-Bell led two more flights, each of seven IIDs, to overlap with the CO's returning flight and to keep up pressure on the enemy. Fg Off Howard Clark was part of this second wave, flying in HW251, and the attack was without doubt an ordeal of fire. He came through it unscathed, as did all his compatriots, who together had played havoc with the enemy's armour. The enemy retreated and it may well have been the first time that an armoured force was turned back in its tracks solely by air action. The tally for the day was: six tanks, five half-tracks, thirteen armoured cars, ten lorries, a gun and a wireless van, of which Howard Clark's share was two armoured cars. No Hurricanes were lost, although the flak barrage had been intense. The CO's aircraft returned to base with its main spar almost shot through and two other aircraft were damaged but the squadron was rightly elated with its return to the fray. It should be added that there were other RAF units, including Hurri-bombers, involved in this rout of the enemy but the particularly close-quarter action by the 'Flying Tin-Openers' of No 6 came in for the most praise. Congratulations flowed in from recently promoted Air Marshal Coningham, General Montgomery and a much-relieved General Leclerc. Next day, a flight of six aircraft was sent to Bou Grara airstrip on the coast where they stood by for action in case the enemy had another go, but there was no more action for a while and the squadron moved westward once more, this time to Senem airfield, 10 miles west of Medenines – well inside Tunisia.

Preceded by several days of squally rain and high winds – Howard, writing on what he described as 'captured Italian note paper', said: 'It is blowing like the very devil at the moment and my tent is due to go airborne at any moment' – Montgomery began his offensive against the Mareth Line on 20 March and met with stiff resistance. The ferocity of the air to ground battle was already being felt, as first the losses of aircraft then pilots began to mount.

On the morning of the 24th Howard Clark, flying HW251, was back in action as one of twelve Hurricane IIDs that set about a formation of twenty enemy tanks and other assorted vehicles near El Hamma. It was not all one way this time. Two Hurricanes were shot down: one pilot, WO Mercer, was found safe by New Zealand soldiers, but the other, Flt Sgt Frank Harris, was killed, his grave being found later by the squadron. During that afternoon seven more Hurricanes went after the same target with some success, but lost two more aircraft, this time to Bf 109s from I./JG 27 that penetrated the top cover. In addition to the deadly light flak barrages encountered, Bf 109s and Macchi 202s of the German and Italian Air Forces were hotly contesting the intense Allied fighter and ground attack operations by Spitfires, Airacobras, Kittyhawks and Hurri-bombers against the Mareth Line and any movement in its vicinity.

Howard did not fly during the following day when ten IIDs attacked a force of fifty tanks near Kebili, destroying eleven and damaging six, but again the price was heavy. Six IIDs were shot down by flak and the pilots had to crash-land. All six aircraft were Cat B damaged but miraculously only one pilot was slightly wounded. Next day, with top cover provided by twenty-one Kittyhawks from Nos 3 (RAAF) and 250 Squadrons, the CO led eleven aircraft on a hunt for tanks near Djebel Tebaga, but only derelict vehicles were seen. Two Hurricane IIDs were shot down but both pilots escaped to NZ army lines. Although pilot losses were light, No 6 had lost no fewer than sixteen IIDs in the past five days of operations from Senem. The co-operation between Allied tanks, infantry, artillery and aircraft worked well and on 27 March Montgomery's forces breached the Mareth Line in the Djebel Tebaga and Djebel Melab areas. By the end of the month they were advancing on Gabes. In the meantime, No 6 had to replace its heavy losses before it was able to re-enter operations, so it had IIDs flown in from Helwan.

On 3 April, with the Eighth Army pushing the Germans back towards the sea, No 6 Squadron moved forward to Gabes airfield, sharing it with No 601 and No 40 (SAAF) Squadrons. Next day was taken up with a visit by the 'top brass': ACM Tedder, AVM Broadhurst and Lt Gen Carl Spaatz of the USAAF. Tedder spoke at length with the pilots and assured them that when it came to 'tank-busting', No 6 had proved its value, and that of the role, and the

Howard Clark, fighter pilot, in the cockpit of his Hurricane IID. (Clark Collection)

squadron would be equipped with any new anti-tank air weapon or aircraft that might be developed. He said that the objective of present operations was not to frighten the enemy out of this zone but to trap him in the area and completely destroy him. It would take two or three months yet. On 5 April Howard wrote to his parents:

> Up here we haven't got anything to drink at all, not even lemonade or soft drinks and the beer ran out a week ago when we were down to one bottle each per week! We are also on very strict rations. We have been pretty busy lately but being right on the coast can go for a swim when not on standby. I hope that it won't take much longer to clear the war up in N. Africa, I am ready for some leave. It was last September the last time I had any proper leave …

In the early hours of 6 April 1943, assisted by an intense Allied air bombardment, the Eighth Army opened up a new offensive against the Axis Wadi Akarit Line. Italian defences crumbled quickly but heavy fighting broke out when the Germans counter-attacked. High above the land forces and ground attack aircraft, fierce dogfights took place over the Cekhira (or La Skira) area, while Hurricane IIDs of No 6 Squadron were back in action in support of the Eighth Army in what became the battle for the harbour town of Sfax.

Three separate operations were mounted by No 6 in support of the army on 6 April. First away at 12.25 were thirteen aircraft led by the CO and including

Fg Off Clark in HV594. They searched for sixteen tanks reported in the Sfax area but after hunting for fifteen minutes at low level, running the gauntlet of intense light flak, the CO called off the strike. In the meantime, the flak had claimed three Hurricanes from which two pilots, Fg Off Petersen and Flt Sgt Hastings, found their way back to the squadron, while the third, Fg Off Marcel Zillessen, was missing, believed killed. In fact, Zillessen survived his crash-landing but was captured and made a POW, spending the rest of the war in Stalag Luft III.

That afternoon, a second operation had eight Hurricane IIDs from No 6 and twelve Kittyhawks from No 3 (RAAF) Squadrons, escorted by twelve Spitfires from No 601 Squadron, on the lookout for more tanks and infantry around Cekhira. Again no targets were found, but the Spitfires engaged ten-plus Bf 109s at 10,000ft, driving them off and claiming two. For the Kittyhawks, it was their fifth mission of the day, this time dive-bombing a troop build-up near Wadi Akarit. They mixed it with some Italian Macchi 202s and claimed one shot down for the loss of one of their own. On the way back to base the Hurricane IIDs ran across some enemy motor transports and left four lorries destroyed. Although the flak over the target was intense, no Hurricanes were lost. In the third operation late that afternoon, which did not involve Fg Off Clark, six aircraft took off to hunt for eight tanks. One Mk III Special Tank was hit by four pairs of 40mm AP shells and a semi-tracked troop carrier by two pairs of shells. Several lorries were also destroyed. This was a day when the air action was fast and furious, lasting well into the late afternoon when

Rare image of No 6 Squadron Hurricane IIDs, with Spitfire escort, taking off on the operation that Howard Clark flew from Gabes, Tunisia, on 6 April 1943. (Via Martyn Chorlton)

Wg Cdr Ian Gleed led Nos 92 and 145 Squadrons' Spitfires and a small number of Polish Spitfires in a patrol over the Djebel Tebaga area. They successfully engaged more Bf 109s over Cekhira, but the day had its downside, with the US 52nd Fighter Group in particular taking a beating, losing six of their Spitfires in combat during the day. The duration of the Hurricane IID sorties was about one hour.

The battle for Sfax was still raging when disaster struck the next day, 7 April 1943. Axis troops began to retreat from Wadi Akarit and the British entered Mezzouna. The US First Army opened up an offensive to try to link up with the Eighth Army, but met with stiff resistance trying to capture Djebel Aouareb. Late in the day, No 6 was ordered to mount a strike against a large concentration of enemy tanks. Eleven Hurricane IIDs from the squadron, including Howard Clark in KW704, took off from Gabes at 18.20 led by Sqn Ldr Weston-Burt. The enemy tanks were found in the Cekhira area and on approaching the target the Hurricanes were met with an intense barrage of anti-aircraft fire. Many low-level firing runs were made on the tanks but the flak was so 'hot' that no fewer than six Hurricane IIDs were hit and shot down. From these six aircraft, three pilots were able to crash-land and emerge safely, but the other three pilots were killed. Among those pilots sadly lost was Fg Off Howard Clark.

The tide of battle ebbed and flowed over the following days and there was no opportunity to search for the missing airmen for another two days. On 9 April Flt Lt Morrison-Bell and Fg Off Lee flew a sortie over the Cekhira area in an endeavour to locate the crashed aircraft. They spotted what appeared to be a Hurricane undercarriage leg beside a burned-out wreckage near a track adjacent to La Skira LG (landing ground). Next day, Flt Lts Hudson (adjutant) and Marchant (MO), together with Plt Off Freeland, took a vehicle to reconnoitre the area around La Skira LG more closely. They discovered a grave with a marker bearing the name of Fg Off Clark, at map ref. Sfax T(Z) 2379. Some members of the 1st Royal Tank Regiment who were still in the vicinity said that they had buried a pilot, whose description matched that of Fg Off Clark, near the burned-out wreckage of his aircraft. Howard Clark had apparently been shot down in flames but was probably dead before he hit the ground since the soldiers said a 0.5in bullet wound had been found in his head. The serial number of the Hurricane IID was that flown by Clark. A few miles away the search party found another grave near the wreckage of a Hurricane IID. This was Flt Sgt Eric Hastings. The search for the third missing pilot was abandoned as darkness fell over that lonely place. Another search party went out to La Skira LG the next day and found the undercarriage leg and burned-out wreckage. Here they found a grave with the identity discs of

Fg Off John Walter DFC attached to the improvised cross. They had now found the graves of all three missing airmen.

Amidst all these frantic battles there had been an important birthday for Howard and his mother sent him an airmail letter in anticipation of that event.

March 30, 1943

My dearest Howard,

The day before your [21st] birthday and again I wish you every happiness and all the luck in the world. I must admit I feel much better myself than I did 21 years ago today … there should be several cables on their way [from well-wishers] … The news is wonderful. The Hurricanes got a very good press in *The Times* and also the *Daily Mail*, explaining what they did … The daffodils are all out on the bank and there are lots of violets and the wall-flowers are beginning to show flower – the almond is out and though we have had some frosts and morning fog, Spring is here …

Poignantly, this letter was returned to his mother marked: 'Return to sender on Air Ministry Instructions.'

At the close of that momentous day, No 6 Squadron received orders to move from Gabes to Sfax (El Maou LG); on 16 April the squadron moved on again, this time to Bou Goubrine LG. With the end of the campaign in sight, on 5 May it was déjà vu for the squadron when its senior personnel were moved on. Sqn Ldr Weston-Burt relinquished command to newly promoted Sqn Ldr Morrison-Bell and went to command No 260 Squadron, while Flt Lt Bluett and Fg Off Hearn were posted to No 112 Squadron. No 6's days of tank-busting, 40mm-style, were over. The anti-tank 40mm cannon was shortly to be superseded by the rocket projectile. The battle for control of the port of Sfax was over when the Eighth Army captured it on 10 June. Although there were more battles to be won, one month later, German forces in Tunisia finally capitulated and the North African campaign was over.

First during the Egypt (forty-five tanks destroyed) and then the Libya/Tunisia (forty-six tanks) battles, No 6 Squadron, with its Hurricane IIDs, claimed to have knocked out over ninety tanks and destroyed a host of other vehicles. To achieve this valuable contribution, the IID, armed with its potent 40mm cannon, was obliged to make long, very low approach runs on its targets and thus it became a sitting duck for any and every type and calibre of anti-aircraft fire. During the Tunisian action from 9 March to 8 April 1943, the squadron flew 120 sorties, fired 1,230 40mm shells and claimed forty-six tanks and thirty-seven other guns and vehicles. It lost twenty-five aircraft but miraculously, and often simply due to the ability of the Hurricane to absorb massive punishment, it lost only four pilots, even though twice it had six IIDs shot down – with one of these occasions sadly being the day Fg Off Clark lost his life, almost within sight of the final victory in the Western Desert campaign.

Flying Officer Alfred Howard Mayhew Clark is remembered with pride and deep affection by his family, who arranged for a memorial consisting of oak panels, carved and inscribed with his name, to be erected inside the chapel in the centre of the village of Moulton, where there is also a road named Cekhira Avenue in his honour. Howard is also commemorated on the Ashdown House and Uppingham Rolls of Honour.

2

TRAIN-BUSTING OVER THE REICH

Flying Officer Jack Cheney

Jack Cheney was born in Spalding on 31 December 1921. Living at Pansy Cottage – no longer standing – in Haverfield Road, his primary education was at Spalding Parish Church Day School, where he showed such promise that, aged 11, he was awarded a governors' free scholarship to Spalding Grammar School, which happened to be located just across the road from his home. The governors' faith was not misplaced since, by the time he left school in July 1940, he was a senior sixth-former, school prefect, vice-captain of the 1st XV with his rugby colours, member of the school cricket 1st XI and captain of Gamlyn House. He gained his School Certificate, an intermediate scholarship and his matriculation in July 1938. Jack left the school in July 1940 and three months later he was in the RAF, having volunteered and been accepted for pilot training.

In October 1940, 18-year-old Jack Cheney began the transition from sixth-form schoolboy at Spalding Grammar to night-fighter pilot in the RAF, with a first operational posting at RAF Wittering. Jack entered the RAF in November 1940 as an airman in No 5 Flight of 'C' Squadron at No 7 Initial Training Wing (7 ITW) in Newquay. Posted to No 1 Elementary Flying Training School (1 EFTS) at Desford in March 1941, he underwent basic flying instruction on the DH82A Tiger Moth, then moved on, in May 1941, to No 15 Service Flying Training School (15 SFTS) at Kidlington where he converted to the Airspeed Oxford trainer. In August 1941 Jack was posted to No 54 Operational Training Unit (54 OTU) at RAF Church Fenton, which was the main RAF night-fighter training unit at that time, and operated the Bristol Blenheim Mk I fitted with Airborne Interception Type 4 (AI Mk IV)

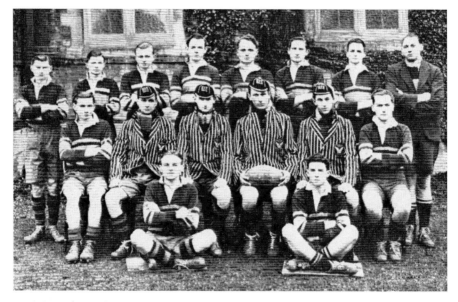

Seated second on the left, wearing Spalding Grammar School rugby colours, Jack Cheney as a schoolboy in March 1940. (Spalding Grammar School)

Foreground, in flying suit with parachute slung nonchalantly over his shoulder, pilot under training Jack Cheney at EFTS Desford in March 1941. (J. Cheney Collection)

radar equipment. From there, now paired up with his radar operator, he moved to his first operational posting with No 1432 (Air Target Illumination) Flight based at RAF Collyweston/Wittering. He spent a substantial part of his operational career patrolling the night sky above the East Midlands and this chapter describes, in his own words, his experiences while training to become a night-fighter pilot, his involvement with one of the more unusual aircraft used in the quest for supremacy of the wartime night sky, and flying intruder operations over Germany in the superb DH Mosquito NFII:

After three glorious weeks of leave at home in Spalding, looking up old friends, putting my feet up and sampling home cooking with my mother and three sisters, I was summoned to No 54 Operational Training Unit (54 OTU) at RAF Church Fenton in Yorkshire. This was to be the last stage of my training as a night-fighter pilot and I arrived at the station on 3 August 1941. I was not immediately impressed by what I saw of the base but later that day, I met up with 'Tosh' Bramley, Jimmy Smith, Arthur Howard and 'Hammy' Hamilton, all of whom had been with me on No 22 Course at No 7 Service Flying Training School, Kidlington (Oxford airport). Life, it seemed, would not be quite so bad after all. Church Fenton was considered to be the crack night-fighter OTU in the country but we soon discovered it had also earned a reputation as a killer station.

Now designated No 11 Course, we were obliged to do some day flying in the Airspeed Oxford just to get our hand in again. However, before being permitted to fly at Church Fenton at night we first had to go to RAF Catterick and do a few hours at night in Tiger Moths. We were at Catterick for only a week and flew from a satellite landing ground called Forest Farm. What a week that was! It was really great fun being back in the old Tiger again. All too soon though it was back to the serious business at Church Fenton, where night flying dual was carried out in the Oxford, augmented by day solo flights in the ropey old Bristol Blenheim.

September saw the arrival of our observers. For this seemingly important event, the actual teaming up process was, in fact, pretty informal. We were all assembled in a large room and told to get on with it. A fair-haired fellow about my own age, calling himself Sgt Mycock, made the first approach to me. We seemed to hit it off from the start and from that day he became, and still is, my observer. His name is James Kenneth Mycock but from that first day I met him I called him Mike and so it remained.

A tragic blow fell on 2 September, when my pal Arthur Howard and his observer were killed in an Oxford. Blokes were killing themselves right, left and centre in the ropey old Blenheims, which we had now begun to fly at night. At the end of that month, the aircrew sergeants of my course moved out of Church Fenton mess, to be rehoused in an old country house known as Barkston Towers, three miles from the aerodrome. It was a marvellous old place, with ornate gardens and a splendid interior. George, our cook, was in the submarine service in the last war and vowed he would never go near an aeroplane. He was good to us though and served up colossal meals and we lived like kings to the end of the course.

Together now with our observers, we put in a tremendous amount of both day and night flying in an effort to become an efficient team and yet again the end of the course was rushed. It was not the hard work I minded, it was more of a desire to get away from the OTU in general and the CFI [Certified Flight Instructor], Sqn Ldr Aikens, in particular. One week before the course was due to finish, on October 17, another blow fell on my small circle of friends, Sgt T.C. 'Tosh' Bramley was killed during an altitude test at night in Blenheim IV, V5622. He was the fourteenth casualty in three months.

Those of us left in my group of pals said our farewells again and on 28 October 1941, almost one year after I joined up, parted company to go to our respective operational stations. Church Fenton at least had lived up to its grim reputation while I was there. Now I was off to RAF Wittering, not far from my home, for my first operational posting to No 1453 Air Target Illumination (Turbinlite) Flight.

The emergence of the Turbinlite concept has its roots in the air situation following the Battle of Britain. Due to the – not unreasonable – previous concentration on single-seat, high-performance day-fighters, when the Luftwaffe turned to its night offensive there was no suitable specialist RAF night-fighter or control system to take them on. The few airborne radar-equipped (AI or airborne interception) Blenheims that did exist had little success, but like all such ideas, that was more a reflection of the very newness of this particular man/machine system, together with inadequate aircraft, rather than an indication of the true potential of the AI night-fighter concept itself. Lack of results diverted attention away from acceptance that the subject had simply been neglected and that it needed a focused and swift injection of resources. Critics of the system – and there was always competition for resources or competing ideas – were the catalyst for some of these alternative ideas gaining a lot more prominence than their true practicality warranted. Among the latter was the idea to mount a searchlight in the nose of an aeroplane. The RAF had acquired some Douglas Boston aircraft originally destined for the French and this was the most suitable aircraft to hand.

To the modern eye at least, any basic description of the Turbinlite Havoc concept cannot fail to engender incredulity about its practicality. It was based around the American-designed Douglas Boston twin-engine light bomber, designated by the RAF as Havoc I, with its nose compartment removed and replaced by an enormously powerful searchlight.

The idea was the brainchild of Wing Commander W. Helmore and the light, named Turbinlite, was built by the General Electric Company (GEC) in England and powered by forty-eight 12-volt batteries that weighed a total of about 2,000lb. These were stowed away on reinforced flooring in the bomb bay, the batteries themselves being laid out in four banks of twelve with two banks placed in each of the two halves of the bomb bay. They were charged up from an external ground-based source with special attention given to providing forced ventilation inside the aeroplane to avoid the build-up of hydrogen fumes during the charging process. A description of the Turbinlite by a former pilot, Michael Allen DFC**, will convey the sheer power of this airborne searchlight:

Its batteries were capable of producing a current of 1,400 amps and discharging totally in two minutes. The lamp – reputed to be the most powerful in the world at that time – produced a beam from mechanically adjusted carbon rods located in front of a para-elliptical mirror reflector with a small frontal area approximating to the size of that cross-section of the forward fuselage. The light thus produced had an illumination intensity of over 800,000 watts [try to imagine 8,000 x 100 watt domestic light bulbs] and blazed out as a horizontal, sausage-shaped, beam of light that illuminated an area 950 yards wide at one mile range. It was not, however, simply a case of detecting a target then throwing a light-switch! The carbon rods took some seconds to bring the arc-light to full power during which time, in order to avoid a situation where the beam was not at full strength but nevertheless provided an enemy with a juicy light to fire at, the light source and reflector were hidden behind shutter doors on the inner surface of the lamp glass. Only when maximum luminosity was achieved [code name: Boiling!] did the pilot open the shutters, expose the beam and [hopefully] pinpoint the target like a blinded moth.

Equipped with an AI Mk IV set, with an arrowhead transmitter antenna protruding from each side of the lamp glass, the aeroplane carried a crew of two. The pilot sat in a comfortable single-seat front cockpit and a radar operator occupied the glazed rear compartment, originally intended for a gunner. But in this AI configuration the Boston carried no armament, because with the

The design team in front of the Douglas Turbinlite Havoc prototype after its first flight. From left to right: Dick Becker, Dennis Roberts, Leslie Baynes, Bruce Benson. (Courtesy of Paul R. Becker)

weight of the batteries, light and radar there was no spare capacity for guns and ammunition! Despite this peculiar arrangement and – as will be seen – the lack of combat success, it nevertheless provided night-fighter crews with many months of valuable – if boring – night flying and radar interception practice. This was to stand them in good stead when the Luftwaffe stepped up its activity over Britain later and also when RAF night-fighters carried the fight to continental and other skies.

One of an eventual ten such units in Fighter Command's 11 and 12 Groups, No 1453 Air Target Illumination Flight, to give it its full title, formed at RAF Wittering in July 1941 from elements of 1451 Flight which was based at RAF Hunsdon. The commanding officer of the new flight was Sqn Ldr Kenneth Blair DFC, who had seen active service both in France with No 85 Squadron and in the Battle of Britain, and was transferred from No 151 Squadron based at Wittering at the time. These Havocs co-operated with one or more single-engine fighters, usually Hurricanes, but on occasion Defiants or even Spitfires are recorded as taking on the role of satellite fighter. Take-off would be carried out in close company, with the Hurricane keeping formation to the rear of the Havoc by reference to a few tiny, variable-intensity lights playing over broad white paint stripes on the upper and lower rear surface of the wings.

Of course, to assemble in this manner at night would have been no mean feat in itself, but how was this unwieldy group going to bring the enemy into combat? The scenario goes like this: ground control would vector the Havoc on to a bandit to a point where the AI operator could take over and use airborne radar to try to pick up the target. If a target was found the AI operator guided his pilot towards visual range. The pilot might, of course, be fortunate to get a visual contact first but the whole idea was to bring the Havoc within searchlight range – without needing to rely on a visual sighting – and that was when the Turbinlite would be switched on. The pilot of the satellite fighter was supposed to spot the enemy in the beam, move in and shoot it down. There were many imponderables that could affect the success of this sequence of events – not least that it was highly unlikely that an enemy aircraft so illuminated would stay mesmerised in the beam long enough for the satellite fighter to catch it! Or that either of the two RAF pilots would not have their night vision ruined by the sudden intense light. So far, successful interceptions had been a quite rare event.

It was in July 1941 that No 151 Squadron began co-operating with the Turbinlite Havoc unit at Wittering. As a first step, several of its aircraft and pilots were sent to RAF Hunsdon to learn the ropes from one of the first Havoc units formed. When they returned to Wittering, almost all flying in August, September and much of October was devoted to training with No 1453 Flight.

As the flight was more or less up to personnel strength, training started in earnest with the Hurricane and Defiant boys from No 151 Squadron. It was recorded in No 151 Squadron's Operational Record Book that: 'on October 22, Pilot Officers Stevens in Hurricane Z3261 and McRitchie in Defiant AA431 carried out a pukka Turbinlite patrol for the first time.' It also records that: 'Plt Off Stevens broke away and independently destroyed an enemy aircraft.'

Jack Cheney continues:

The weather deteriorated into December but practice interceptions continued whenever there was a break. Despite the cold, our dispersal was very comfortable during the bad spells and we sat around line-shooting whenever there was little else to do. However, the calm was quickly shattered when, on 18 December, Sgt James Sudders, who had been with us at Church Fenton and posted in during October, spun in and crashed his Havoc at Stowgate railway crossing, between Crowland and Market Deeping (Lincs). At this time radio observers outnumbered pilots so it was quite usual for a pilot to have two observers attached to him. On this occasion, Sudders had both Sgt Eric Welch, his regular RO, and Sgt William Fradley, a spare RO, in the back of BD120 and they were all killed in the accident.

Later on in December there were a few sorties in company with Hurricanes of 151 Squadron to try out a new wheeze. The Havocs were to fly around at 5,000 feet dropping flares on possible targets as an alternative method of illuminating the enemy. Bit of a shambles all round! Since the flares were loaded in the bomb bay, the Havocs used for these sorties were the battery-less non-Turbinlite aircraft that the squadron had on charge for crew training purposes. As we were not yet declared fully operational, the whole flight was allowed Christmas leave, which suited me down to the ground being so near to home. There was precious little flying for us in January 1942 and we were still 'non-op'. The bad weather made our other activities scarce but we played several ice hockey matches on the frozen Whitewater lake at the edge of the airfield. There was also bags of snow clearing to be done and it was both back-breaking and heart-breaking as, every time an area was cleared, it snowed up very soon after. The CO was dead keen on playing soldiers so, when flying was scrubbed, we used up many Very cartridges and thunder-flashes on these ground exercises.

In February the snow abated a little and although it was still cold enough to keep skating, we were able to put some flying in too. My pride took a bit of a blow when I taxied a Havoc into one of the dispersal bay walls. The brakes failed and the starboard engine cowling was a trifle bent but there was no serious damage and I got away with it. The station dance, held on 17 February in Stamford Grammar School, was a good opportunity to give Flt Lt George Turner, one of 1453's original pilots, a good send-off. He was being posted to RAF West Malling and a replacement crew arrived from 51 OTU Cranfield even before he had left.

A milestone was also reached before the end of that month when the flight was, at long last, declared operational. Night readiness routine was started, with bags of panic, Mae Wests and things. Despite all this readiness routine though there was not much trade and the only excitement occurred during the night flying tests [NFT], when one could indulge in a spot of low-level work over the wide-open space of the Fens. I was warned off doing this after word got back to the CO about my regular aerial visits over my home in Spalding, which also happened to be just across the road from my old school. My mother – and of course the boys of the school – got an enormous kick from the sight of my big black Havoc thundering down the school road just above rooftop height. But it had obviously upset someone and they reported me!

Shortly before the end of March the flight was re-equipped with Douglas Boston III aircraft to replace the lower powered Havoc Is. These new mounts were handled gingerly at first, in view of the extra power but when we got used to them they were found to be aces up on the old Havocs. Two new crews arrived from Cranfield on April 7 but sadly only one week later one of these was lost in an accident. Plt Off Jacques Henri Horrell [English father, French mother] and Sgt Samuel Capewell were on an NFT with Plt Off Frank Darycott BSc, the flight's special signals [radar] expert also on board. An enquiry into the crash suggested that Horrell became aware that two unidentified Spitfires were diving on him from astern. It was surmised that he took violent evasive action and fell into a spin from which he could not recover, the aeroplane crashing at Aldwincle St Peters in Northamptonshire.

Now that the weather was getting better, our thoughts turned to outdoor pursuits to relieve the waiting. Someone had the bright idea that we should take up sailing on the lake near dispersal, so a sailing dinghy was purchased from the aircrew fund. The first trips were made, a bit too daringly and in the strong April winds quite a few duckings followed, including Mike who tried to go solo too soon.

Flying livened up a bit in May when mine was one of three crews detached for readiness duty at RAF Swanton Morley, Norfolk. Each day the detachment took off at dusk for Swanton and returned to Wittering at dawn the next morning. 151 Squadron had by now exchanged its Hurricanes for Mosquitoes so the flight was now co-operating with 486 (New Zealand) Squadron instead. Another change of scene occurred in the middle of this month, too, when I underwent a blind approach course with 1529 BAT Flight at Collyweston, Wittering's second satellite. It was a pleasant change to fly a single-engine aeroplane again, this time the Miles Master II. Upon my return to the fold I continued to do readiness at Swanton but there was precious little doing because

Night-fighter crew member Mike Mycock, with Jack Cheney behind him, relaxing on Whitewater Lake, RAF Wittering, 1942. (J. Cheney Collection)

Jerry just didn't show up much. Plt Off Gallagher got a scramble one night and chased an unidentified target until it was discovered to be a friendly aircraft. That was the only chase during the month but it did at least relieve the monotony of the continual waiting.

Late in the month my pride and joy, Boston Z2184, went u/s [unserviceable] with a radio fault. It had only flown once with the flight and was practically brand new. It was, however, repaired by the 30th, just in time to fly Sgt Dave Glen to RAF Church Fenton to start his leave. I found that the station had changed considerably since my time there. The OTU had disappeared and night-fighter operations had taken its place with the return of 25 Squadron from RAF Ballyhalbert in Northern Ireland.

Detached aircrews continued to go regularly to Swanton Morley well into June but there were no more scrambles. There was plenty of activity, though, on the night of the thousand bomber raid on Germany at the end of May. Both Swanton and Wittering were littered with our bombers coming back in one piece or in several pieces. At the end of the month our flying from Swanton Morley was washed out. July got off to a good start, though, as the flight was one year old and it was decided to have a party to celebrate. All the aircrews and many of the technical NCOs were invited to Pilsgate, the CO's house near Stamford, where copious quantities of strawberries and cream were consumed and the beer flowed freely. When the CO persuaded us to leave, the party departed in two cars (eighteen in the Humber!) to continue the merry-making at the White Hart in nearby Ufford, before finally retiring somewhat worse for wear for a nightcap in the mess. Standing patrols began at Wittering during this month but though these were flown regularly, no trade came our way. No 486 Squadron converted to Typhoons but still kept a few Hurricanes to co-operate with us.

On 26 July 1942 the flight upped sticks to go on detachment to RAF Hibaldstow, eight miles south of Scunthorpe, to reinforce No 1459 Flight and maintain standing patrols co-operating with the Hurricanes of No 253 (Hyderabad) Squadron. This was all very well but still no trade came our way. The 'conventional' night-fighters usually had first bite of the cherry at any trade that came over England these days. Aircrew were billeted at RAF Kirton Lindsey and we had the bind of travelling daily to and from Hibaldstow to do our flying. The dispersal at Hibaldstow was definitely ropey compared to the comfort of Wittering and the food was lousy, too. But, you can get used to anything eventually and after a few days this was no exception. Kirton Lindsey Mess was full of Polish Spitfire pilots from 303 Squadron led by Sqn Ldr Jan Zumbach and I was very envious of their cannon-armed Spitfires.

Turbinlite standing patrols from Hibaldstow continued into August and things began to hot up a bit as most crews began to get their share of scrambles. Nobby Clarke got two head-on interceptions one night over Hull but was unable to turn quickly enough to follow them up. Jerry Clymer had the most atrocious bad luck. Almost invariably, when he got the order to scramble his engines would refuse to start, or he would be recalled before he could get off the deck. Mike and I chased an unidentified aircraft and almost came within range, only to be told it was a friendly.

On August 24 Mike and I were sent off on yet another detachment, this time to RAF Coltishall with Havoc BJ467 and a ground crew of six. We stayed three days doing some ground control exercises for Fighter Command under the watchful eye of Flt Lt Derek Jackson, a university don and electronics boffin. There were endless snags between Coltishall and Wittering control and I was heartily fed up with the job by the time we left for home. No sooner had we arrived back at Kirton Lindsey than I was told to report back to Coltishall on the 31st. Another binding few days!

The pace of life took another upward turn on September 3 1942, when 1453 Flight was re-formed as No 532 Squadron. A number of Hurricanes were sent to us and pilots for them were drawn from 486 Squadron and from various OTUs. The idea now was for the squadron to become self-

'A' Flight of No 532 Squadron. Jack Cheney is seated second from the left; Mike Mycock is standing second from the left. (J. Cheney Collection)

contained, in that it comprised 'A' flight with Havocs (Boston III) and 'B' flight with the Hurricanes. The other good news was that we were to return to Wittering on the 6th.

Back at Wittering, the first two days were spent rearranging and clearing up our old Whitewater dispersal. Training under the new structure began immediately but after only two days, would you believe it, it was all change again and off we went back to Hibaldstow. In order to become operational there, it was necessary to borrow three Hurricane pilots from 486 Squadron at Wittering, which was now fully fledged on Typhoons. Does anyone really know what they are doing in this war?

Once the move to Hibaldstow was complete we settled down to get the new Hurricane pilots operational, so that the 486 chaps could return to their squadron. Just before they left we had the only scramble of the month. At 21.30 on the 19th, Sgt Preston, one of the 486 boys and I took off to intercept a bogey. We were airborne for only forty minutes though before the hated recall came through. The Hun had gone further north and some of the squadrons in that direction took over the hunt. That was the nearest any of us got to the Hun in September. For the rest of the month we got stuck into our training programme in order to become fully operational, spending much of the time on instrument tests, since the artificial horizons in the Havocs were playing up at this time.

A change of command brought the month to a close. We bid a boozy farewell to John Willie Blair, posted out to 51 OTU Cranfield and an equally rousing celebration for his deputy Flt Lt C.L.W. Stewart on his appointment as the new CO. Needless to say this historic occasion was dealt with in style and lunch that day finished at 16.00 hours. At 17.00 that same afternoon I flew Sgt Joe Gunnill down to Wittering to attend the Beam Approach Training School and I don't think I have flown a steadier course in my life!

With the coming of the moon period in mid-October the weather turned duff and night flying was reduced to practically zero and it was not until the 24th that the weather decided to clear. Although the squadron was on readiness and could only put up one Boston at a time, Mike and I managed to jam in six and a half hours of night flying, the first for a fortnight. I crawled into bed at 08.00 next morning well satisfied after such a splendid session. The weather clamped down yet again so odd jobs were the order of the day. The latest wheeze is for us to scrape off the matt black dope from the Havocs in order to get the new grey and green camouflage on in the specified time. Well, at least it's warm and useful work, though some of the aircraft began to resemble patchwork quilts.

In general terms, up to November 1940 aeroplanes used for night operations were painted in the standard RAF day paint scheme. When night-fighter operations became common it was felt that black or a dark colour might be the most suitable for camouflage at night. As a result, a black paint with an almost 'fuzzy' finish to it called 'Special Night' or 'RDM2' was applied first to under-surfaces from September 1940, then overall by about mid-November 1940. However, by the time the Blitz ended, Special Night was considered not to be the best colour for night-fighters – a conclusion that had already been discovered in the First World War! Flying experiments showed that it tended to turn a fighter into a dark silhouette and rather than the aircraft merging with the darkness, it could, under certain conditions and at reducing ranges, actually become more visible. Unfortunately, no one seemed to have an alternative and it took many more experiments and almost eighteen months before a replacement colour scheme was settled upon. It seemed that, contrary to expectations, disruptive patterns of grey rendered aeroplanes less visible under most conditions, including the night sky. Thus, in October 1942 night-fighters were to be painted medium sea grey overall with a disruptive pattern of dark green on upper surfaces – hence the hard work referred to by Jack Cheney:

On my day off Joe Gunnill flew my beloved Z2184 on an NFT and over Goole the port fuel pump packed up. By a clever bit of juggling with the inter-feeds he managed to keep the port engine running and brought it back all in one piece.

Wonder of wonders, on October 31 the weather cleared up and patrols were on again. Three of the others were detailed for these while I was briefed to carry out a bomber affiliation sortie with a Lancaster from 44 Squadron at Waddington. Everything had been previously arranged with the Lancaster crew who were word perfect, so I cracked off at 19.05 to rendezvous with them. By that time there was quite a haze over the aerodrome and the lights were very dim, even in the circuit.

To start with, the Lanc took off before it should have done but luckily I caught a glimpse of its lights as it left the ground. There then followed the most gruelling time I have had for many a long time as far as night flying goes. The Lanc proceeded to do turns, with about forty degrees of bank on, around the aerodrome at low speed. I must say the Boston stood up to it very well even though I must have been very close to stalling many times. Unfortunately I was unable to get to the exact range to carry out my orders and after an hour of trying I gave up in disgust and went home. I found out later that, although I was burning all my lights, not one of the bomber crew ever saw me even though I was in visual range all the time. That seems to augur well for our night-fighters – but not so good for the bomber boys!

Douglas Turbinlite Boston III (Havoc), Z2184, was flown by Jack Cheney during 1942. (J. Cheney Collection)

What with the weather being u/s as well as the aircraft we are doing an awful lot of Link trainer time these days. On the 4th visibility rose to all of 2 yards so how appropriate it was that we were assembled for a lecture on new blind flying techniques. By mid-day visibility had risen to 10 yards but it is so cold here now that Jimmy Green had to put his feet into my hot bath to get them warm!

Life at the dispersal gets very boring with no aeroplanes to fly, even if the weather is so duff. Fortunately I managed to wangle some leave again and while I was away things livened up again with a few incidents. One afternoon the whole of 'A' flight – with the sole exception of Sgt Gunnill – and most of 'B' flight took off on NFTs. While they were airborne, the weather clamped in and our aircraft were scattered to the four corners of 12 Group. Some got down at Church Fenton, some at Coleby Grange and a few at Wittering and they just had to stay put overnight. Poor old Joe Gunnill was left holding the fort at Hibaldstow with just one aircraft and the AOC was tearing his hair out.

On the 7th Sgt Carter wrote off Hurricane BE581 when he crash-landed on a Q-site a mile west of Mablethorpe. It burst into flames and he was damned lucky to get out alive and only with cuts and bruises. The very next day one of our sister 538 Squadron Havocs taxied very prettily into Church Fenton's telephone exchange. I have never seen a taxiing accident look so much like the result of spiralling in from 20,000 feet in my life. Both main-planes had at least fifty degrees of dihedral and the rest of the machine is a complete write-off. Sgt Lowndes, the unfortunate pilot, was injured in the prang, which was attributed to the windscreen completely misting up and poor lighting on the peri-track.

I managed to get airborne for the first time this month for an NFT on the 13th but it was only for ten minutes before the inevitable bad weather closed in. Hibaldstow is a helluva place for lousy weather! It was another week before I put in more night hours and even then I had to turn back early with a spot of engine trouble. I managed to squeeze in another sortie at 04.00 and it was wizard to have that peace and quiet of the last patrol of the night. Except for the odd NFT, flying was washed out for the rest of the month and the monotony was only relieved by the bind of the group captain's inspection of dispersals and being invited to attend a colossal binge at Wittering's annual dance. On 1 December the squadron's official photographs were taken and the rain just held off until they were completed. The weather is marginally better now, allowing all NFTs to be got in and a session of night flying until about midnight but it is exceedingly cold up there now and there is not much sign of the Hun.

As December wore on it was back to foul weather again and I had to wait until the 10th before getting airborne again. At long last the Hun decided to liven things up a bit and twelve enemy aircraft came over on a mine laying sortie. Just our luck that they were too far north for us to co-operate successfully against them. It was the 20th before the enemy sent another foray but 532 was not on readiness that night so 538 scrambled a couple of aircraft with bags of flap all round but no result.

For once no one moaned when the weather went delightfully non-op for four whole days from Christmas Eve. From teatime on the 24th until the early hours of the 28th everyone, almost without exception, was gloriously tight. There were dances in the various messes and the WAAFs were on top line all the time. What a smashing party and it lasted four whole days! There were many sore heads and lively stomachs when flying resumed on the 29th, although the first snow of the winter soon put paid to that. It was my 21st birthday on the 31st and I went home on a week's pass. January 1943 and back at Hibaldstow we passed the time snow clearing mostly but I did manage to put in some night flying on the 9th. Between then and the 18th little flying of any sort took place and the only event of note was that my promotion to flying officer came through.

Well, it looks like the writing is on the wall for the squadron because No 12 Group declared us non-operational on 18 January 1943 with big changes rumoured. A hint of what was in the wind came when the CO went over to Wittering to test the new Mosquito night-fighter.

Back at Hibaldstow, the news was out that 532 and all the other Turbinlite units are disbanded with effect from 25th January and all personnel are to be posted. Most of us in 'A' flight, including Mike and I, will go to No 25 Squadron to fly Mosquitoes at RAF Church Fenton. 'B' flight is being split up among various single-engine fighter squadrons, with a few of the boys choosing to go to OTU to convert to twins. The Turbinlite scheme is finished and I can't say I'm very sorry about it but the pity is that the squadron has to break up as a result.

It was lunchtime of 29 January 1943, when I set out by train for RAF Church Fenton to embark on this next phase of my flying career. I was delighted to find a familiar face upon my arrival, for none other than my former CO, John Willie Blair, is now the senior controller at the station. Fg Off Jimmy Wootton, who was with me at 54 OTU, was another welcome sight together with several old pals who should make the squadron quite lively.

At a meeting next morning all the new arrivals at Church Fenton were introduced to the Squadron Commander, Wg Cdr E.G. Watkins AFC, who spelled out why we were here and what was expected of us. He explained that, back in 1942, moves were made to use Mossies on Intruder operations, as a more effective replacement for the Douglas Bostons then in service. Supply of Mosquitoes for this purpose was, however, slow and only a handful were made available for intruding by the close of that year. First priority was given to the night-fighter defence force but in the light of a decline in the enemy's night-time forays, in December 1942 the role of the Mosquito night-fighting force was revised and it was decided to allocate more aircraft for offensive work.

Wg Cdr Watkins went on to outline how the crews of No 25 Squadron were to intensify their training with the objective of undertaking freelance sorties known as 'Rangers'. No 12 Group, into which RAF Church Fenton fell, was allocated northern Germany as its 'patch' and the intruder sorties would be operated from forward aerodromes at RAF Coltishall in Norfolk and RAF Castle Camps in Suffolk.

Night Rangers were sorties against transport targets, mounted during the moon periods when it was possible to see the ground more clearly. Intruder sorties, on the other hand, were those made in the dark periods, involving patrols in the vicinity of one or more enemy airfields and setting off at predetermined times. At set times other aircraft would take over from those despatched earlier, so that a constant patrol could be maintained in order to restrict enemy aircraft movements. The whole idea was to keep the Hun on his toes all the time, to disrupt his communications and destroy aircraft and other transport in the process. One Flight would fly Rangers on moonlight nights while the other would still be required to put up the usual defensive patrols.

It all sounded terrific stuff and was aces up on the monotonous bind we had endured with the Turbinlite patrols on our previous squadron. Mike and I were allocated to 'A' flight and during the afternoon we new boys were given the gen on the Mosquito by the flight commander Sqn Ldr Bill Carnaby. I finished off that busy day by swotting up Pilot's Notes on the Mossie during the evening and again the next morning.

Early on February 1st there were the first of many lectures on navigation to a level essential for swanning about over northern Europe and about mid-morning Vic Hester did a spot of flying in a Mosquito, the first of my crowd to get his hands on one. This milestone raised our hopes for some real flying but these were soon dashed when no one else was briefed to go. It looks as if it's going to take us a long time to become operational with such a shortage of spare aircraft and some bad serviceability just now. Rather than let us get idle, the CO decided that exercise was the answer and I had my first dose of PT in a long time, under the eagle eye of Sgt Finch, the PTI from Hibaldstow.

At long last my opportunity to fly came on the 5th. The deputy 'A' flight commander, Flt Lt Joe Singleton, took me up in DZ688 to give me my first taste of the Mosquito – and it was absolutely wizard! Nothing to touch it so far, it is light on the controls, has an excellent stall and is good on one engine. Somehow during the thirty minute flight Joe and I contrived to change seats while airborne and so I was at last able to get my hand in. Unfortunately the aircraft went u/s later so I could not go up on my own. Gally [Flt Lt Gallagher] went off solo in DD733 in the afternoon and caused quite a commotion when he developed a bad swing on landing, resulting in a jolly good prang. The poor fellow wrote off the undercart and damaged a wing tip, the props and the undercarriage doors. It might have been something to smile about except that it just happened to be the CO's machine – and he was not best pleased about it.

It was back to PT again on the 6th, then everyone rushed down to dispersal to see what chance there was of flying. Sqn Ldr Carnaby dropped the bombshell that the CO had decided that, in view of Gally's fearful efforts, we must all have more dual before being sent off solo. Cries of 'shame!' and poor old Gally is none too popular now. I was, however, promised a quick whip round tomorrow and as I had already had one trip, I would then be allowed to go off on my own.

This promise was soon short-lived, though, when Joe Singleton apologised and said he really could not send me off as the CO had put his foot down

Fg Off Jack Cheney, pilot with No 25 Squadron, at Church Fenton, 1943. (J. Cheney Collection)

Flt Sgt James Kenneth 'Mike' Mycock, navigator/radar operator. (J. Cheney Collection)

very firmly about us having to have more dual. Bill Mallett managed to get a short trip with Joe but we are still dogged by un-serviceability. Vic Hester was asked to fly down to Wittering today, presumably to test the Turbinlite version of the Mosquito, as he was the only bloke with time on both types. There was one good piece of news, though, for today Mike's commission came through at last and we were able to be together, now he is a shiny new Pilot Officer in the officer's mess.

Next few days were duff as far as flying was concerned, since the dual-control Mosquito is still u/s and there were yet more lectures. Why the hell must we have all this dual? I'm getting browned off just sitting on the ground. The boredom is only relieved by PT, sunray lamp sessions and time in the Link [pilot] and Hunt [gunnery] trainers.

The dual Mosquito was declared serviceable at last on the 11th and Johnny Limbert went up first. Our luck ran out though when the wind rose to gale force and all Mosquitoes were called back, so he was unable to go solo. Everyone is pretty well browned off by now. Boredom turned into mischief that evening and a mild drinking session turned into a small riot. Joe Gunnill, just back from leave, Bill Mallet, Mike and I started a game of table tennis, liberally interspersed with beer. The table, always a little shaky on its legs, ended up as a pile of twisted debris on the hall floor as the result of bodily contact with several players hurtling to get at the ball. We four collapsed into a heap on top, laughing like drains. There was another wild do a couple of days later to celebrate Joe Gunnill's departure for RAF Charterhall [a night-fighter training unit]. Tables and chairs were stacked up so that he could write his name on the ceiling but in the process two inkwells were knocked over, spilling their contents all over the anteroom carpet. Black number two! This orgy of bedlam came to an end with me cannoning into a wall and splitting my head open. I awoke next morning with trip hammers going full blast in my head, my hair matted and the pillow covered in blood. The Squadron Leader (Admin), a strict disciplinarian of First World War vintage, dished out numerous severe wiggings and the Doc cut off practically half my hair and covered my head with plaster. To cap it all the dual Mosquito, HJ862, pranged into a dispersal bay and was once more u/s, so everyone put in for a 48-hour pass.

For a few days after my return from leave there was lots of fog about and still no flying, what a bind. However, on February 25th, Johnny and Gally were first off and they got their long awaited first solos in the Mosquito. I waited, keyed up, all afternoon for an aircraft and was finally rewarded after tea. Well, having gone solo in the Mossie, maybe now we can get cracking. The next couple of weeks, in fact, livened up considerably as I spent the days

A dual-control Mosquito TIII, HJ866, as used to train No 25 Squadron pilots during conversion to the NFII. (J. Cheney Collection)

and nights clocking up practice hours, NFTs and starting on the defensive patrol roster.

There was not much enemy activity on the patrols during March. We flew on the 6th in DD754 and on the 7th in DZ655, both under Roecliffe GCI, but spent the two-and-a-half-hour sorties doing practice interceptions which, in truth, didn't go too well. The enemy sent a raid over on evening of March 9th and our squadron put up seven Mosquitoes between 19.00 and midnight. Easington Chain Home Low [CHL] radar station vectored Mike and I, in DZ688, towards an unidentified aircraft, which turned out to be a friendly. Later in our patrol we chased an enemy aircraft and Mike held a contact on our AI for about seven seconds but the target was going too fast to bring into range. We were put on to another EA [enemy aircraft] but could not turn that into a contact either. Only one of our crews managed to turn a contact into a visual on a Dornier Do 217 but were frustrated by searchlights. Mike and I did six more defensive patrols, in DZ655 and HJ914, during the first half of April but the Hun came nowhere near our patch so the patrol time was occupied in exercising with ground radar stations or searchlights.

The second half of April was quite different though. It saw the start of the offensive intruder operations, called Ranger, by No 25 Squadron, using Mosquito NFIIs with the AI radar removed and a Gee navigation set installed. Mike and I got our first taste of the action on the 20th. The sky was clear, with a brilliant moon. 'B' flight flew all their defensive patrols while three of 'A' flight's Ranger aircraft – including mine – were active from Coltishall and made a great killing.

Fg Off Jimmy Wootton and his navigator, Plt Off John Dymock, were sent off first, to the Osnabrück area, then Mike and I went off at 22.40 on 20th April 1943. Manor 24 (our call-sign) was airborne from Coltishall in bright moonlight, with no cloud and visibility of four miles. We crossed the North Sea at 200 feet and after pin-pointing the island of Vlieland to starboard we climbed to 4,500 feet. I altered course for the Zuider Zee dam and crossed the mainland coast at Makkum where a prominent jetty made another good pin-point. From there Mike gave me a course for Assen and thence to Aschendorf, which was reached just before midnight.

We followed some railway lines to Papenburg and Leer, encountering moderate flak and searchlight activity on the way. A train was spotted entering Leer from the south and with a quickening of the pulse, I turned into the attack. Just as I did so, the Mossie was illuminated by the glare of three searchlights for about half a minute. Considerable light flak, again pretty accurate, was thrown up at us and I had to break off the attack with some violent evasive action.

Having succeeded in dodging the lights, we set course for Zwischenaur Lake, to the west of Bremen where, further along the same railway lines a fast-moving train was spotted. I pushed the stick gently forward and made a head-on pass at it, starting at 1,300 feet range and with Mike shouting out the altitude readings as I concentrated on the train, the gun sight and firing the guns. I kept my thumb on the button in a five second burst as we closed to 400 feet range and I could see cannon strikes all over the locomotive as I broke away and headed off in the direction of Cloppenburg.

Following the railway tracks south towards Quackenbruck airfield and Furstenau we soon came upon another train near Bippen. This time I attacked from astern and to starboard, opening up with a long, six-second burst. The slow-moving train was hit in a concentrated strike and the flash from the explosions was quite blinding. The locomotive became enveloped in clouds of steam and smoke, grinding to a halt and lit up by a vivid red glow.

Our fuel state showed it was time to go home. The course took us over Lingen where considerable light flak came up from the town and from other isolated gun posts on the outskirts. Over the Zuider Zee, then across the Dutch coast at Ijmuiden and then it was down on the deck all the way across the North Sea. We made landfall at Great Yarmouth some thirty minutes later and touched down on Coltishall's runway at 01.15. Despite attention from the German flak, my Mossie sustained no hits nor, for that matter, did any of the other Ranger aircraft that night. Thus ended my first taste of the real action. There was no great feeling of elation, just relief that it had gone off well and being pleased at having a crack at the Hun on his home ground. The four 20mm cannon in our Mosquitoes were each loaded with 250 rounds of a mixture of HE [High Explosive], incendiary, ball and armour-piercing rounds. Although, of course, the four .303in Browning machine guns were also available, I had used only the cannon on this sortie as they were the more effective for these strafing runs. The two trains we attacked had been given a combined dose of 340 rounds.

Later that day it was back to Church Fenton and a routine of NFTs and defensive night patrols for the next three weeks but Jerry didn't bother us much. Then the moon and weather became ideal for more Ranger activity so we could get to grips with the enemy once again.

On May 15th the defensive patrols were still having no luck, although both friendly and hostile contacts were being chased. Meanwhile, Mike and I were destined to be in the thick of the action again when we took off from our forward base at Coltishall at 23.10 to seek out more transportation targets on what was designated Long Ranger Route No 1.

A large convoy of ships was seen off Vlieland and I overflew them in a diving turn without stirring up a nasty greeting, before crossing the Dutch coast a few minutes later. We reached the familiar pin point at Makkum then headed for the Diepholtz area where I orbited the airfield looking for trade. After stooging around for ten minutes without any sign of life, Mike spotted a train entering the town from the south. I peeled off into a shallow dive from abeam and raked it with a three-second burst of cannon fire, breaking off at 500 feet with strikes being seen all over the coaches. It was essential for Mike to keep calling out the altitude during the diving attacks as it was quite impossible to concentrate on the gunsight and the target and watch our height all at the same time, for one could become quite mesmerised by the kaleidoscope of dials, flashes and explosions.

Turning away now towards Steinhuder Lake, lights could be seen at Lengenhagen aerodrome on the outskirts of Hanover but we were out of luck, for no aeroplane activity could be detected there. Two searchlights probed the sky from Burgdorf aerodrome in an effort to catch us but they did not illuminate our aircraft. Shortly after this, two trains were sighted near Gifhorn and I hammered both these one after the other in beam attacks using raking three-second bursts from the cannon only. Several strikes were observed on both locomotives and after the second pass, the sky was lit up by a satisfying red glow as we left them behind.

We pressed on towards Gardelegen airfield, only seventy miles short of Berlin and en route, surprised another train west of Fallersleben. I made two runs on this one, firing a short burst on the first pass from astern then whipping hard round and pouring a longer burst from all eight guns along the whole length of the train, watching the cannon shells hitting the coaches and loco on each pass. During the second attack there was moderate but accurate light flak coming at us from the nearby town, so we sheered off and set course for Salzwedel airfield. A few minutes later, yet another train was spotted near Wieren and I made two head-on attacks with the cannon, producing strikes on the locomotive both times.

Now we turned north in the general direction of Hamburg. A couple of minutes after passing over Ulzen a train hove into view at outside Unterlutz. I made a run in from astern this time, giving it a three-second burst from the machine guns only and I hung on so long in the dive that the Mossie was almost skimming the rear end of the train by the time I hauled the nose up. Good hits were seen on the leading coaches and the loco.

After this last attack the windscreen of the Mosquito misted over on the outside, which made navigation difficult so, since our ammo was just about finished, Mike gave me a course for base via the Zuider Zee at Aarderwijk and the Dutch coast at Ijmuiden. The return was uneventful and we touched down at Coltishall at 03.20 to claim in our four-hour sortie five locomotives and an unknown quantity of coaches on which I had expended 700 rounds of 20mm and 1,000 rounds of .303in ammo. Two other Ranger crews also claimed a further four trains between them but No 25 Squadron's two Intruder sorties to the Soesterberg and Deelen airfield areas each drew a blank. On the whole it had been a productive night though and I slept the sleep of the exhausted.

Four nights later Mike and I were off again, this time allocated to Ranger Route No 19. We were second away, after Fg Off Davies who went to the Drentewede area. Keeping low over the North Sea, then climbing to 4,500 feet to cross the coast at Terschelling at midnight, Mike gave me a course for Assen, Aschendorf, Syke and Drackenburg and skirting round the hot spot of Bremen. Searching in a north-east direction we sighted a train a few miles east of Visselhovede and I immediately dived at it head-on, letting go with a three-second burst of cannon. This hit the locomotive which promptly rolled to a stop emitting lovely dense clouds of smoke and steam. One down! We turned away for Soltau then headed east to Ulzen, attacking a southbound train near Bevensen. This loco was hammered with cannon fire and it, too, was left stationary, in clouds of steam lit up by a dull red glow.

We took time now to patrol up and down the Ulzen to Hannover railway line looking for 'trade'. Our luck was in since, before long, we were rewarded by the sight of no fewer than *three* trains near Celle. No time to dither. I hit the first loco with cannon fire in a head-on attack and the second, a few miles behind it and travelling in the same direction, was given the same treatment. Quickly hauling the Mossie round in a tight turn I overtook the third train from astern and raked its whole length with a four-second burst from the combined fire power of the cannon and Brownings. This loco was hit and ground to a halt, erupting in large clouds of steam and smoke.

This area was proving very fruitful as yet another train was observed five miles away puffing serenely towards Celle. I dived on this one from head-on, firing at it with machine guns only and hits seemed to pepper the loco and set fire to some of the coaches, which were burning furiously as the train came to a halt.

Having stirred up a hornet's nest Mike, always on top of our position, gave me a course to steer for base. As we flew over Steinhuder Lake, sadly low on fuel and ammunition, some ten miles or so to the north could be seen what appeared to be an aerodrome with signs of a visual Lorenz lighting system. However, keeping on track we came across another train on the outskirts of Lemforde and with some ammunition to spare it was too good a target to overlook. I dived straight at it and let fly a concentrated burst with the remaining Browning ammo, which produced the usual clouds of steam and a satisfying red glow. Time to go home.

The rest of the flight back had to be by dead reckoning as the compass packed up after the last attack. We must have wandered off course a bit near Utrecht because the aircraft was suddenly coned by about twelve searchlights. They held us for a couple of minutes before I could throw them off with violent evasive action. The lights were followed up by a barrage of intense and pretty accurate light flak but we emerged unscathed. Ten minutes later, as we crossed the Dutch coast, we were picked up by two more searchlights on the island of Overflakee. They held us for about a minute and it was only by more violent manoeuvres and then diving full pelt to the deck that they were shaken off. I kept down low over the North Sea and we landed at Coltishall at 03.35 after another four hours of working up quite a sweat. This time our claim was for seven locomotives and an unknown number of coaches set on fire. [Seven locos by one crew in one night sortie was a squadron record and remained unbeaten by any squadron.]

Wing Commander Simon Maude – squadron CO since March – was one of the other Ranger crews that night. He had been busy in the Bremen area, claiming one train and starting fires in a factory and rail yard during his sortie. In contrast, Sqn Ldr Brinsden saw no activity whatsoever and his description of his own sortie was highly original, in that he became the first pilot to complain of boredom on a Ranger operation!

During the next few days the weather remained warm and although visibility decreased and Ranger operations were cancelled, the full night defensive programme was still flown every night and Mike and I were detailed to do our share of this. We actually got a bit of excitement on the 23rd when, flying DZ655, we were vectored onto a contact and pursued a retreating Hun two thirds of the way to Holland but sadly were unable to bring him into range.

Things remained quiet until June 4th when orders were received for three crews and aircraft to be despatched for special duties at RAF Predannack in Cornwall. This mysterious project captured everyone's imagination and the crews selected were mine, Flt Lt Joe Singleton with Fg Off Geoff Haslam (Nav) and Fg Off Jimmy Wootton with Plt Off John Dymock (Nav). That same day was spent in preparing ourselves and our aircraft to leave but rain and low cloud prevented departure.

Much of the following day was spent swinging the compasses and re-harmonising the guns of DZ688, DZ685 and DD757 (my aircraft), the Mosquitoes assigned to the Predannack operation. These aircraft were from among those employed on the Ranger operations so they had had the AI equipment removed and a Gee navigation aid installed. By teatime on the 5th the wind had freshened somewhat and the clouds had lifted sufficiently to allow us to embark on our detachment to No 264 Squadron's base.

It was made clear on our arrival at Predannack that the main task of these composite squadron operations, code-named Instep, is to patrol the Bay of Biscay in an attempt to intercept and destroy enemy aircraft – notably Junkers Ju 88s – that were interfering with Coastal Command's anti-submarine patrols. No time was lost and we began operations immediately. At 18.00 in the evening of June 7th Joe Singleton with his navigator Geoff Haslam and me with Mike, took off in company with two other Mossies from the Australian No 456 Squadron and headed south across the wide open spaces of the Bay of Biscay.

It was strange flying over an expanse of sea, out of sight of land for so long, heading ever further south towards the north coast of Spain. After an uneventful flight in loose formation we turned at the end of the patrol line at latitude 46.00N, longitude 04.15W. Coming round onto the northerly heading I spotted a smudge of smoke to starboard and reported it to Joe who

DH Mosquito NFII, DD739, of No 456 Squadron as used on Instep patrols in 1943 with AI MkV radar removed from the nose, but wing antennae retained. (J. Cheney Collection)

was formation leader. Course was altered and our formation came up with a fishing vessel that was identified as a French trawler named *Tadorne*. We had been briefed to watch out for such ships, as they were suspected of passing on information about Coastal Command aircraft to the Ju 88 squadrons. Since all fishing vessels had been warned by leaflet drops to keep out of the area Joe had no hesitation in going in to attack.

Ordering me and one of the 456 boys to orbit as top cover, Joe told Plt Off John Newell (with Nav Flt Sgt Allen Keating) of 456 to go line astern and follow him down to attack. They each carried out two strafing runs on the vessel and hits were registered all over the centre of the target, which stopped dead in the water, on fire and with clouds of smoke and steam billowing from it. We reformed on Joe's aircraft and returned to Predannack without further incident. [Research later revealed that the Vichy vessel *Tadorne* operated from La Rochelle and was pressed into German navy service as UJ-2218 in the role of an armed auxiliary sub-hunter. The attack took place 110 nautical miles west of La Pallice, during which the trawler was badly damaged with casualties of three dead and five injured, but despite this damage the vessel managed to return to La Rochelle.]

There was yet more excitement a couple of days later when I was part of a patrol that made contact with five Ju 88 long-range fighters over the Bay. In the ensuing fracas, one Ju 88 was destroyed by Joe Singleton: the first 'kill' by a No 25 Squadron Mosquito.

Our patrol of six Mosquitoes, led by Joe, took off from Predannack during the afternoon of June 11th. Jimmy Wootton was flying as No 2; I was No 3 and three of the 456 crews made up the second section. Shortly after takeoff, Flt Lt Gordon Panitz (with Nav Fg Off Richard Williams) of 456 had to break away and return to base with engine trouble, while the rest of us continued on our way in a loose vic formation at sea level. When nearing the end of the outward leg, about 130 miles off the north-west tip of Spain, Jimmy spotted a formation of five Ju 88s through the broken cloud. They were flying in loose echelon at 5,000 feet almost directly above us. Well, this was what we had come for!

Immediately, Joe ordered our formation to close up and started a climb up-sun of the enemy. He called for Jimmy Wootton (25) and John Newell (456) to stay with him and for me to take Flt Sgt Richardson (456) and operate as a separate section and keep an eye out for the Ju 88s' top cover element. However, at this point my radio decided to pack up so, although Richardson closed up on me, we were unable to make contact with the enemy before the Ju 88s broke off the engagement. When we reached base again, Joe told me what happened.

He said his section was seen by the enemy early in the climb to get up-sun. The 88s started a climbing orbit in loose line astern, firing off a burst of red star flares as they did so. Joe replied by firing off his own Very pistol in the hope of adding to the confusion and gain time to claw more height. Both formations tried to turn up-sun of each other and when the enemy aircraft were about 2,000 feet above, he gave the order to break formation and for everyone to choose their own target. Several of the enemy opened fire and Joe, selecting the rearmost, turned inside it and opened fire with a full deflection shot from 800 yards range. The burst hit the Ju's port engine and thick smoke poured out. Further bursts of cannon brought even more flames and smoke and the enemy aircraft turned slowly over onto its back and dived into the sea, where a large oil patch marked its entry. Jimmy Wootton and John Newell between them claimed three more as damaged before they hightailed it off home.

The next day, officialdom caught up with Joe Singleton. He was declared 'tour expired' and returned with Geoff Haslam in DD757 to Church Fenton where they received a great welcome as a result of their success. They were replaced at Predannack by 'B' flight commander, Flt Lt Baillie and his navigator, Plt Off Burrow in Mosquito DD738.

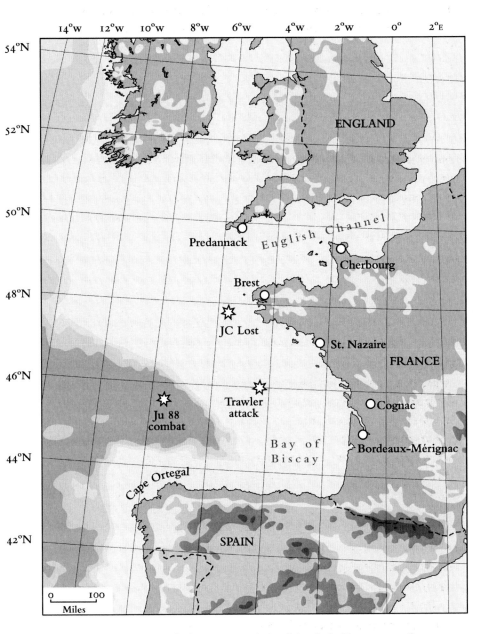

Map of the Biscay area in which Instep patrols, involving Jack Cheney, were flown, June 1943. (Author)

It was on 13 June 1943 that disaster overtook Jack Cheney and the following entry from No 25 Squadron Operations Record Book (Form 540) reveals what happened:

> Late today unpleasant news was received from Predannack. Two crews, Fg Off J.E. Wootton with his navigator Plt Off J.M. Dymock and Fg Off J. Cheney with his navigator Plt Off J.K. Mycock, are reported missing following an engagement while patrolling over the Bay of Biscay. Four Mosquitoes, piloted by Flt Lt Baillie, Fg Offs Wootton and Cheney and Fg Off Reg Harris from the Canadian No 410 Squadron were airborne at 12.59 on a composite Instep patrol.
>
> During the patrol four Ju 88s were sighted at 7,000 feet. There was patchy cloud at 5,000 feet and a thin continuous layer at 8,000 feet and when spotted, the enemy aircraft broke formation and climbed into the higher cloud. Flt Lt Baillie followed but lost sight of the enemy. On coming down out of the higher cloud he saw one of his section below and soon afterwards saw the other two at sea level. Some little time later he saw all three Mosquitoes well ahead of him but was unable to catch up. He did not want to break radio silence for them to rejoin and he soon lost them from sight. Flt Lt Baillie returned to Predannack, landing at 17.50.
>
> Between 17.10 and 17.25, Fg Off Jimmy Wootton was heard calling for an emergency homing to Predannack and a further transmission from one of the missing aircraft stated they were being chased by Focke Wulf Fw 190s.
>
> These three aircraft, DZ688, 'V' [Cheney – in which Jack had made his first Mosquito flight]; DZ685, 'J' [Wootton] and DZ753 [Fg Off Reg Harris and Sgt Edward Skeel of 410 Squadron], failed to return and no other details are known of their fate. It would seem that there is little hope of their survival and that the squadron must necessarily face the loss of two very capable crews and four officers for whom we hold a high regard.

Postscript

It is believed that the enemy aircraft first encountered were Ju 88C-6s of *FlFu Atlantik* (a German naval *Luftflotte*), V/KG40, commanded by Major Alfred Hemm. *Gruppe* HQ was at Kerlin near Lorient and *Staffeln* were dispersed at Mérignac and Cognac airfields, regularly carrying out sweeps over the Bay of Biscay out to longitude 10W and occasionally to 15W. The Ju 88s carried a crew of three and were armed with a battery of three 7.9mm machine guns and three 20mm cannon fixed to fire forward and located under the cockpit.

These guns were under the control of the pilot while the navigator and radio operator each had access to 7.9mm machine guns free-mounted to cover attacks on the rear of the aircraft. The Junkers were heavier, slower and less agile than the Mosquito, but the Junkers could out-dive a Mosquito and since the German formations operated with a couple of Ju 88s acting as spotters flying above the main group, the Mosquito crews had to be careful not to get caught by a 'spotter' section diving down on them.

The Instep Mosquitoes from Predannack usually took a dogleg course around the Brest peninsula and maintained strict radio silence for as long as possible. It needed only a short transmission for the enemy to gain a fix and alert his own single-seat fighters, who would be waiting to pounce when the Mosquitoes came within range. On this last patrol the outward leg would be made at sea level, flying for economy, but once the enemy had been spotted, precious fuel would be consumed rapidly during combat manoeuvring. After over four and a half hours in the air, low on fuel and apparently unsure of their position after the brush with the Ju 88s, these pilots may have been flying perilously close to the Brest peninsula on that return leg.

The Luftwaffe Command diary records that on the following day, General Adolf Galland reported personally to Hitler that a force of Mosquitoes had been engaged over the Bay of Biscay and four [*sic*] of them had been shot down. Post-war research by the eminent aviation historian Chris Goss established that the Mosquitoes were 'bounced' by Fw 190s of 8/JG 2. Oberfeldwebel (Ofw) Friedrich May is credited with shooting down two and Feldwebel (Fw) Alois Schnöll claimed a third. Fw Schnöll was himself killed in action on 22 August 1943, while Ofw May died in action on 20 October 1943.

Some of the others mentioned in Jack Cheney's Instep patrols also failed to survive the war. Australians Gordon Panitz and his navigator/radar operator Richard Williams were both later awarded the DFC; Panitz rose to the rank of wing commander as OC No 464 Squadron, but both were killed in action on 22 August 1944. Australian Flt Lt John Newell lost his life in an aeroplane accident on 5 March 1945 while serving with No 256 Squadron.

Fg Off Jack Cheney is remembered on the war memorial in Spalding Parish Church and on the Roll of Honour in Spalding Grammar School. Both he and Plt Off Mycock are also recorded on the Runnymede Memorial to the Missing.

3

THE FLYING FARMER

Wing Commander Walter Dring

When the Second World War broke out, Walter Dring was 23 years old and farming land at Westfield Farm, Pinchbeck West, near Spalding in Lincolnshire. His father, also named Walter, and mother Ethel ran Woad Farm, the main family business near Weston, where the younger Walter was born on 14 July 1916. Walter junior was educated locally at Moulton Grammar School before joining the family business. Although not particularly academically inclined, he was nevertheless a very articulate man and partial to reading poetry. As a young working man, however, Walter lived for farming and sport, excelling at both. He played cricket, in which he was considered a good batsman, and rugby for Spalding. According to his cousin Peter, Walter was energetic and gregarious by nature, but a moderate drinker who did not feel the need to bolster his sometimes enthusiastic socialising by such means. He held firm views about right and wrong and, while he did not force his opinions upon others, he expected his friends to be loyal and did not hesitate to reciprocate this loyalty – backed up if necessary by his strong physique. Walter had supreme confidence in his own abilities yet was perfectly at ease and utterly reliable as a member of any team and he would follow any leader in whom he could believe or respect. Family correspondence shows he was also a modest and thoughtful man. All these attributes stood him in good stead in his work, social and sporting activities and they certainly provided a sound basis for his future flying career.

According to his brother Harold, Walter went to live with another family on the Pinchbeck farm in 1937 because he was such a go-ahead person; this caused arguments with his father who – while being a brilliant businessman

– was more for taking his time over things. Walter would not be tied down to conventional ways of doing things, and out on his own he soon proved himself to be both a good farmer and a popular employer.

Throughout 1939, well aware of the world situation, Walter did not like what he saw as aggressive bullying by the Nazi regime. His spirit of fair play and adventure was stirred and he decided he would leave what could have been a secure reserved occupation and volunteer for the RAF. He put in his application and was called – actually the day before his twenty-fourth birthday – to attend No 3 Recruit Centre at RAF Padgate, where he was inducted as an aircraftman in the RAF Volunteer Reserve (RAFVR) for training as potential aircrew. Walter wrote later:

It was in the memorable heat of 1940 when the RAF finally decided they could use my body. I had fought hard for a long time to get my release from farming but the Ministry of Labour saw fit to keep me, as food became more problematic. So, while the Spitfire squadrons moved up and down the country, usually flying over my farm, I stood and waved – but my determination to fly increased.

I remember on 4 September 1939, I had rung up my nearest recruiting centre and had been told 'nothing doing!' However, after continually arguing, I was called for my medical. During the cold winter of 1939/40 I had skated on the flooded fields of Cowbit Wash. I had danced and played rugger and all the time I was getting restless with people who did not bother about the war. I lost interest in my farm, which would carry on alright and I spent my time brushing up my geometry and getting really fit to pass the required tests when they should arrive.

It was in July 1940 – I remember the men were hoeing sugar beet and the women were weeding – when eventually I received the blue envelope. I was told to report to Padgate on the 13th. I remember going back to the work in hand and telling my men – who seemed dubious of my capabilities of flying! I always had a touch of drama about myself and now saw myself as a young farmer going off to war. It went down fairly well.

Having made this commitment, he was placed on the reserve pool, returning home to await the call to arms. This duly arrived and, leaving his farm in the capable hands of brother Harold, LAC Walter Dring reported for duty at the RAF Receiving Unit in Torquay on 27 September 1940. After two weeks of induction he was posted to No 6 Initial Training Wing (ITW) in Aberystwyth. Here, for the next three months, aspiring pilots and observers were taught the necessities of service life and the basics of, in Walter's

LAC Walter Dring on the ice-encrusted deck of the ship taking him to Canada, February 1941. (John & Susan Rowe, Dring Collection)

case, pilot ground school training. His first posting was to No 18 Course at No 22 Elementary Flying Training School (22 EFTS), a unit operated by Marshalls Ltd at Cambridge airfield, where his aptitude for pilot training was first assessed, then – being considered suitable – continued in the DH Tiger Moth. It was on 29 December that he made his first flight in T5634 under the watchful eye of Sgt Smullian who remained his instructor for most of his flying at the school. In quite rapid time, Walter 'went solo' in T5634 on 12 January 1941 after just seven hours fifty minutes dual instruction. More intensive training followed until, having accumulated twenty-one hours dual and thirty-two hours solo, and assessed as 'above average' as a pupil pilot, he set out by ship on 24 February to Canada for further pilot training. Walter was posted to No 31 Service Flying Training School (SFTS) located at Collins Bay, near Kingston, Ontario, from 11 March 1941. This unit was part of the British Commonwealth Air Training Plan (BCATP) and while Walter was there, he operated the Fairey Battle as a trainer. Walter went solo in Battle (T) R7471 on 25 April, recalling: 'Forgot the undercart until I was on final approach!' Five months later, now with 140 hours in his logbook, having scored top marks both in dive-bombing (a portent of his future?) and in his final exam, he was awarded his 'Wings' as a 'single-engine' pilot. Walter was posted back to England, arriving at No 3 Personnel Reception Centre, Bournemouth, on 21 August to await his next duty.

LAC Dring climbs into the cockpit of a Fairey Battle Trainer at No 31 SFTS Collins Bay, Canada, April 1941. (John & Susan Rowe, Dring Collection)

By July 1941, having successfully completed his pilot training and been promoted to temporary sergeant, in August Walter was commissioned as a pilot officer and selected for operational service on single-engine fighters. On 27 August this saw him reporting to No 11 Course at No 58 Operational Training Unit (58 OTU), a day-fighter training unit equipped with the Supermarine Spitfire based at Grangemouth, near Falkirk in Scotland. Following a few hours dual in a Miles Master, he was allowed to go solo in a Spitfire for the first time, taking up P9543 for an hour, after which he wrote in his logbook: 'absolutely the cat's whiskers.' Over the next six weeks Walter practised hard in the Spitfire, carrying out circuits and landings, navigation and formation exercises, air gunnery, aerobatics and instrument flying until, on 6 October 1941, assessed as 'above average', he was posted to his first operational squadron, No 56 (Punjab) Squadron at RAF Duxford.

When he joined the squadron it was commanded by ace Battle of France veteran Sqn Ldr Peter 'Prosser' Hanks DFC and currently using the Hawker Hurricane IIB, but it was in the process of re-equipping with the Hawker Typhoon IA. It was on 27 October that Walter Dring made his first flight with the squadron, a sector recco (reconnaissance) in Hurricane II, Z3082 – 'bags of panic!' After that it was mostly a daily routine of familiarisation with the new Typhoon and – when there were enough serviceable aircraft – flying practice interceptions. Failing that, the pilots fell back on the trusty Hurricane to keep

No 11 Course, No 58 OTU, RAF Grangemouth; Plt Off Dring is seated third from the left on the front row, September 1941. (John & Susan Rowe, Dring Collection)

their hand in and Walter, a member of 'A' Flight, only made his first flight in a Typhoon (R7597) on 10 December 1941.

The Hawker Typhoon was being rushed into service in an effort to counter a new German fighter: the Focke-Wulf Fw 190. In September 1941, No 56 was the first squadron to receive Typhoons, but such were the problems encountered that the squadron was not declared fully operational until 30 May 1942, nine months after receiving its first aircraft. It was with the Typhoon, though, that Walter Dring would remain associated for the whole of his operational RAF career and indeed would emerge as one of the leading exponents of Typhoon tactics during the next three years. Initially, No 56 was equipped with the Typhoon IA, such as R7586, R7589, R7591 and R7641, the version fitted with twelve .303in Browning machine guns, but this model was soon superseded by the Typhoon IB, which was armed with four 20mm cannon. For a time the squadron operated a mixture of Typhoons and Hurricanes because low serviceability caused by problems with the former meant the latter were needed to fulfil the squadron's readiness commitments.

Conceived as a medium- to high-level interceptor to replace the Hurricane, when it was found that the Typhoon's Napier Sabre engine and its thick wing section produced a disappointing rate of climb and poor manoeuvring performance at altitudes above 18,000ft – coupled with the catalogue of teething problems – there was some talk about withdrawing it from service altogether. Even though more and more squadrons were being re-equipped with this aircraft, its real salvation came when experienced squadron commanders, such as No 609's Roland Beamont, recognised its potential for ground attack and close support fighter-bomber operations. Like Hugh Dundas, of whom we shall hear more later, Beamont was given an opportunity to present his views on the aircraft at a key meeting – where scrapping was indeed a serious item on the agenda. He was tenacious and persuasive in his defence of the Typhoon as a ground attack fighter; indeed to the extent that it was not scrapped. The interceptor role would have to be addressed by the RAF in a different way because from 1943 onwards, the name Typhoon became synonymous with ground attack, a role in which it was supreme and to which, in no small way, Walter Dring contributed in due course.

In December 1941 Prosser Hanks was promoted to wing commander, remaining at Duxford to command the embryonic Duxford Typhoon wing, while command of No 56 Squadron passed to another Battle of Britain ace, Sqn Ldr Hugh 'Cocky' Dundas DFC. His job was not only to ensure that the many technical issues were resolved and to bring the squadron to a state of operational readiness, but also to lift the morale of the squadron by raising its pilots' belief in their aircraft. After his first flight in a Typhoon, Dundas had no hesitation in addressing immediately the poor rear view which, from his combat experience, he saw as a potential pilot killer. In his autobiography *Flying Start* (Stanley Paul, 1988), he wrote:

> When I was called upon to give my views I stated simply that if I had been asked to go to war in 1940 and 1941 in an aircraft with similarly restricted rear view I should have been dead long ago. I said that I did not believe that any experienced fighter pilot would disagree with me in stating that the matter must be put right before we were made operational.

His vociferous representations to higher authority were acted upon and the rear end of the 'car-door' cockpit was rapidly redesigned and retrofitted by the manufacturers, who subsequently went further by developing a bubble canopy for this aircraft.

Meanwhile, throughout the winter of 1942, the pilots of No 56, including Walter Dring, worked hard with whatever serviceable aircraft they had, but on 20 January the last of their Hurricanes was flown out to RAF High Ercall and the squadron was declared non-operational. It would remain so until they had ironed out all the issues with their Typhoons, something which everyone was keen to do as quickly as possible. In the meantime, it relieved the pilots of the bind of readiness duty.

Severe overnight frost made the airfield surface serviceable on 14 February, allowing a lot of flying practice to be put in. A practice sweep to Hull by eight Typhoons, including that flown by Plt Off Walter Dring, was led by Sqn Ldr Dundas. During February, four of No 56 Squadron's pilots flew to Brockworth to ferry new Typhoons from the factory to Duxford for eventual use by No 266 Squadron. When the second and third squadrons to be equipped with the Typhoon, Nos 266 and 609, actually moved into Duxford, No 56 moved out to Snailwell on 30 March 1942, from where 'A' Flight operated, while 'B' Flight used RAF Ludham. No 56 shared Snailwell with No 137 Squadron (Westland Whirlwind) and No 268 (AC) Squadron (NA Mustang I). By the middle of April, with the squadron now entirely equipped at Snailwell with 'modified' Mk IB aircraft, the squadron diarist was moved to write: 'Everyone in a very cheerful mood. The squadron has already done 240 hours of practice flying in Typhoons this month. Serviceability is improving and there are hopes that the squadron will be operational soon.'

All of the practice flying was directed at bringing all pilots to a high state of expertise on the Typhoon and thus be declared operational once more. It was natural, therefore, that the full squadron formation flying practised during April would eventually lead to trial wing formations in company with Nos 266 and 609 Squadrons. The first of these took place on 17 April when No 56 flew as top cover to No 266, the whole formation being led by Wg Cdr Denys Gillam DSO, DFC★, AFC, who was now the Duxford wing leader. Spitfires of No 616 Squadron intercepted 266 but failed to spot No 56 Squadron and were themselves 'bounced' by the joyous Typhoon pilots.

Now promoted to flying officer, as a squadron pilot trying to come to terms with this potent aircraft Walter Dring was actively involved with all these issues

Hawker Typhoon fighters of No 56 Squadron. (Author's Collection)

and events. It was on 18 August, just after the squadron moved to Matlaske, that an unusual coincidence occurred involving the loss of Typhoon IB, R7644, and its New Zealand pilot, Sgt James Jones. A squadron formation, including Walter, made a practice sweep across the Fens from Matlaske. Reaching the vicinity of Moulton, near Spalding, at about 12.45, this aircraft dived towards the ground and was seen to break up in the air and crash. It came down on Gibson's Farm, Spalding Gate, Moulton, near the Dring family home. Whether any high spirits were involved in the incident is not known, but Walter wrote later: '[I] did a fairly steep dive; Sgt Jones followed but failed to pull out and went in about half a mile from my home.'

Despite the optimism expressed by the squadron diarist, during May aircraft serviceability took a nose dive. Several new engines had to be fitted that month and there were some days when the squadron could muster only two aircraft to fly. However, by the end of the month serviceability rose once more and everyone was somewhat cheered by rumours of an impending return to operational status. Rumour became reality on 29 May 1942 when Gp Capt John Grandy, Duxford's station commander, visited Snailwell to break the news that the AOC had approved operational status for the squadron. Furthermore, he announced that one flight of four Typhoons was to be detached to the Westhampnett satellite of RAF Tangmere and another flight of four aircraft to RAF Manston. The Typhoon was to be pitted immediately against the bomb-carrying, tip-and-run Messerschmitt Bf 109s harassing land and shipping targets along the south coast. Although they had first been noted in January 1942, these raids began in earnest from about March 1942 and continued until June 1943. The Typhoon pilots were buzzing with expectation and raring to get a crack at the enemy – and they did not have long to wait since these detachments were implemented the very next day.

With Wg Cdr Gillam scenting the prospect of a fight on his old stamping ground at Manston, he flew off to the Kent airfield with 'A' Flight, comprising himself, Flt Lt Ronald Fokes and Fg Offs Robert Deugo and Walter Dring, where they arrived at 11.40. No 56's CO, Sqn Ldr Dundas, took 'B' Flight to Westhampnett in company with Plt Offs Doniger, Pollack and Coombes. Spare pilots followed in a Handley Page Harrow, which dropped off Flt Sgt Myall and Sgt Stuart-Turner together with ground crews at Manston, before flying on to Tangmere with Plt Offs MacDonald and Reed (USA) with the remaining ground crews and the intelligence officer.

Sqn Ldr Dundas was keen to get the job under way and as soon as the pilots had fixed up dispersal and accommodation with the resident No 129 Squadron (Spitfire) boys, he scheduled a sortie for 17.30 that day. Thus the first operational sortie by Typhoons was made by Sqn Ldr Hugh Dundas and Plt Off Norman Doniger, who patrolled – uneventfully – from Selsey Bill to St Catherines Head on the Isle of Wight, landing back at Westhampnett at 18.50. This pair were relieved by Plt Offs Pollack and Coombes, who patrolled at heights between 300 and 3,000ft over the same route. Twice they were vectored on to an X-raid, but despite seeing vapour trails they were unable to make contact. Over at Manston, Plt Off Dring, from 'A' Flight, was quickly off the mark as he was airborne for one of two similar patrols flown in that sector. Next day, the 31st, the Manston Flight put up three patrols of two aircraft each but without success. During the day 'A' Flight was joined by three more Typhoons flown in by Plt Offs Mause and Poulter and Sgt Stimpson, while 'B' Flight also flew two patrols and was joined by Sgts Storey and Woodhouse.

When action finally came, sadly it was for all the wrong reasons. The first day of June dawned a fine clear summer's day with wispy high cirrus cloud and good visibility. During the afternoon 'A' Flight despatched Plt Off Robert Deugo and Sgt Keith Stuart-Turner from Manston to intercept a raid off Dover. Two Spitfires from No 401 Squadron based at Gravesend were also vectored on to the same raid. Plt Off Deugo said later that he followed the vectors (courses) given by the controller, climbing as instructed to 17,000ft to orbit just off Dover. He identified two Spitfires approaching above his section, close enough to see their roundels very clearly. Thinking no more of it, he watched these Spitfires as they curved in towards the Typhoons. Likewise, the Spitfire pilots had spotted the Typhoons but mistook them for Fw 190s and opened fire simultaneously on both aircraft. Sgt Stuart-Turner's aircraft was hit and he must have died instantly because his aircraft turned over on to its back and dived vertically into the sea in flames. Deugo's aircraft was also severely hit but he was able to turn it upside down and bale out. Coming down in the sea he inflated his life raft and spent the next couple of hours bobbing around until picked up by an RAF rescue launch and taken to Dover, where he was admitted to hospital with burns and gunshot wounds. Sadly, this would not be the last case of mistaken identity for Typhoon squadrons.

Patrols along the south coast by section pairs of aircraft continued every day until 7 June 1942, by which time the enemy had still not been brought to battle. Walter Dring, for example, was airborne with Wg Cdr Gillam during the evening of the 5th when they were vectored on to an incoming Ju 88, but returned to Manston without seeing a thing. When the No 56 Squadron detachments were brought to an end, both flights returned to Snailwell.

In addition to carrying out readiness duties and standing patrols, activity was now generally directed at exercising the three-squadron Typhoon wing

Pilots of 'A' Flight, No 56 Squadron at Matlaske, December 1942. From left to right: Sgt E.A. Magee, Plt Off C.T. Stimpson, Fg Off G. Myall, Fg Off A.G.H. Rouse, Fg Off R. Poulter, Fg Off R. Deugo, Sgt F.A. Sullivan. (Ken Ellis Collection)

and although everyone was airborne to this end whenever there was suitable weather, there was much debate at all levels of command on just what type of operation the Typhoon was best suited to. This all came to a head in a meeting held at Duxford on 10 June, chaired by Air Marshal Sholto Douglas, at which Sqn Ldr Dundas presented his own ideas – persuasively – once again. His view was not to exclude the Typhoon from the current concept of offensive sweeps because of its altitude performance limitations, but rather to capital-ise upon its particular strengths within those large-scale operations. Hugh Dundas wrote:

> I proposed, for instance, that an ideal way of using the [Typhoon] Wing would be to send it in for a high-speed sweep round the rear of the main formations as they were withdrawing. We could go in at about 21,000 feet, gradually losing height as we swept around, so that we would be at optimum altitude during the critical stages of our passage. We would attack anything we saw ... not sticking around for dogfights ... but taking advantage of our superior speed to pounce and get away.

The first of these Typhoon wing operations came on 20 June 1942. Wg Cdr Denys Gillam led eleven aircraft from No 56, including Walter Dring, together with a similar number from No 266 Squadron, from Duxford at 15.12 to sweep along the enemy coast from Dunkirk to Boulogne. The wing's third squadron, No 609, was not included in this particular operation. No 56 landed back at Snailwell at 16.20 without having seen any action. The wing continued with this type of operation along the coast of northern France and Belgium at intervals throughout June, July and August 1942, sometimes moving to a forward base on the south coast, but the results were always inconclusive. When any Fw 190s were spotted they always seemed to beat a hasty retreat. Visiting RAF Sutton Bridge for some air-firing practice on 12 July, Walter's ebullience got the better of him when he 'shot up place, by doing one upward roll – practically court-martialled!' It was nearly 'curtains' though on 19 July. Flying R7854, Walter was returning from a wing sweep around Le Touquet when, over mid-Channel, he was attacked by Spitfires. He wrote: 'Section of Spitfires did perfect attack on me. F/O Rouse saw cannons firing as I broke away. No hits.' Walter had seen their intentions just in time.

It was at 06.00 on 30 July that No 56 left Snailwell for RAF West Malling to undertake another of these offensive operations. At 12.20 the whole squadron left West Malling and flew to Gravelines, then along the coast to Cap Gris Nez and thence back to Snailwell. Walter wrote:

We were at 20,000 feet over Calais when suddenly there was a terrific bang and a whoosh of air. I sat panic stricken for a brief moment and thought 'I'm hit' and waited for developments while losing height and turning. I was scared absolutely stiff until I realised my [cockpit] door had blown open, then I calmed down. Coming back over the Channel, one of the new boys, Norwegian Fg Off Erik Haabjørn, reported engine trouble and he slowed to 160mph. Struggling to keep airborne he was down to 2,000 feet, ten miles from the English coast when he was attacked by Spits and shot to hell. Fortunately Haabjørn was unhurt and baled out, spending just fifteen minutes in his life raft before being hauled out by an air-sea rescue launch. It has now developed into a war between 11 Group and 12 Group. As a Belgian in 609 said: 'the Nazis don't need to attack us, they leave it to the Spits!'

Walter took some leave at this point but was back in time for the biggest 'show' so far for the Typhoons and indeed Walter himself (three one-hour sorties). This came on 19 August 1942 when the Typhoon wing was involved in Operation Jubilee: the Dieppe Raid. The RAF committed forty-nine fighter squadrons

to this operation against which the Luftwaffe put up 115 fighters. The scheduled 'dawn show' was cancelled and the first sweep of the day was made from
Duxford at 11.15 when No 56 Squadron Typhoons flew towards Ostend. Ten
miles from the Belgian coast the squadron turned south and followed the coast
down to Mardyck before heading back to West Malling without seeing any
'trade'. 'We had a quick beer and swallowed lunch almost whole and the call
came to attack the bombers that were going for the returning convoy. What
luck, just what our machines are suited for,' wrote Walter later.

Refuelled, the squadron took off from West Malling at 14.00, this time
heading for Le Treport intending to make a sweep back towards Le Touquet.
Flying at 20,000ft altitude, No 56 was acting as top cover for the Duxford
Wing, with No 266 squadron a couple of thousand feet below and No 609
Squadron at 15,000ft.

As the wing approached the coast the leader was advised of enemy bombers coming from Douai to attack British ships heading for home. Nos 266
and 609 Squadrons went for the three Dornier Do 217 bombers and a dozen
Fw 190s escorting them. No 56 stayed at 17,000ft as top cover, holding off
several diving attacks by more groups of Fw 190s coming out of the sun
from about 5,000ft higher and keeping the sky clear until the lower squadrons withdrew. The wing landed back at West Malling satisfied that this first
engagement had shown that the Typhoon could compete with the Fw 190
at medium altitudes, even though it might not be able to outmanoeuvre the
enemy fighter. The squadron was airborne again at 17.00, making a sweep with
No 266 Squadron from Le Touquet to Boulogne for an hour before returning
to Snailwell. Next day No 56 was on top cover duty at 24,000ft as the wing
swept from Dunkirk to Cap Gris Nez, again without drawing German fighters in the vicinity into battle. In the air battle over Dieppe, in addition to the
bomber aircraft committed on both sides, the RAF lost eighty-eight fighter
aircraft compared to the Luftwaffe's twenty-three.

The remainder of August was spent moving the squadron to Matlaske airfield in Norfolk, from where daily readiness and convoy patrols began on the
25th. Walter, in philosophical mood, recalled:

The officers' mess is in a delightful old watermill converted into a modern
house. The stream flows underneath with lots of trout in it. It is miles from
anywhere and on leaving the aerodrome there is complete peace and rustic-
ity far away from the crowd. I have not known such peace of mind since I
joined the RAF. Life is doubly enhanced when there is a danger of losing
the things we like, such as the other pilots' comradeship and the happiness of
squadron life. It seems now that life is rich and full.

Back to reality, the next day saw the squadron airborne at 06.50 to fly over to Duxford for a wing briefing before the three squadrons, including Walter Dring, took off at 08.15 on a low-level sweep from Dunkirk to St Omer and Boulogne – still without provoking any enemy response. The enemy also refused the obvious invitation to come up and fight on 3 September when a Typhoon wing sweep, as top cover to Westland Whirlwinds acting as bombers, was mounted from Duxford. The Typhoons joined a Spitfire wing and swept from Nieuwpoort on a broad front down to Marck, but saw no German activity whatsoever. There was a slightly more aggressive response on the 6th when No 56 sent nine Typhoons to Thorney Island to join the wing on a sweep over Dieppe and Abbeville. Four Fw 190s dived on No 56 Squadron from above and up-sun but broke away without completing an attack. Later, off Boulogne, as the squadron was heading home, more Fw 190s approached but did not attack. The squadron landed at Snailwell to refuel then flew back to Matlaske. The enemy seemed particularly cagey about tangling with Typhoons.

Among the usual patrols and inconclusive scrambles from Matlaske, Walter Dring and Fg Off Aldwyn Rouse had a late scramble at 19.50 on the 8th, becoming airborne in a record one and a half minutes from receiving the order! They chased a Hun out over the North Sea but darkness prevented them finding it, so they returned twenty-five minutes later. Sector Ops was not happy about this early return but night-landing a Typhoon on an unlit airfield was no easy task. A few days later Walter led the dawn patrol and was taxiing along the perimeter track followed by Plt Off Myall. Juggling throttle and brakes while weaving behind that enormous engine cowling, 'Myall taxied right up my backside,' said Walter, 'and his prop completely severed the rear fuselage of what was the CO's machine, badly damaging his own aircraft in the process.' Two more Typhoons out of action!

The squadron chalked up its first 'kill' with a Typhoon on 14 September 1942, when Green Section – Flt Lt Michael Ingle-Finch and Plt Off Wally Coombes – claimed a Ju 88 shot down in the sea off the north Norfolk coast. Interestingly, Wally Coombes was flying a Mk IA armed with twelve machine guns and Ingle-Finch was in a IB with four cannon.

At 13.45 the following day Walter Dring and nine other Typhoons, including the CO's, flew down to Exeter for a 17.00 take-off on a wing sweep at 15,000ft over the Cherbourg peninsula. Once again there was no air or ground opposition and the wing returned to Warmwell for refuelling and No 56 got back to Matlaske at 19.00.

Ever since re-equipping with the Typhoon the squadron had suffered a litany of crashes in addition to the unserviceability caused by technical problems. Walter Dring added to the list on 16 September by severely damaging his aircraft during a bad landing: 'the undercarriage collapsed and I slewed along the ground to a standstill. I sat in the cockpit wishing the earth would open up and swallow me up.'

At that date his was the eighth such accident to 'A' Flight aircraft and it was becoming a touchy subject among all the pilots. The situation came to a head when Gp Capt George Harvey, Coltishall station commander (Matlaske came under Coltishall control), visited the squadron on 21 September. He gathered all pilots at 'B' Flight dispersal to give them a stern talking-to about the numerous 'prangs', and according to the squadron diary: 'meted out justice to some of the more outstanding sinners.' By general discussion he was also trying to find out the real reasons for the mishaps and to discover a cure for them, even by improving the airfield if necessary. Walter Dring spoke up, saying he thought the chief trouble lay in the fact that when they were coming in to land, subconsciously they were all thinking they must not overshoot and several pilots agreed with him. The flight commanders, on the other hand, said they thought the problem was 'overconfidence'.

They were now operating less as a wing. Officialdom seemed to have decided that the Typhoon was neither an effective sweeper nor fighter-vs-fighter aircraft so the Typhoon wing was in effect broken up, with squadrons such as No 56 now operating as individual units. It was around this point that the Typhoon began to be regarded as more suited to the ground attack role with an alternative role as a bomber interceptor. It was in the latter role, though, that the squadron was occupied for the most part.

The weather turned rainy towards the end of the month but there were frequent inconclusive scrambles and on 27 September Walter Dring acted as number two in a section convoy patrol with his 'A' Flight commander, Norwegian Capt (Flt Lt) Gunnar Piltingsrud. It was mid-October before Jerry started to come over more often, with single raiders all over Coltishall sector during the morning of the 19th. Morale flagged somewhat now that the Typhoon wing was disbanded, even though during October the squadron had thirty-five scrambles, carried out thirty-seven shipping and 'stooge' patrols and had started night flying training. However, on 27 October the CO received orders to start flying offensive air-to-ground and low-level air-to-air operations, called 'Rhubarb', so things were looking like they might hot up.

A Rhubarb was the smallest of the operations carried out by RAF fighters over France and the Low Countries. It usually required cloud cover over or near the target and could be authorised at squadron or flight level and flown by up to four aircraft, but generally these sorties were made by only two aircraft. Pilots involved could attack targets of opportunity, which meant they could pounce on just about anything that moved on land, sea or in the air, and

'The Flying Farmer', Flt Lt Walter Dring, No 183 Squadron, 1943. (John & Susan Rowe, Dring Collection)

on any building or structure that seemed to have some military importance. The first successful Rhubarb by the Typhoon pilots of No 56 Squadron was carried out on 17 November 1942.

Things were happening fast on the personnel front in November. First, on the 11th, Sqn Ldr Dundas was promoted to wing commander and posted to Duxford to command a (non-existent) wing of Typhoon bombers. Before the wing could be formed he found himself posted again, this time to a Spitfire wing in North Africa! On the 19th, Battle of Britain veteran Flt Lt Arthur ('Gus') Gowers DFC was promoted to squadron leader and posted away to become CO of No 183 Squadron, at that time in the process of forming as a new Typhoon bomber squadron at RAF Church Fenton. On 24 November, now with 516 hours in his logbook and once again assessed as an 'above average' fighter pilot, Fg Off Walter Dring started his rapid rise upwards with promotion to flight lieutenant and an appointment as a flight commander with No 183 Squadron. His promotion was duly celebrated in the mess and the next day, 25 November 1942, he prepared to take up his new responsibilities at Church Fenton and open a new chapter in his flying career.

No 183 Squadron began its Second World War life on 1 November 1942, marked by the arrival of its first aircraft, a Typhoon Mk IA, R7649, transferred from No 181 Squadron. Flt Lt Dring arrived on 30 November and new pilots began arriving from No 59 OTU. They had to wait a month before more Typhoons were slowly allotted from various sources. Mk IA, R7631 was transferred from No 181 on 1 December and the next day three Mk IBs arrived from No 13 MU: DN273, DN275 and DN297. These were soon followed by Mk IA, R7869 from No 56 Squadron and a Hurricane I, R2680 was flown in from No 32 Squadron. There now followed an intense work-up period of formation, low-flying, aerobatics, cloud-flying, air-firing, bombing and some

No 183 Squadron, Church Fenton, December 1942. Flt Lt Dring (middle row, third from the left), next to Act Sqn Ldr A.V. Gowers (centre). (John & Susan Rowe, Dring Collection)

dogfighting practices. Walter Dring became 'B' Flight commander and worked his new pilots hard whenever the weather allowed.

It was while he was at Church Fenton that Walter met the lady who would become his wife. Section Officer Sheila Coggins was in charge of the station cipher room and, having spotted this attractive young WAAF in the foyer of the cipher office one day, Walter decided he would like to get to know her better. Sheila described how it all began:

> There was a tap on the cipher office door and the same pilot appeared in the doorway. My colleague asked him what he wanted and he replied he just wanted to talk to the other cipher officer. He was told no one was allowed into the office because of the secret nature of its contents but he laughed and came in anyway. He introduced himself as: 'String, because I am a ropey type.' We all had a cup of coffee and biscuits and he told me all about himself. He asked me out for a meal in York and turned up at the WAAF officers mess in an old sports car and we went out and talked about each other's troubles.

'String' was the nickname by which he was known among his RAF contemporaries.

★ ★ ★

More Typhoons arrived in January and February 1943, including DN242, DN249, DN253, DN257, DN271, P8944, R8884, R8885, R8886 and R8933. The actual availability of Typhoons for the practice programme during these early months was constantly diminished by the need to send all of them, in small quantities, to No 13 MU at RAF Henlow for what was said to be 'modification', but what this actually meant was not detailed.

Flt Lt Dring, always at the forefront of things during this intense period, suffered his fair share of problems. He was obliged to make forced landings on 27 January, due to engine failure, and on 9 February when he could only get one wheel of the undercarriage down. He pulled off a successful one-wheeled landing, but caused category 'B' damage to Typhoon DN297; so that was another two aircraft missing for a while. He had engine failures on 18 and 26 February, managing to land intact on both occasions, but had to belly-land when his throttle seized up on 11 March.

By 25 February 1943, equipment and organisation had settled down and the squadron was put on a 'war footing'. For No 183 Squadron there followed a highly mobile existence, in the form of 'exercises' involving carefully detailed moves of the squadron's aircraft and ground support to new locations, from where it was to launch dive-bombing 'attacks' against other RAF airfields. This mobility was what Walter Dring's air war was going to be all about from now on.

It began on 1 March when a convoy of lorries set off with the ground crews and support staff from the Yorkshire base, bound for RAF Cranfield in Bedfordshire, 150 miles to the south. At 08.20 the air component of twelve Typhoons made the transit in slick formation with the CO leading. Two days were allowed for all personnel to settle in and for the pilots to familiarise themselves with maps of the area. At 07.30 on the 4th, eight Typhoons, led by the CO, were despatched to 'attack' RAF Chilbolton, 4 miles south-east of Andover in Hampshire, a flying distance of about 75 miles. The 'attack' was deemed successful and all aircraft returned to Cranfield by 08.55. At 11.55 another eight aircraft were ordered off for a dive-bombing and machine-gun attack on RAF Ibsley, 2 miles north of Ringwood, Hampshire, this time about 100 miles distant. All aircraft returned to Cranfield at 12.30, having had a grand old time beating up all the buildings and the Spitfires and Hurricanes parked out on its airfield. There was no let-up and at 15.34 Flt Lt Walter Dring led a force of eight Typhoons to 'attack' RAF Stoney Cross, 4 miles north-west of Lyndhurst in the New Forest. This frantic war-game programme continued for a few more days until the squadron was moved to RAF Colerne, near Bath, during March 1943.

Little operational flying was undertaken from Colerne and on 8 March it was all change again, now to RAF Gatwick where a unit known as No 123

Airfield was based and No 183 was to join that organisation. No 123 Airfield was the slightly strange collective name given to encompass the three squadrons now based on the airfield. Such units were highly mobile and would act like a completely mobile 'airfield', moving from place to place in convoy, taking with them literally every facility that several squadrons could normally expect to find on a permanent airfield. In the midst of all this to-ing and fro-ing, with the help of a borrowed Hurricane, Walter flew from Colerne to RAF Peterhead to spend a precious, all-too-short couple of days with the love of his life, Sheila, who had been posted to that far distant corner of the land.

Meanwhile, back at Gatwick, there were no more 'war games'. On 17 April No 183 Squadron's war began for real. Ten Typhoons were bombed up and detached to RAF Ford on the Sussex coast for the first operation against a German target across the Channel, but bad weather delayed the operation until the 19th. Take-off was 07.50 and the target was the power station at Yainville, on a prominent bend in the River Seine west of Rouen. Eight Typhoons would make the attack, four armed with 250lb general-purpose (GP) bombs – these aircraft were now being referred to as 'Bombphoons' – and four Typhoons would act as close cover with their cannon only. The No 183 Squadron formation was escorted to and from the target by No IX (Spitfire) Wing from Kenley, led by the illustrious Wg Cdr J.E. 'Johnnie' Johnson. The attack went reasonably well, with the bombers diving at the target from the direction of the nearby town of Duclair and scoring near misses. They made their escape at low level. Two of the escorting Typhoons had a crack with their cannon at a train, while Walter Dring, during his one-hour sortie in DN273, attacked and damaged an army truck. No more offensive operations were mounted during the rest of April and most of the time was spent on more training sorties.

One of the last events the squadron undertook at Gatwick was to join in the celebrations on 1 May to mark the marriage of Flt Lt Walter Dring to Section Officer Sheila Coggins in Christ Church, Banbury. Most of the squadron were able to get to the ceremony and the subsequent party, the squadron diarist noted: 'Judging by their appearance next morning, was a bit of a whizzer!' While Walter and his new bride were on leave, the squadron moved to RAF Lasham, 6 miles south of Basingstoke in Hampshire, on 3 May.

Walter was back with No 183 Squadron on 14 May, just in time to take part in the squadron's second operational sortie. Led by Sqn Ldr Gowers, the target for eight Bombphoons was Triqueville aerodrome, south-east of the Seine estuary, and Walter Dring flew DN408 on this operation. The weather clamped in on the target and it could not be located, so the pilots dumped their bombs and returned to base. Plt Off Berrisford failed to return from this sortie and became the squadron's first operational loss. The squadron moved

A page from Walter Dring's logbook with a photo of him, his bride Sheila and their wedding party on 1 May 1943 pasted in between bombing sorties. (John & Susan Rowe, Dring Collection)

back to Colerne on 30 May but was there less than a week before it was moved to RAF Harrowbeer, 6 miles south of Tavistock in Devon, on 5 June. It was certainly learning about mobility!

Four aircraft were bombed up on 15 June and at 05.30 were escorted by eight others for an armed shipping recco. They all returned due to bad weather but had another go at 09.30; this was also aborted. The weather improved so they were airborne again at 17.00, but since no target was kind enough to present itself they brought the bombs back to base. It was much the same result when four Bombphoons went looking for shipping the following day, but they dumped their bombs before returning to base.

Walter Dring scheduled a Bombphoon Rhubarb sortie for himself and Polish Fg Off Eugeniusz 'Gott' Gottowt on the morning of 17 June, but they had to abandon it when they reached the Sept-Îles off the north coast of Brittany because of insufficient cloud cover. Gottowt had to make a wheels-up landing back at Harrowbeer but he was uninjured. Walter and Gott tried again on the 19th with a bit more success. Making landfall on the Brest peninsula, they skirted the Brest balloon barrage and found two merchant ships anchored in the Goulet. They attacked both vessels in turn at mast-top height, scoring very near misses, believing one bomb to have actually struck one of the ships. One of Gott's bombs failed to release and he was very annoyed that he had to bring it home.

July 1943 saw the Typhoon IBs of No 183 Squadron going out regularly from Harrowbeer on armed shipping recco sorties. These operations involved varying numbers of aircraft but Walter Dring flew always in JP402, which appears to have become 'his' aircraft. For example, on 2 July four Bombphoons, each carrying two 250lb GP bombs, set out for the Brittany coast looking for enemy shipping. Two more of the squadron's Typhoons flew with six from No 193 Squadron which acted as their escort. They flew at sea level to Bréhat, turned west and along the coast to the Sept-Îles, flying at about 3,500ft, 3 miles offshore. Nothing was seen so they all returned to base an hour and a half later. This process was repeated on the 4th, 6th and 8th along the same stretch of the French coast but with the same result – nothing seen to attack.

Yet another movement order was received and on 2 August the squadron was busy packing up to move to RAF Tangmere on the Sussex coast. Walter Dring was given a spot of leave at this point and spent a precious few days with his new wife. He returned to Tangmere on the 8th, when fighter readiness was the pattern for the next couple of weeks, with just a few scrambles to lighten the constant routine of practice flying.

Things hotted up on 16 August, when No 183 Squadron took ten Typhoons, including Walter Dring in JP402, to RAF West Malling in Kent to take part in a Ramrod operation with Nos 197 and 486 Squadrons. Led by Sqn Ldr Gowers, take-off was at 17.10 and No 183 acted as top cover, but this wing operation to the St Pol area was led by Sqn Ldr Desmond Scott of 486 (NZ) Squadron. A number of Fw 190s were seen but were not engaged by No 183 because of the commitment to closely escort the bombers. All of the RAF aircraft returned safely at 18.35.

Next day, in fine weather, the squadron, with Flt Lt Walter Dring in JP368, sent eight aircraft to bomb Poix aerodrome, west of Amiens. Along with Caen-Carpiquet, Poix aerodrome was just about the hottest spot on the Continent for flak at this time. No 183's aircraft were armed with bombs and were covered by twelve fighters from No 486 Squadron. Take-off was at 12.05 and over the aerodrome they encountered considerable flak. Three aircraft sustained hits during the dive-bombing attacks, but two bombs fell on the runway, while the rest fell among the fuel dumps and parked aircraft. All aircraft returned safely.

The Typhoon wing made a fighter sweep under the command of Sqn Ldr Desmond Scott on the 19th and Walter Dring was flying JP368 with seven other aircraft from No 183. The wing made landfall near Trouville at 6,000ft but ran into 10/10ths cloud, so the wing flew back out to sea, then re-crossed the coast near Caen where the weather was clearer. The Typhoons made a wide orbit around Caen and flew down to Bayeux before re-crossing the coast outbound at 4,500ft near Ouistreham. No enemy aircraft were seen, nor was there any sign of flak during the whole of the sortie.

Walter's next sortie came on the evening of 31 August when, flying JP402, he was one of eight Bombphoons that set out to attack Monchy-Breton aerodrome. The bombers were escorted by no fewer than eighteen Typhoons from Nos 197 and 486 Squadrons, but the formation ran into 10/10ths cloud at 4,000–6,000ft mid-Channel and as it stretched well inland, the operation was abandoned.

By way of a change, Walter Dring, in JP402, was one of eight Typhoons from 183 and two from 197 that flew a shipping protection sortie over the English Channel on 2 September 1943. The aircraft took off at 15.00 and flew at 1,500ft on a course of 100° until they reached the patrol line some 10 miles off Dungeness. They patrolled from there on a line taking them to 12 miles off Boulogne, with No 197 Squadron's Typhoons 'on the deck' and the 183 boys at 3,000ft. No enemy aircraft appeared and the patrol was back at Tangmere at 17.00.

At 18.00 two days later, Walter, in JP402 again, and nine others of No 183 flew an escort operation to a force of eighteen NA B-25 Mitchell light bombers attacking Boulogne harbour. They made a perfect rendezvous with the bombers and despite encountering heavy, accurate flak the attack went according to plan and everyone returned safely an hour later. No 486 Squadron was also part of the same escorting force and Sqn Ldr Scott recalled: 'The flak was murderous. When you can hear flak, then you know it is getting close!'

It was back to Bombphoon duty for Walter again on 6 September when he and seven other aircraft, escorted by Typhoons from Nos 197 and 486 Squadrons, dive-bombed the railway marshalling yard at Serquex, near Dieppe. They reckoned 80 per cent of the bombs hit rail tracks and locomotive sheds, at a cost of only one aircraft slightly damaged by light flak. Some aircraft from the other squadrons involved were shot down.

This was the last of the action for Walter in September, but there was always lots of non-op flying going on in the form of air tests, formation, dogfighting and bombing practice; there was no let-up in the quest to keep pilots sharp. The squadron was on the move again, this time to RAF Perranporth, a cliff-top airfield on the north coast of Cornwall. One of the more interesting aspects of this airfield was that if one landed towards the sea and ran out of runway there was no run-off area – just an 80ft sheer drop on to the beach below! With the onset of autumn the weather turned sour and curtailed flying activities.

On 3 October 1943, Flt Lt Walter Dring shot down his own and No 183's first enemy aircraft. The weather had picked up and Walter, flying his trusty JP402 'S' (now with 'Sheila' painted on the cowling), was leading eight Typhoons from No 183 as fighter escort to some Mosquito bombers that were attacking a target at Guerlédan, near Pontivy in central Brittany. Take-off was at 13.05 and No 183 Squadron was to act as forward cover to the Mosquitoes

Flt Lt Walter Dring of No 183 Squadron standing on the wing of his Hawker Typhoon, R8884, RAF Gatwick, April 1943. (John & Susan Rowe, Dring Collection)

as they left France. While the attack was taking place, the Typhoons swept around the exit route then found the Mosquitoes, which were approaching the coast at 1,000ft. The Typhoons were on the port side and about 1,000ft above the bombers when they were engaged by six enemy aircraft (E/A). Walter's combat report describes what happened next:

I was leading Jungle Green section on Ramrod 90 as forward cover to Mosquitoes. We had completed our sweep and were re-crossing the French coast at 6,000 feet, flying above cloud and diving gently to locate the returning bombers. On breaking cloud, I saw the Mosquitoes going west. As we were about to turn in order to form up on them, I saw Blue section being attacked head-on by six E/A, five Fw 190s and one Me 109. They made a zoom attack from the cloud base and climbed back into the cloud base again. Blue section positioned themselves on the port side of the bombers and about 1,000 feet above. I stayed on the starboard side and slightly above. After flying about a mile on a northerly course I saw Blue section being attacked by an E/A. I called Blue section to break and turned port into the attack. I saw an aircraft coming towards and above me. It then pulled into a climb and, in plain view, I clearly recognised it as an Fw 190. I opened

fire with a one-second burst from 350 yards range with full deflection. The
Fw 190 continued his climbing turn to starboard, enabling me to close in to
line astern at about 500 feet altitude. I gave him 3 one-second bursts, closing
from 300 to 150 yards as I did so. The final burst was a no-deflection burst in
dead line astern. I saw what looked like black oil pouring from the aircraft.
I then broke off my attack, as I knew there were more enemy aircraft behind.
Suddenly I saw the Fw 190 dive steeply towards the sea and as it was about
to hit the water I saw the hood fly off. It hit the sea and disappeared immediately. There was no sign of the pilot and I heard 'Moocher' Leader (Sqn Ldr
Fokes of 257 Sqn) say that he had seen the E/A go in. I found myself alone
and joined up with another Typhoon which proved to be Blue 4 and we
returned to base as a section.

Walter Dring's victory was confirmed as a Fw 190 destroyed for the expendi-
ture of 120 rounds of 20mm cannon ammunition. Post-war research by
aviation historian Chris Goss revealed the Luftwaffe aircraft to be Fw 190
A-5, Wk Nr 7288, from II./JG 2, based at Cormeilles airfield and flown by
Lt Johann-Heinrich Achenbach.

Fg Off J.E. Mitchell of 'A' Flight also claimed a Fw 190 as destroyed and
although that was confirmed at the time, post-war research shows it did not
actually crash. All in all, it had been a good day for the squadron and a grand
celebration was held at The Stork pub that evening where the CO split a prize
of £5 – promised for the first E/A destroyed – between Dring and Mitchell.

Ramrod and Circus operations were being mounted almost daily by the
RAF over occupied territory and No 183 Squadron was called upon from time
to time to provide high cover to the participating bombers. On 8 October
Walter Dring led eight Typhoons as high cover to Boston bombers and their
close escort. Take-off from Perranporth was at 14.50 and, setting course from
the Lizard, they joined the formation ten minutes later as it crossed the French
coast at 18,000ft, east of Ushant. They were over the target of Poulmic at 15.33
and after completion of that action the wing followed the bombers out, crossing the coast at Plouescat, near Roscoff, at 13,000ft. No enemy air activity was
seen and everyone returned safely to Perranporth by 16.15. A similar operation was mounted next day as high cover to Mitchells from No 10 Group for
Ramrod 92. Walter was flying his usual JP402, one of eight Typhoons from
No 183 Squadron. They met up with eight more Typhoons from No 257
Squadron and set course from Start Point to the French coast at Lesneven, west
of Morlaix. After cruising around the target area of Brest/Guipavas airfield, for
about eight minutes without sighting either the bombers or the enemy, the
Typhoons withdrew and flew back to Perranporth.

By 14 October the squadron had moved again, this time to RAF Predannack on the Lizard in Cornwall. The first operation from the new base was an early morning shipping strike mounted that day to the Goulet estuary at Brest. Led by Flt Lt McAdam, three fighters, including Walter in JP402, and four Bombphoons took off from Predannack at 07.23 and flew in formation to the target area. Two small ships were found off Pointe de St Mathieu in the Iroise and Walter and the other two fighters immediately attacked these, raking them with cannon fire. As the fighters broke away, one pair of bombers dived on each ship and scored several near misses with their 250lb bombs. Two Typhoons were slightly damaged by light flak but no one was hurt and all the aircraft were safely back at Predannack by 08.35.

Enemy light flak was by far the biggest menace for a fighter-bomber pilot and it was inevitable that the more sorties one did, the greater the risk was of being hit. Walter Dring's flying career took another major turn on 24 October as the result of an attack on the blockade runner *Munsterland*, laden with tungsten ore, in Cherbourg harbour. During this one-hour operation No 183 Squadron suffered its most serious losses to date. The CO, Sqn Ldr Arthur Gowers DFC, flying JP396, was seen to go down in flames just outside the mole of the harbour, while Fg Off Gerry Rawson and Fg Off P.W.B. Timms did not return either. One of the latter was seen to bale out but Gowers was posted as missing in action. 'Gus' Gowers had been with the squadron since its formation and the high morale prevailing was due to his excellent leadership and example. Gerald 'Gerry' Rawson was later posted as missing in action, while 'Timmy' Timms was the one who baled out. He was picked up by the Germans and spent the rest of the war as a prisoner in Stalag Luft I. Fg Off Munrowd's aircraft also took a bad flak hit in the tail and he had to nurse the Typhoon back to England where he made a perfect belly landing at RAF Warmwell. The heavy flak encountered, together with the general melee, had split up the squadron and aircraft landed back at various airfields: Warmwell, Ibsley and Tarrant Rushton. It took the whole of the next day to get them all back to Predannack.

Walter Dring had come a long way in a short time and on 25 October he found himself promoted to acting squadron leader and placed in charge of No 183 – the best choice according to all the pilots.

After the recent losses it was vital that Walter should get the squadron focused squarely on the job in hand so, on 26 October, he scheduled a full squadron formation practice during the morning and a dive-bombing attack on Poulmic/ Lanveoc seaplane base, on the south side of the Brest estuary, that afternoon. With Walter leading, take-off was at 13.45 and course was set from the Lizard. The formation of eight Bombphoons skimmed the waves for twenty minutes, then climbed to 13,000ft to cross the French coast at Cameret-sur-Mer, west of Crozon, a few miles from the target. Flying across the target in echelon, they each peeled off and dived to 5,000ft, released their bombs and zoomed back up to 8,000ft to reform. Thirteen bombs were seen to explode around the hangars, mess buildings and workshops, with dust and debris rising to 1,000ft. Flak was heavy and pretty accurate for the height but fortunately no one was hit. Walter led the squadron away from the Brest defences and on the way out, swept the area Sizun-Landerneau-Landivisiau searching for enemy aircraft. None was seen and all aircraft returned to Predannack at 15.15.

★ ★ ★

Typhoon squadron commanders were constantly reviewing their techniques for carrying out these ground attack sorties. Some months earlier, the optimum size for a Typhoon formation was found to be eight aircraft. Current practice for dive-bombing attacks, such as the one mentioned above, was to do a maximum-rate 'battle-climb' – at around 185mph – from 'the deck' to the planned attack altitude of around 12–13,000ft. Sqn Ldr Dring would then order his aircraft into echelon – he preferred port echelon but it depended on circumstances – and with each pilot knowing his position in the line it was imperative – and expected – that this manoeuvre would be carried out slickly and quickly while the CO kept his eye on the target. As the formation changed to echelon the order was also given to arm the bombs. Walter would watch the target position change until it passed beneath his starboard wing, then call: 'Target 3 o'clock below, diving now!' Moving the control column firmly to the right and back, right rudder on, with about 130° bank his Typhoon went down in an almost vertical attack dive, nose pointing at the target – and everyone followed him at one-second intervals. Those with the hardest job were the pilots in the positions furthest from the formation leader, as the target went well past them by the time it was the last one's turn to wing-over – and any flak gunners had had good practice on those going down before him! The 7-ton Typhoon built up speed rapidly and could exceed 400mph by the time the bomb release altitude, at say 4,000ft, was reached. Bringing the nose of the aircraft on to the aiming point, the pilot pressed the bomb release button on the end of the throttle lever and pulled back on the control column to get out of the dive and climb back up to rejoin the formation at the designated altitude. It was at this point that, depending on the severity of the pull-out, the G-force exerted enormous pressure on the pilot. On these operations it was quite normal for the more experienced pilots to pull as much 'G' as they could stand, often holding their breath and pulling in their stomach muscles tightly to keep the blood in their upper half, teetering on the edge of or just losing their vision, but not their consciousness, in order to regain height and get out of the worst of the flak as quickly as possible. The Typhoon was tough enough to take more G-force than its pilots could handle.

Always concerned for his pilots' welfare and ensuring they were rested and did not do every 'show', Walter Dring pushed himself hard, personally leading most of the difficult operations carried out by No 183 Squadron. On 28 October, eight aircraft led by Walter flew to RAF Warmwell to mount another attack on Nos 5 and 6 dry docks at Cherbourg, where the 6,000-ton ship, attacked previously, was reported to be berthed. This operation was to coincide with attacks by Whirlwind and Boston bombers, and the Typhoons, armed with two 500lb GP bombs, were to bomb five minutes after the Whirlwinds. Take-off from Warmwell was at 14.30. Standard dive-bombing procedure was carried out from 12,000ft, with bomb release at 7,000ft, but with heavy flak coming up, no direct hits on the ship were observed. On the next day, the 29th, Dring led eight Bombphoons across the Channel, this time to hit Brest/Guipavas aerodrome with two 500lb bombs each.

A big operation was mounted on 2 November with Walter leading a formation of ten aircraft – six Bombphoons and four fighters for flak suppression – on a shipping strike to Ushant. Here, flying at about 250ft between the island and the mainland, and 5 miles west of Camaret, they sighted two merchant vessels of 2,000 tons and 800 tons, steaming westwards in line astern. Walter ordered the anti-flak fighters to attack the larger vessel, while he split up the

bombers into two groups to make runs on both ships simultaneously. The bombing runs were made at wave-top height, aiming the aircraft directly at the ship's side, and all aircraft were met with a hail of 20mm flak fired at them from both ships. With tracer zipping almost like a funnel towards each attacker, the judgement of when to hit the release button or pull up to clear the masts and

Photo portrait of Sqn Ldr Walter Dring DFC when CO of No 183 Squadron, 1944. (John & Susan Rowe, Dring Collection)

superstructure was far from easy. Walter led the way in and then circled while the rest made their runs. Someone must have judged it right because the larger ship was seen on fire and possibly sinking, while the smaller one was enveloped in smoke. However, JP184 flown by Fg Off Allan Palmer was hit by flak. Palmer's wingman saw the aircraft pull up to about 200ft, then the port wing dropped and it crashed into the sea. Palmer's body was not recovered.

On 5 November Walter Dring was in JP136 leading a dive-bombing attack on Poulmic airfield near Brest. Armed with two 500lb bombs each, his eight aircraft flew at low level towards the French coast but when they were about to climb to altitude they entered 10/10ths cloud at 2,000ft with the top at 4,500ft. Walter decided it was impossible to bomb at that level and aborted the show. Bomb-arming switches were turned off and the bombs released into the sea but Plt Off Arthur Napier, flying as No 3 in the leading flight, nearly went the same way as the bombs. He was flying so close to the surface of the sea that his prop blades hit the water and he was engulfed by a cloud of spray. He managed to stay airborne and landed at Predannack with bent prop-tips, damaged bomb racks and loads of vibration.

Having been flying almost constantly up to this point Walter decided it was time to let someone else lead some operations for a change. In Flt Lt Allan McAdam AFC, Walter had a worthy deputy who could be relied upon to lead the squadron in an equally aggressive way. Walter returned to the fray on 21 November in JP128, leading eight Bombphoons and two anti-flak fighters on an unproductive armed shipping recco to the Ushant area.

It seems likely during the short period Walter was not flying ops that he was away getting the latest information about the use of rocket-powered projectiles (RPs) for the Typhoon. The standard RP eventually used by Typhoons consisted of a metal warhead, 6in in diameter, filled with high explosive weighing 60lb, fitted to one end of a 3in metal tube packed with cordite propellant that was fired by an electrical circuit. Around the rear or exhaust end of the tube were four small stabilising fins. When ignited electrically, the cordite burned to produce a jet of rapidly expanding gas that forced the projectile to slide off its rail at ever-increasing speed through the air, until all the propellant was burned up. The Typhoon was fitted with four rails under each wing to carry the RPs, one per rail. Being propelled by a rocket, the force of impact was greater than that achieved by a conventional bomb. The rocket principle also caused no recoil effect on the aeroplane and together with its four 20mm cannon, an RP-equipped Typhoon represented a highly manoeuvrable and potent aerial artillery platform. It took some skill to aim the projectiles properly. The cockpit reflector sight had two settings, one of which allowed for the RPs to be positioned lower than the guns, but the pilot also had to make allowance for trajectory drop after firing.

No 183 Squadron had its first opportunity to try out this new weapon on 22 November 1943 when Walter Dring, flying RP-armed JP136, led ten aircraft on an armed shipping recco sortie to the area of Pointe du Raz. Plt Off Harbutt was in the only other RP-armed Typhoon, JP213, while the remaining eight acted as fighter cover. The crossing to Ushant was made down on the deck and the formation turned east, soon coming across a juicy target. One mile west of Cap de la Chevre, a 4,000-ton vessel was sighted sailing south-south-west escorted by no fewer than seven minesweepers. With visibility deteriorating, 7/10ths cloud at 1,000ft lowering to 600ft and with frequent heavy rain, Walter ordered the fighters to circle out of range while he and Harbutt each dived at the merchant ship firing all their RPs in a single pass. During the dives, flak of all calibres came up at them from every vessel, but probably because the Typhoons had come upon the convoy so rapidly, its gunners were out of luck and the two Typhoons escaped unscathed. Equally, no RP hits were seen either and the Typhoons disappeared into the murk heading for home.

Keen to get the hang of the RPs, Sqn Ldr Dring went out at 08.15 the next morning to the same area off Ushant, leading eight Typhoons in JP209. Two Typhoons were armed with RPs – one of which was Walter's – while the rest acted as anti-flak cover. Turning towards the French coast, two ships of about 4,000 tons each were sighted. These looked like flak-ships and when intense gunfire started to come up, this was quickly confirmed. Everything from multiple pom-poms, 20mm and even 3.7in shells made the attack a dangerous enterprise, but flanked by fighters making cannon-strafe passes, the two RP aircraft fired their projectiles and everyone emerged unharmed. Neither was any damage done to the flak-ships. An attempt was made to repeat this scenario during the afternoon of the next day, with Walter leading a formation of four Bombphoons and six anti-flak fighters into the Goulet. However, the weather was poor, the sea very rough and there was nothing doing this time, so the formation returned, minus bombs, to base.

November the 26th was a busy day. Taking off at 08.45, Flt Lt McAdam led the squadron back to the Goulet but had no success and was back by 09.50. At 16.40 No 10 Group mounted a Ramrod to bomb Martinvast airfield and No 183 Squadron led by Sqn Ldr Dring provided eight Bombphoons, each armed with two 500lb medium-capacity (MC) bombs with instantaneous fuses. Course was set from Harrowbeer, flying at sea level for twenty minutes, then climbing to 11,000ft over the French coast just south of Cap de Flamanville. Following a railway line the formation reached the target which was dive-bombed from 11,000ft down to 6,000ft amid moderate flak. It was a source of great irritation that despite all bombs falling within the target area, all failed to explode! Flt Lt McAdam took the squadron back to the Goulet next day and had better success against a couple of minesweepers, both of which were strafed and one hit on the waterline.

Two 45-gallon drop tanks were fitted to each of No 183's six Typhoon fighters for a long-range Rodeo sortie to the Kerlin-Bastard area of the Bay of Biscay. In company with ten Typhoons from No 257 Squadron, and two Spitfire squadrons making up the wing formation, it was an operation designed to tempt the Luftwaffe into the air for a fight. Taking off at 14.00, the Typhoons flew in two groups of eight aircraft at sea level until they reached the target area, then climbed to 8,000ft where, with visibility of 25 miles, they circled in the crisp, clear air while increasing their altitude to 12,000ft. The Spitfires provided top cover at 20,000ft waiting for the opportunity to drop on the enemy should he be so bold as to appear. In the event it all fizzled out and apart from seeing a couple of Me 410s on the airfield and a stationary 8,000-ton merchant vessel near Île de Groix, no enemy aircraft came anywhere near the Typhoons and all returned safely to base. Actually, the outward journey itself was not without incident. There was no cockpit fuel gauge for the drop tanks, so after taking off on main tanks, a signal was given in the air for everyone to switch to the first drop tank and run on it for a pre-briefed period of time. Another signal from the formation leader prompted a switch-over to the second tank, which would again be used for the set period of time. At a third signal the pilots would switch to the main tank and jettison the drop tanks. This latter point was reached near Lorient and the wing leader, Wg Cdr Denys Gillam, duly gave the order to drop the tanks. This was all very well but he seemed to have forgotten that eight aircraft of No 257 Squadron were in front of and slightly above the formation of six 183 plus two 257 aircraft. On his signal, sixteen drop tanks from the first group whizzed back towards the second group, which had to take rapid and violent evasive manoeuvres to miss these incoming aluminium missiles! The leader of the second formation was Walter Dring in JR128 'S', who turned the air blue with his protest to the Wingco at this bombardment. The Wingco at least had the good grace to apologise.

Things looked up on 18 December when Sqn Ldr Dring led eight Typhoon fighters with drop tanks on a long-range escort sortie to Concarneau in the Bay of Biscay. Take-off was at 11.05 and the Typhoons met up with a squadron of torpedo-carrying Beaufighters from Coastal Command. The Beaufighters took up line astern and the Typhoons flew four on each side of the line. Under a 3,000ft overcast sky with rain showers, keeping station on the slower and heavily laden torpedo bombers was tricky, and being responsible for navigation, the bombers took a wide course around Brest to the west of Ushant to approach Concarneau at 800ft from the south-west. The target was a convoy creeping along close inshore, comprising a 6,000-ton merchant vessel escorted by two destroyers and two E-boats. The Beaufighters attacked the merchant vessel and two torpedo hits were seen. Going in with the first of the bombers, Flt Lt S.J. Lovell and Fg Off Peter Brett attacked the ship with cannon fire and broke away when the torpedoes exploded, while the rest of the squadron made dummy passes at the targets as each of the other Beaufighters made their runs. This tactic was successful in putting off the enemy gunners because, despite being fired upon from all the ships and from gun emplacements behind Concarneau town, none of the attackers was shot down, although Fg Off C.N. Walley made a wheels-up landing back at Predannack because he had a flak hole through his wing and thought a tyre had burst. This sortie lasted two hours and thirty-five minutes.

'No-Ball' was the code name for V-1 launch sites in the occupied countries. These launch sites for the Fieseler Fi 103 (V-1) pulse-jet-propelled missile, colloquially known as a 'Doodlebug' or 'Buzz-bomb', were relatively small constructions often built in wooded areas for concealment, making them difficult to spot from the air. The sites contained a concrete, ski-shaped missile launch ramp and associated buildings, and No 186 Squadron, among others, was tasked several times to make dive-bomb attacks on some sites under construction. The missiles, Hitler's first 'V' weapon, had a warhead of 1,900lb of explosive, a range of 150 miles and the ramps were directed mainly – although not entirely – at England and London in particular. The first V-1 missiles were not launched against England until 13 June 1944, but sites were being built prolifically along the Channel strip of France, Belgium and Holland many months prior to operational use. Once this new weapon had been identified and linked with the construction sites discovered in France, it became a target for Allied bombers of all types.

One such operation was mounted on 22 December, when Walter Dring, flying JR128 'S', personally led two sorties that day to one of these 'ski' sites being built near Cherbourg. Taking off from RAF Harrowbeer, to which the squadron had flown for the operation, at 11.00, leading a formation of seven Bombphoons from No 183 Squadron, Walter reached and, in a clear sky, identified the No-Ball target near Maupertus at 11.32. With No 193 Squadron acting as top cover, Walter ordered his squadron into echelon at 10,000ft altitude and led the wing-over on to the target. He released his two 500-pounders at 5,000ft in a dive before zooming back up to reform his aircraft for the trip home. German flak was sporadic and inaccurate but only one bomb-burst in the target area was spotted. They landed back at 12.25 and after a debrief, a second sortie was planned against a different No-Ball target in the same area, this time at full wing strength. No 183 supplied eleven Bombphoons and

No 164 a further five, while Nos 193 and 266 Squadrons provided sixteen fighters to act as top cover for the bombers. Take-off was at 15.00.

The weather was fine until the French coast when 8/10ths to 10/10ths cloud south of Cherbourg made it impossible to identify the new target. Turning the formation westwards, Walter Dring spotted, through a gap in the clouds, the construction site he had bombed that morning and decided to bomb that instead. One of the pilots flying with Walter on that op, Fg Off Peter Brett, wrote a vivid description of the dive-bombing attack:

As we approached the target area, the cloud cover was almost complete. However the CO [Dring] put us in echelon port and then started a slow turn to starboard to see if he could pick up the target. He managed to spot what we were aiming for through a small hole in the clouds and tightened up his turn to keep it in sight, as he called the 'arm bombs' and 'diving now' orders. I was flying at number two to the leader of the second four of the second squadron [eight Typhoon aircraft was, in the light of practical experience, considered to be the optimum number for a 'squadron' formation; therefore, for the duration of this op, for example, Peter Brett in JR145 'A', Fg Off Foster in JP973 'E' and Flt Sgt Grant in JP601 'L', all from 183 Squadron, became temporarily attached to the five Typhoons from No 193 Squadron, referred to here as the 'second squadron'.] which made me fourteenth of the sixteen aircraft to dive. It also meant that I had to keep on opening up the throttle in order to keep up as I was on the far left hand end of a string of aircraft turning right. By the time that the aircraft in front of me peeled off into the dive, I was nearly at full throttle and banked steeply to keep in formation. I just managed to glimpse the target through the small hole in the cloud as I peeled over into the dive but had to pull over almost inverted to get round on to the line of the bombing dive. As soon as I was in the dive I realised that I was going much too fast but there was nothing I could do except throttle back in fine pitch and hope that the following pilot would be able to keep clear. I concentrated on lining up with the target, released my bombs and pulled out. By this time I was experienced enough to pull the maximum 'G' I could stand and had learned that this could be increased by putting my feet up on the 'high' rudder pedals, curling up into a ball and yelling as loudly as possible. All of which tended to push blood up into the head and thus help counteract the effects of 'G' force. Even so, my vision went immediately and I blacked out almost completely. When my vision returned I was going almost straight up and just had time to see my airspeed was well over 450mph, before I was back in cloud. Before I had time to settle onto instruments I was through the cloud layer and found I was shooting up past the rest of the formation, although my airspeed was bleeding off rapidly and I quickly rejoined. The trip back was uneventful but I was unsure whether I had been hit by flak or not. The aircraft seemed noisier than usual and I was having to use very slightly more throttle and higher revs to keep station. On landing at Harrowbeer, the local ground crew drew my attention to the undersides of both wings. Several rivets had 'popped' at the point where the wing 'cranked' and this had allowed the metal skinning to pull away from the rib and left a gap of a centimetre. This had been enough to cause a slight increase in drag and change the noise and feel of the aircraft in flight. As far as anybody could tell, the only way this could have happened is that I had far exceeded the maximum speed and consequently the maximum 'G' on pullout, which had actually bent the wings! I was considered to be extremely lucky to have survived.

Despite accurate medium and heavy flak, on this occasion several bombs were seen to fall in the target area.

There was no operational let-up over Christmas 1943. At 12.30 on Christmas Eve, Flt Lt Lovell led six aircraft to dive-bomb Guipavas airfield. This was followed at 16.35 by Walter Dring leading four Bombphoons on an armed shipping recco to the favourite hunting ground around Ushant, the Goulet and Batz, but nothing was sighted and the aircraft were back by 18.00. Christmas Day did indeed bring a present for Sqn Ldr Dring, in the form of a shared claim (one-third) for an enemy aircraft shot down during a long-range fighter sweep to Kerlin-Bastard airfield. Walter took off at 14.00 in JR128 'S' with four other aircraft, arriving over the target at an altitude of 5,000ft. He spotted an enemy aircraft taxiing on to the runway below and while orbiting the airfield watched it take off. In his combat report he described what happened next:

[As Blue leader] I gave the order to my section to go in line astern and doing a half-roll, I dived on the aircraft which was then at a height of 500 feet, closing in on it at a speed of 380–400mph. At a range of about 400 yards I gave it a short burst, following this with another at 300 yards and giving a final burst from about 200–150 yards. I gave 30° deflection on the port side and estimate the e/a [enemy aircraft] was doing about 140mph. I saw strikes in the front of the e/a and on the port engines, the outer engine being set on fire. Return fire was experienced from the dorsal turret ahead of the tail. After my attack I broke away to port to avoid hitting the e/a and looking over my shoulder, saw that my numbers 2 and 3 had delivered their attacks and that the e/a was going down in flames in a 45° dive. I saw no one get out and later saw it burning on the ground, with smoke rising to about 500 feet.

Flt Lt Raymond Hartley, on his first operational sortie with the squadron, described his part in the action:

> I was flying as No 2 to Blue Leader. As we arrived over the target I heard the order to go into line astern. We were then at 5,000 feet and I saw Blue Leader begin his attack on the e/a from astern. I followed him down and as he began to break away, succeeded in getting in a burst closing in from about 450 yards to 250 yards, with 5° deflection changing to dead astern. I saw one of the starboard engines burst into flames and then I broke away to starboard almost passing over the e/a. I turned and followed Blue Leader and rejoined the rest of the formation. During my attack I experienced return fire from the dorsal turret.

No 183 Squadron's operational diary recorded this aircraft as 'an FW 200K', but post-war research by historian Chris Goss identified it as Heinkel He 177A-3 bomber, Werk Nummer 535672, operated by 6/KG 40. When attacked by Walter Dring it was about to fly from Kerlin-Bastard airfield at Lorient to Bordeaux-Mérignac airfield and was destroyed in the attack. The crew of four, Ofw Hans Behr, Fw Werner Götze, Ofw Kurt Wyborny and Ofw Paul Herzog, all died when the He 177 came down in La Fontaine de Kériaquel in the village of Pont Scorff, about 4 miles north of the airfield.

Walter Dring led armed shipping, fighter sweep and dive-bombing operations – usually in JR 128 – to the Brest area on 27, 28, 30 and 31 December 1943, with the squadron often flying two such operations in a day. He always led from the front and, while sparing neither himself nor his pilots in this constant harrying of the enemy airfields, rocket installations and shipping movements, he remained a popular and inspiring CO. In his letters home, Walter said that as an officer having command he must be in the lead and do the leading, and even though he might come in for some criticism, he just had to get on with it. He said: 'Responsibility makes character.' He pushed his pilots hard but found it easy to mix with them and he looked after them. Fg Off Peter Brett, for example, recalled that the CO always arranged things so that pilots going on leave could fly an aircraft to an airfield near their destination which would then be picked up and flown back by another pilot returning from leave, thus saving them a lot of travelling time. New Year's Day 1944 brought recognition of Walter's efforts with the award of a DFC. The citation read:

> This officer has completed much operational flying and has displayed great skill and fine fighting qualities throughout. He is a most efficient squadron commander and recently he has led his formation in a series of successful

attacks on airfields and shipping. On one of the latter occasions, hits were obtained on two merchant vessels. Squadron Leader Dring has displayed great leadership and determination. He has destroyed one enemy aircraft.

With the New Year celebrations over it was back to attacks on airfields, shipping and high-priority No-Ball targets in the Cherbourg area. On 4 January Walter led two pairs of Bombphoons on dive-bomb attacks against two separate flying bomb sites. Taking off from Harrowbeer and returning to Predannack, the results were inconclusive and the squadron went back twice on the 6th for another go.

At first light, Walter Dring, in JR 128, took ten aircraft over to Harrowbeer and from there at 10.40, led eight aircraft to the site south-west of Cherbourg. The weather was much better this time and the target was clearly identified. In what was now the squadron's 'standard' procedure, the Bombphoons dived in two sections of four from 9,000ft, releasing their 500lb bombs at 4,000ft before zooming to reform. Bomb-bursts were well concentrated in the target area but damage could not be assessed due to the amount of smoke billowing up. The formation landed back at Harrowbeer at 11.45 to refuel, rearm and grab a bite to eat before take-off at 14.55 for the same target. Once again, Walter led the squadron and the bombs were seen to fall right in the target area or very close to it. Flak on both occasions had been light to moderate, coming up mainly from Cherbourg itself, and this was thought to be due to the No-Ball site being still under construction and not yet protected by its own guns; both sorties were considered to have been successful.

Since the turn of the year it was becoming obvious that the pressure on all squadrons was being ratcheted up, with two operations a day now becoming a regular occurrence. Walter Dring saw it as his duty to lead from the

Portrait of 'String': Sqn Ldr Walter Dring, OC No 183 Squadron, drawn and signed by Cuthbert Orde on 28 August 1943. (John & Susan Rowe, Dring Collection)

front, so running a squadron and flying ground attack operations day after day no doubt had a cumulative effect on him; in those days little was known about combat stress, and neither was there much time to dwell on it.

On the 7th, Walter, still using JR128, led eight Typhoon fighters on an uneventful fighter sweep over the Cherbourg peninsula. Taking off from Predannack at 09.40 they were back at 11.15 to refuel and have bomb racks and 500-pounders attached, grab lunch and get briefed for a dive-bombing sortie to the No-Ball site near Cherbourg. Following the same routine as before, the target was plastered but Flt Sgt Grant in JP973 took a hit in one wing and had to be escorted by his section directly to RAF Warmwell where he landed safely. The rest of the squadron landed back at Predannack at 16.45.

Orders were received to have another crack at Kerlin-Bastard airfield near Lorient, so long-range petrol tanks were fitted on the 8th. Take-off was at 15.35 and Walter Dring led eight Typhoons at wave-top height out to the west of Ushant, making landfall over Îles de Glénan where they were greeted by light flak. The weather was poor, with cloud base at 2,000ft and frequent rainstorms, so they kept down low until near the target. Climbing to 1,000ft over the airfield, they swept around the area but no enemy aircraft were seen, so a course was set for home. Four vessels of about 3–4,000 tons each were spotted creeping along the coast and sporadic flak came up from them. As the Typhoons flew over Île de Groix, a 400-ton coaster was seen more or less on their track, about 6 miles south-west of the island, so Flt Lt McAdam made a firing pass at it, scoring hits on the bridge and superstructure. The formation then turned north at 500ft and, with a calm, grey sea and an equally grey, low cloud base, everyone was concentrating on finding and keeping some sort of horizon and maintaining the formation – no easy task with visibility not much more than 3 miles. Everyone landed safely at 17.45.

For nearly a week there was little flying due to poor weather, but by the 14th it had improved and the Cherbourg No-Ball site came in for more attention. At first light, twelve Bombphoons flew to Harrowbeer and Walter led two sorties, the first at 12.10 and the second at 15.45. The Germans seemed to have woken up somewhat at this construction site and flak was heavy and quite accurate during both operations. The site was dive-bombed from 11,000ft down to bomb release at 5,000ft, with hits seen on buildings all over the target area. During the second attack the squadron suffered the loss of Flt Lt Allan McAdam DFC, AFC, who was last seen going down in his dive and is believed to have been hit by the intense flak barrage.

The weather towards the end of January was good enough for a series of long-range fighter sweeps to the Kerlin-Bastard airfield area. Walter flew JP385 for sorties on 27, 28 and 29 January, during which two flights of three

Typhoons skirted Ushant below the cloud base at 2,000ft before sweeping in from the Bay of Biscay to attack the aerodrome with cannon fire from all sides. They then hurtled away across the Brest peninsula at 'zero' feet. Flt Lt Lord led the second sortie against the airfield on the afternoon of the 28th. During the return leg, Flt Sgt Robin Philipps' engine overheated and he ditched in JP402. The formation circled the spot but there was no sign of the pilot and the Trinidadian was posted as missing in action, and is remembered on Runnymede Memorial.

On the 29th, the following day, Walter Dring led two long-range sorties, the first of which was a more adventurous, low-level operation than those previously undertaken. Taking off at 10.10, he led a formation of six Typhoons across the Channel to make landfall at Vierge, then on to shoot up Guipavas airfield. A new course took them to Kerlin-Bastard which, because there was no sign of any aircraft or activity, was left untouched. Now the formation flew on towards Vannes airfield, but low cloud caused Walter to alter course to St Brieuc airfield, where buildings, bowsers and gun positions were liberally sprayed with cannon fire. Any likely target, such as a lorry or railway locomotive, was given a quick 'squirt' by the Typhoons as they roared over them, hugging contours en route to Morlaix airfield. This, too, showed no signs of activity so, with ammunition to spare, Walter led the formation back to have another go at Guipavas. Flak at all the airfields was intense, especially the light-calibre stuff, and none more so than at Guipavas where the formation paid a high price. Flt Lt Stuart Lovell, in MM970, was hit and seen to crash in flames, while Sgt Sidney Smith, Lovell's wingman, in JP382, disappeared without anyone seeing what happened. It was later established that both pilots died when they went down for a second pass. Flt Lt Lovell flew so low that he hit the building he was firing at with his prop and he cartwheeled in; it is thought that Sgt Smith, following up behind, may have been hit by flak or possibly flying debris. Both airmen are buried in Brest-Kerfautras cemetery.

Back at base by 12.10, there was no time for recriminations: just refuel, rearm and have a bite to eat. Then Walter, this time in JR427, led five aircraft at 14.30 on another two-and-a-half-hour sortie to Kerlin, where the formation swept in line abreast at 300mph below a 1,000ft cloud base all along the coast from Lorient back to Ushant. Six ships, of between 500 and 3,000 tons, were seen but not attacked and no enemy aircraft challenged the formation.

A similar operation was mounted on 31 January with little productive outcome, but another pilot, Fg Off Dickie Foster, a close friend of Walter's, was lost to ground fire as the formation pulled out across the Brest peninsula. Walter wrote an evocative account of this operation later that tells us much about his inner feelings:

We approached the French coast, lying low and sinister, north of Lorient. Six aeroplanes in perfect line abreast doing 300mph right on the water, so low that the shadows of our aircraft almost touched and we pulled up to avoid odd seagulls or cormorants. Suddenly a large rocket rose from the shore; we had been spotted. Automatically I turn my gun button to 'Fire'.

We were close in now and I counted the ships in between the Isle de Gloic and Lorient for 'Spy's' [squadron intelligence officer] benefit when we returned. I recognised the landfall, slightly north of the aerodrome there and taking a look around, my heart filled with pride. There away on the left was Eric, always in position, never speaking but seeing everything. Next to him was Brian leading my other section and his No 2 Arthur, always ready to go looking for trouble. On my right was Pete, a newcomer to ops, then on my left was Dickie, a cool old hand aged twenty, flying lower than anyone else in a wizard position. I felt proud of these boys I had personally trained. They knew their stuff alright, having learned it in one of the most difficult jobs in the RAF. So I felt proud and confident, which almost made me arrogant as we crossed the coast, skimming houses, trees and breakwaters.

No flak – we've caught them by surprise. No aircraft either, damn it. Blast Pete! In his inexperience he's going too close to the 'drome. 'Pete, port for Christ's sake!' Look starboard. Blue section alright. A little flak now. What's that? Oh hell, a 20mm shell has struck Dickie's starboard petrol tank. He doesn't realise. The flames lick spasmodically back under the wing. It's all up. I yell: 'Dickie, bale out', knowing the cloud base is only 500 feet but it's his only hope now. We fly on for what seems an age but was only five seconds. I pull up close to Dickie. I begin to think he may be alright. Ah, there goes the hood. Oh God, the flames! They surge in a wild rush in the upcurrent from the bottom of the cockpit, so thick I can hardly see him. He's getting out, head and shoulders above the fuselage, oh but he's burning now, he's chok-ing. My friend Dickie is burning before my eyes. He's leaning back along the fuselage to try to escape the flames but they are growing. He forgets to get out or probably can't see. Oh dear me, he's shoving the stick forward uncon-sciously. He's going down now, black smoke, flames, death itself right beside me. I go down, saying to myself: 'he can't get out now, it's too late. Dickie's had it; my God: Dickie.' As if, because he is my friend, he should have been free to fly through flak unscathed. I realise I'm heading for the trees and pull out hard, as Dickie's machine hits the earth. I twitch as it explodes and the engine leaps out and careers along the ground. I feel sick, but where are the others? What course am I steering? 000°? That's no use. Turn on to 065° you fool. 'Blue section, over on my port, line abreast, come on now, quickly! 065°; steady.' I look behind, no fighters, only a pall of smoke reaching into the sky, black oily smoke, Dickie's pyre. We are in line abreast; good old Eric over on the left, Dickie's best friend and fellow humourist. He told me afterwards that he cried in his cockpit. Arthur: I know, with murder in his eyes wanting to turn round and kill all the gunners for miles around, as he sobs in agony. Pete: shaken; getting in my way flying badly. He'll be alright. Myself, moaning away, steering 065° for Gael aerodrome and Fw 190s. Remembering how Dickie loved making fires. The irony of Fate. How, before today the Hun had no guns there at all. Thinking: why isn't it me and why I have to go back and face his oldest friends and be hard and apparently unfeeling. There they are, four loyal friends, trusting me implicitly. We are fighting fit, in fighting aeroplanes, in fighting formation and in four minutes we'll be over Gael. Look behind. No fighters, no smoke. Look ahead: there's Gael …

In his logbook Walter noted that January was the worst month for the squadron, losing six pilots, and morale was badly shaken.

Events were moving apace now and No 183 Squadron was moving with them. At the end of January 1944 the squadron transferred from Predannack in No 10 Group to RAF Tangmere in No 11 Group. At Tangmere, No 183 Squadron became part of the three-squadron No 136 Wing under the command of Wg Cdr Denys Gillam. Dive-bombing was still on the menu but the squadron's targets were now airfields, transportation, radar and V-weapon sites along and inland from the Channel coast between Cherbourg and the Pas de Calais.

There was no time to admire the new surroundings. The first operation under the new 'boss' was mounted at 09.00 on 1 February when Nos 183, led by Walter Dring in JR385, Nos 193 and 257 Squadrons went for a No-Ball site in the Pas de Calais. Low cloud obscured the primary target so the formation dive-bombed the alternative at Zudausques, 5 miles west of St Omer, with good results. During the afternoon, Walter was in the air again, leading the squadron in a wing attack on another site 10 miles south of Abbeville. Some direct hits were seen and, although flak was heavy during both operations, there were no casualties.

Always looking for better ways of plastering a target – particularly the difficult No-Ball sites – on 13 February Walter, in MN197, and his wingman Fg Off Arthur Napier, in MN144, tried out a method of target marking. The pair flew slightly ahead of the main formation with the task of accurately identifying the target. It was felt that just two aircraft appearing over a target area was less likely to 'spook' the flak defences quite so much as a larger force with more obvious intentions. Having located the target, they acted as 'pathfinders' by dropping their bombs and calling in the rest of the formation to aim at the smoke generated. This pair raked the target with cannon fire to distract the gunners, observed where the bombs fell and adjusted aiming points for the other pilots. On this occasion the results were recorded as 'excellent'. Walter led a similar dive-bombing operation on the 15th, with equally good results, but this 'pathfinder' method does not seem to have been used much thereafter. Peter Brett wrote that flak encountered during dive-bombing operations was becoming more concentrated and more accurate. German gunners had worked out that if they spotted a large group of aircraft, such as Typhoons, in their vicinity, when the group changed into an echelon formation it almost certainly meant that a target was about to be attacked and, forewarned, the gunners were ready to draw a bead on each diving aircraft. Walter Dring came up with what was considered a better way of getting all the squadron's aircraft down on a target in the shortest time possible. Generally, flying in 'squadron' formation to a target area involved two flights, one behind the other, each of four aircraft flying in a 'finger-four' formation. Walter reckoned German gunners could be deceived by not changing to a large echelon formation as they passed the target area. Instead he kept the two flights intact and made the attack dives as follows, from Peter Brett's recollection. Walter would fly past the target, call 'ready, steady, GO', and on 'GO' the CO half-rolled into a looping dive from which he would pull out on the bombing dive angle. He would be followed immediately by the rest of his own four in the order 3, 4, 2. As soon as the leader of the second four saw the CO's number 2 start his roll, he would follow with his four in the same order. This manoeuvre was practised many times before being tried out on ops and it was found that it took just six or seven seconds to get all eight aircraft diving at the same time. This meant that, on dive-bomb runs, the aircraft were closer to each other but their exposure to flak was minimised, giving the gunners little opportunity to pick out one particular aircraft and having to make do with putting up a barrage instead. Accuracy of bombing was maintained and 'all you had to do was make sure that you did not start your pull-out before the chap in front because if you did, he could then have pulled out into you!'

The following day Sqn Ldr Dring, in MN144, led a flight of four aircraft as part of a wing operation. The attack was intended to be against a No-Ball site, but due to low cloud, poor visibility and a strong wind that blew the formation well off-course, an alternative target consisting of some buildings west of a wood near the village of Herbouville was bombed instead.

During March 1944 most of the squadron's operations were dive-bombing attacks against No-Ball targets, lasting one to one and a half hours. Several times Walter Dring led his squadron in full-strength formation as part of wing operations, such as one mounted against a V-1 site at St Martin l'Hortier near Foucarment, 18 miles south-east of Dieppe, and another as part of a wing dive-bombing attack in support of a force of B-25 Mitchells against a V-1 target near Fruges St Pols.

But it was this month, too, that saw Walter's flying career take another significant change of direction. On 15 March 1944, No 183 Squadron was transferred to the burgeoning 2nd Tactical Air Force (2 TAF) organisation and moved to No 123 Airfield, RAF Manston. Walter was still OC No 183 and the squadron's Operations Record Book contains an entry dated 21 March which shows him still 'leading the charge' on one of the first two operations from the new base. The ORB entries, however, also suggest that a change of command was in the offing, since the first six aircraft that took off at 14.25 were led by Sqn Ldr Remy van Lierde. This group flew to Holland on a low-level Ranger sweep of the Twente–Enschede area, encountering thick snow clouds and losing Flt Lt Peter Raw DFC to flak into the bargain. Sqn Ldr Dring led another six Typhoons on the second Ranger sweep to Northern France/Belgium, first to the Montdidier–Florennes area and then around the Brussels–Louvain–St Trond–Florennes area between 15.50 and 17.25 hours. No enemy air activity was seen, but 4 miles from Louvain the formation was targeted by a heavy flak barrage. Walter's aircraft MN246 was hit in two or three places, including one of his drop tanks, which he had to jettison.

During March 1944, all the wing's Typhoons had gradually been replaced by aircraft that were built with, or modified to, a bubble canopy. This vastly improved all-round visibility but as pilot Sgt Ken Adams, formerly of No 609 Squadron, explained:

[If] a tyre burst on take-off or landing [which] resulted in the Typhoon flipping over on its back ... it nearly always proved fatal because of a broken neck. Remember, we were sitting with our head above the fuselage under a Perspex canopy.

No 609 Squadron's MO, Fg Off George Bell, also observed:

When you got within sight of an upturned Typhoon your heart sank. It was such a heavy aeroplane and when it overturned it invariably caused the tail fin to collapse. The cockpit structure was unable to take any great force at all. The result was that the pilot's head took the crush in either flexion or extension. In many cases this meant that he sustained a broken neck and invariably death. To others, it meant quadriplegia with the rest of their life in a wheelchair.

These observations would come back to haunt the squadron.

★ ★ ★

Walter Dring was undoubtedly being groomed for higher command within
No 2 TAF and both he and his future now came under its authority. Having
been flying operationally for nearly two years, between 25 March and 31 May
Walter found himself posted to No 3 Air Support training course at the Fighter
Leader's School (FLS) at RAF Milfield, near Berwick in Northumberland.
Here he learned about tactics and methods of providing air support to the
army – no doubt with the impending invasion in mind. Upon completion of
the Milfield course he was posted to No 84 Group Support Unit (84 GSU)
at Aston Down near Cirencester, Gloucestershire. Things had come a long
way since the days of 1942 when No 56 Squadron had to learn all about the
Typhoon by trial and error, and having grown up with the Typhoon, Walter
was ideally placed to pass on his hard-earned knowledge and experience to
pilots he might have to work with in the near future. He put in some flying
time in the unit's Spitfires and Typhoons to demonstrate his ideas and even
managed a first solo in an Auster.

With an eye to the air support of fast-moving ground warfare envisaged
when the proposed Allied invasion of Europe took place, No 2 TAF was created in mid-1943. By the beginning of 1944 a clearer idea of what this might
entail had been worked out and one of No 2 TAF's key operational mantras
would be 'mobility'. In November 1943, Nos 83 and 84 Groups were created as the main fighter, fighter-bomber and reconnaissance composite groups
within No 2 TAF. To this end the concept included a number of mobile
Typhoon wings, such as those formed within No 2 TAF's No 84 Group. With
'mobility' being the watchword, after much to-ing and fro-ing of individual
squadrons between numbered airfield units during March 1944, No 123 Wing
finally settled into its four-Typhoon-squadron configuration: Nos 164, 183,
198 and 609 Squadrons, over which the New Zealander Wg Cdr Desmond
Scott DFC was appointed CO. By 1 April these squadrons had left Manston
and, in the first example of what their life 'on the road' would be like, were
now living under canvas at RAF Thorney Island, near Portsmouth. No 123
Wing was to be completely mobile and self-supporting, with its own servicing
and repair equipment and ground staff, transport, medical staff and facilities,
tented accommodation, field kitchens, armoury and signals section; in fact,
everything that would be customary to support squadrons on a normal aerodrome – but mobile. Even before the Allies landed in Normandy in June 1944,
plans were well in hand to make full use of the Typhoon as a ground attack
fighter in the forthcoming battle and the principal weapon for the Typhoons
of No 123 Wing was to be the airborne RP 3 rocket projectile.

The 3in, 60lb rockets used by Typhoon squadrons to great effect during the Normandy campaign. (Author's Collection)

Walter Dring was attached to No 84 GSU until 9 June 1944 when he was promoted to wing commander and posted to No 20 Sector Headquarters, Thorney Island, as Wg Cdr (Flying). At this time the composition of organisational units, such as airfields, wings, sectors, HQs and their descriptive names, were undergoing an almost constant change. When, on 12 July, No 20 Sector disbanded, Walter's movement card showed his final appointment to No 123 Wing HQ as Wg Cdr (Flying) – the post he held until his death six months later. It seems likely that service personnel records lagged well behind reality since, according to Desmond Scott's memoirs, Walter was selected by Scott to be his deputy and Wg Cdr (Flying) during May. Desmond Scott recalled:

'Farmer' Dring came from Spalding [*sic*] in Lincolnshire and was a true son of the soil. He had served in my wing at Tangmere in 1943, where his rugged exterior, wry smile and dry sense of humour had made him a great favourite with the New Zealand boys. His promotion to be my deputy was the start of an association that was to span the hot dusty days of Normandy, the cooler though hectic days against the Channel ports, the mud of Merville, Ursel airfield in Belgium and Gilze-Rijen in flat, soggy Holland. We were to share the joys, hopes and sorrows of a modern crusade. His part in it began with a flourish, prospered and, when at its peak at the gates of a dying Germany, ended in a crash at Chièvres in the snowbound Ardennes.

The post of Wg Cdr (Flying) involved a great deal of planning, briefings, debriefings and administration, particularly since the wing was not only committed to harrying the Germans from its English base prior to D-Day, but was also preparing to embark for France once the bridgehead was established. Walter now had day-to-day control over four squadrons but still made time – indeed he thought it vital – to fly operations with them to see how they performed, find out what problems they might encounter, review current tactics and to do what he was good at – leading his pilots from the front, usually in MN711.

In the run-up to and on D-Day, No 123 Wing's orders were quite specific: 'Destroy all enemy radar stations between Ostend and the Channel Islands.' These were among the most formidable targets, usually located near the coast, with clear lines of sight all round that made surprise attacks impossible and were thus veritable hornets' nests of light flak. Many pilots and squadron commanders were lost carrying out this vital work. Of D-Day itself, Desmond Scott wrote: 'Dring and the squadrons were coming and going, extremely busy hammering away in support of the Allied landings.' After D-Day, once the bridgehead had stabilised and a more or less clear 'bomb-line' was established, the role changed to interdiction operations and the Typhoon wings went hunting behind the bridgehead for anything that moved by road, rail or river that looked like a threat to Allied forces. If anything was found it was strafed, rocketed or bombed. Seventeen Typhoons were lost on D-Day operations.

By mid-June the Allies had taken enough ground to consider moving elements of No 2 TAF on to French soil. For a short time, therefore, aircraft of No 123 Wing carrying out operations over France were put under the temporary control of No 83 Wing, whose own squadrons had the use of some hastily constructed airfields within the Allied perimeter; for example, B5 (Camilly/Le Fresney), B8 (Sommervieu) and B10 at Plumetot, only 4 miles from enemy-occupied Caen. These airfields were used for refuelling and rearming and were refuges for battle-damaged aircraft.

On 17 July the ground echelon of No 123 Wing embarked on four Landing Ship Tanks (LSTs) at Gosport and sailed for France. Disembarking off Courselles on the 18th, it proceeded in convoy to airfield B7 at Martragny, near Bayeux, where it was joined by No 2703 AA (Anti-Aircraft) Squadron, RAF Regiment, for airfield defence. It speaks volumes for the quality of the organisation that just one day later, the wing was declared fully operational and Nos 164, 198 and 609 Squadrons flew in to B7 to begin operations, being followed by No 183 Squadron on 25 July.

Now all four squadrons were at B7 Walter was keen to get them back on ops quickly and in his inimitable way tried to instil confidence in his pilots by personally leading the first operation. This took place in the afternoon of 26 July when Walter (his Typhoon now coded 'W-D' – the privilege of a wing commander), leading a formation of 'A' Flight from No 609 Squadron and one flight from No 183 Squadron, made an anti-train sweep between Yvetot and Charleville. Spotting a goods train near Merville, the Typhoons dived on it, firing rockets and cannon and leaving it a smoking wreck. In the evening of 30 July sixteen Typhoons, drawn from Nos 609 and 164 Squadrons, took to the air with Wg Cdr Dring leading the formation. Their target was an enemy infantry HQ located in a wood near Caumont. One hundred and twenty-eight RPs slammed into the target area with many direct hits on the main building and the whole site was left on fire and billowing smoke.

There was another side to Walter Dring's job in which he had to draw upon his ability to understand his subordinates and look after their welfare. He had also to find suitable replacements for squadron commanders who were all too frequently being killed on ops. In his capacity as Wg Cdr (Flying) Walter was also aware of the effect of combat fatigue on his squadron commanders and pilots. It was occasionally necessary for him to make hard decisions about a pilot's fitness to continue flying these highly dangerous ground attack operations. He took advice from his squadron medical officers but never shirked his own duty when the final decision had to be made. When he thought one of his 'boys' had gone far enough, he took him off flying, for the man's sake as well as for the squadron's. The CO of No 164 Squadron, Sqn Ldr Percy Beake DFC, for example, had been flying operations since the Battle of Britain and was well into his second tour. After landing at B7 from an armed reconnaissance sortie on 11 August, he recalled:

Walter called me over to his caravan and said: 'Beaky, you have just done your last op. You are not to fly again and that is an order, until you return to England. I am arranging your relief as soon as possible.' I was absolutely stunned. I hated sending up the squadron without myself leading. In the event my relief, Sqn Ldr Ian Waddy, was shot down by flak within two or three days of taking command, so perhaps Wally Dring had some sort of premonition that prompted my grounding.

By way of an example of the risks these pilots were running day after day, between 1 January and 5 June 1944, No 198 Squadron lost twelve aircraft and ten pilots killed, and between 6 June and 31 December 1944 it lost twenty-seven aircraft with twenty pilots killed.

Another view of Walter Dring is provided by former No 183 Squadron pilot Fg Off Peter Brett, of whom we heard earlier. He recalled that when his squadron, No 183, moved to France on 24 July 1944 he did not go with it because he was 'tour-expired' and due for a 'rest posting'. The day after he arrived at his new unit, No 84 GSU at Thruxton, he was dismayed to find he was being posted back to No 123 Wing in France immediately – and not even back to No 183 but to No 198 Squadron instead. He was flown to B7 next day and duly reported to No 198 Squadron CO, Sqn Ldr Paul Ezanno. Ezanno was equally surprised to see him and took him straight to Wg Cdr Dring, who seems to have dealt with the matter in his usual forthright style. Peter Brett said Dring exclaimed: 'Peter, what the hell are you doing here? I sent you on rest! Those idiots at Command don't know what they're doing. You are grounded until I can sort out what has gone wrong. Just make yourself useful in the ops room.' It took a week before the matter was sorted out, then Peter Brett was flown back to England on fourteen days' leave before returning to No 84 GSU as a ferry pilot, relieved that he had survived his first tour.

One day in late July 1944, Wg Cdr Scott came to grief when he fell from a 'liberated' horse that he was riding around the airfield. Its hooves slipped on the steel matting used to form runways and taxiways for the aircraft and the horse fell on top of Desmond Scott, breaking his leg in several places and putting him completely out of action for over three weeks. The leg was also badly lacerated and he was admitted to a local Field Hospital where he was operated upon. Scott was desperate to stay at B7 and not lose command of his wing – for which his promotion to group captain was imminent – by being hospitalised in England, so he pulled every string possible to get ongoing treatment at B7 by a surgeon who happened to be awaiting a posting to England. During his recuperation, though, Scott's wounds became badly infected and it was only by the swift scrounging of the new wonder drug penicillin from a nearby American Field Hospital by No 609's MO, Fg Off George Bell – in exchange for a bottle of whisky – that the threat to Desmond Scott's leg, and possibly his life, was removed. Shortly afterwards, Scott's promotion to group captain was confirmed and he conceded that during his hospitalisation: '"Farmer" Dring had filled my shoes as Airfield Commander and kept me well informed on the activities of the Wing.' It could be a matter for speculation that if, as the Field Hospital had suggested, Wg Cdr Scott had returned to England for treatment, Walter might himself have been promoted to command No 123 Wing.

In August 1944 the names of Mortain and Falaise would become synonymous with the Typhoon and that period might even be seen as the zenith of the Typhoon's chequered and much-maligned career. At the beginning of August, following the devastating effects on the German army of a series of huge air raids by Allied heavy bombers, the British and Canadian armies had at last fought their way through Caen and were now south of the city, poised to push down the road to Falaise, 16 miles distant. The big British push, Operation Totalize, kicked off on 7 August; the same day as Operation Luttich, a German counter-attack – sometimes referred to as the Mortain counter-attack – began. This latter was an attempt by four Panzer divisions, at the western end of the German line of battle, to head for Avranches, through Mortain and cut off Gen Patton's American forces that had broken through to Le Mans. Providing air support for the 21st Army Group, No 2 TAF was brought in to attack the German Panzers around Mortain, and with the 'cab rank' and VCP (Visual Control Post) system working well at squadron strength, 294 Typhoon sorties were flown, resulting in the German attack being crushed with little progress made. No 123 Wing's RP Typhoons knocked out eighty-seven tanks that afternoon.

By 10 August, Totalize in the eastern sector and Luttich in the western sector had both run out of steam. This, however, left the majority of the German Seventh Army and a large Panzer Group in a pocket, almost surrounded by the Americans from the west and south, and the British, Canadians and Poles from the north and east. There was a diminishing 'mouth' to this pocket, located south-east of Falaise.

The Typhoon squadrons had a field day. On the 10th, No 609 Squadron mounted three operations at squadron strength, hitting tanks and motorised troop transport. Walter Dring led the last one at 18.30, going after some tanks in the Vassey area. Dring was airborne again the next day, when the squadron attacked a chateau and other HQ buildings near St Quentin, leaving them blazing from the effects of the rocket attack. Flying sorties almost every day, Walter's logbook notes:

7th. One flamer, one AFV [Armoured Fighting Vehicle], one carrier. 8th. Weather very bad. 9th. Wing total for day: 16 tanks, 85 MET [Mixed Enemy Transport]. 9th. Lost Tolworthy and Thuesby. 10th. Very heavy flak, no tanks visible. 12th. Blew up ammunition trucks, wizard sight. 13th. Clobbered two Tigers. 14th. Two smokers. 17th. Destroyed 17 trucks. 18th. Two trucks destroyed.

Realising the predicament they were in, pressed on all sides and harried constantly from the air, on the 11th the Germans began a major retreat. They made an enormous effort to extract the 7th Army and the Panzers through the mouth of the pocket near Falaise, around Trun and Chambois – the location that became known as the 'Falaise Gap' – and escape to and across the River Seine.

On 12 August, heavy and medium bombers pounded transportation routes out of the Falaise pocket and, by that evening, German manpower and equipment was in full, almost panic-stricken, flight. Thousands of tanks, half-tracks, infantry lorries, petrol and ammunition vehicles, and horse-drawn transports were all being squeezed into an ever-narrowing area measuring about 7 miles by 6 miles. The RP and bomber Typhoons of No 2 TAF hammered the tightly packed roads trying to close the gap. Hobbling on crutches at the base airfield, Desmond Scott wrote:

> The withering, terrifying power of our fighter-bombers and rocket Typhoons began scorching the battle area with methodical ferocity. The Falaise Pocket became the chopping block and graveyard of Hitler's 7th Army. Dring and the No 123 Wing squadrons blasted their way through blazing hot days of maximum activity. The Falaise Gap was closed on 20 August but elements of armoured formations outside the pocket, together with the remains of the German tanks inside, tried desperately to force it open again. This situation caused the [Allied] armies some concern and 123 Wing was called in to tidy it up. It proved to be one of the finest close-support operations in the history of No 84 Group.

This was Walter Dring in his element!

On 18 August a fierce ground battle developed near Chambois, but Canadian troops linked up with the Poles and closed the mouth of the Pocket – although it was still a tenuous situation and the Germans frantically tried to force an opening again. By the 20th, the enemy counter-attacked with tanks and fighting became severe around Vimoutiers, particularly against the Canadian 4th Armoured Division and the Polish Armoured Brigade, who were just 2,000 yards apart on opposite sides of the River Vie and found themselves outnumbered and in a difficult situation. The recommendation for an award of a decoration to Walter Dring, who had by this time flown 245 operational fighter sorties totalling 300 hours, stated:

> The position of our troops was critical and air support was requested. During the confused land battles of the previous two days, friendly aircraft had unfortunately attacked our own troops on a number of occasions and this target was accepted with some misgivings. Wing Commander W. Dring, the Wing Commander Operations of No 123 Wing, was asked whether he regarded it as a practicable operation for RP Typhoons. He undertook it without hesitation and asked if he could lead all the squadrons of his Wing in the attack. Permission was given and orders issued for the attack, which was carried out, in spite of low cloud and intense flak, with faultless precision and timing.

The success of this heavy attack, in which thirteen tanks were destroyed and eleven damaged, carried out in such close proximity to our own troops, did much to restore the Army's confidence in air support and was instrumental in neutralising the enemy counter-attack. No 123 Wing's consistent success in ground attack operations with RP Typhoons is very largely due to Wing Commander Dring's careful planning, thorough briefing and dashing leadership.

At this most crucial point Walter Dring arrived at the head of thirty-two RP Typhoons from Nos 164, 183, 198 and 609 Squadrons. About 100 German tanks and armoured cars were rolling out of a wood and Dring's formation caught them as they emerged. Plt Off W. T. Lawson, one of the attacking pilots, recalled: 'I was flying number two to Dring. He was first to fire his rockets then he orbited the wood giving instructions throughout the attack.' They claimed seventeen 'flamers' and many damaged.

Walter Dring was awarded an immediate DSO and it is well known that the jaws of the trap (the Pocket) remained firmly closed. Inside the Pocket the Germans left behind 1,300 tanks, 1,500 field guns, 20,000 vehicles and 400,000 troops, half of whom were taken prisoner. Remnants of the German 7th Army retreated across the Seine as best they could, harried constantly by No 2 TAF's Typhoons. This action in effect marked the end of the Normandy campaign; Paris was liberated a week later and the advance towards the River Rhine began. Walter Dring's star was at its zenith, too.

★ ★ ★

No 123 Wing's first move from B7 was to airfield B23 at Morainville, south of Evreux, on 3 September, but three days later it made a great leap to airfield B35 at Baromesnil, inland from Le Treport. On the 11th another leap took it to airfield B53 at Merville, near Armentières, a permanent airfield with long concrete runways, recently vacated by the Luftwaffe, where it would be joined by No 135 Wing. In less than a week No 123 Wing had leapfrogged from Bayeux almost to the Belgian border. During this period the four squadrons were still engaged on operations at the call of the army over a wide area, some of these involving ops against German enclaves in the ports of Le Havre, Boulogne, Calais and Dunkirk.

By this time Desmond Scott, his plaster cast removed, was back in full working and flying order and he and Walter Dring – together with their squadrons – were working well as a team in this frantic race to keep up with the army. Desmond Scott spoke of their relationship:

After weathering the triumphs and tragedies of Normandy and the blister-
ing heat of battle, Dring had become my brother. We had always got on well,
even back in our Tangmere days, but now we were veterans, drawn closer
by the forces of survival. We had, in the previous four years, lived through
a thousand lifetimes. We had become the products of the battle skies and
of the cold, hard facts of war. During the day we did not see much of each
other for, unlike the Spitfire squadrons, Typhoons normally ferreted around
in the battle zone in small formations and it was a full-time job for [Dring]
conducting the many briefings that were part of our close-support operations. In front of the squadron personnel I was always 'Sir' and he 'Dring' but
in the evenings, when flying was finished, we would meet in my caravan
to discuss the day's activities on the same level. Then he became 'Dringo'
and I 'Scottie'. A drink or two and [Dringo] seemed to finish back on his
Lincolnshire farm. I, too, had spent most of my childhood surrounded by
sheep and horses and we talked about farming well into the night. It diverted
our minds from the menacing skies, the mud of Merville and the thousand
fears of an unknown future.

During mid-September 1944, much to the disgust of its commanders, No 123
Wing was not called upon to provide close support in the battles raging
around Arnhem. However, the wing became heavily involved in 'clearing-
out' operations against the German army bottled up in the Antwerp area
around the Scheldt. Antwerp was vital to the Allies and it was captured as early
as 4 September, but shipping could not be brought into the port until the
Germans were removed from Walcheren – and the fortifications there were
strong, with well-camouflaged heavy coastal guns and huge bunkers. First
the wing was asked to provide ground attack support for the Canadian army
clearing out the Breskens 'pocket' opposite Flushing. This ground objective
was achieved by 22 October and gave the army a point from which to launch
an attack on the strategic Walcheren Island, a tough nut to crack.

 While all this was going on, No 123 Wing moved to B67 Ursel, west of
Ghent, on 29 October. The amphibious assault on the island began on
1 November, but at Ursel airfield, like all the other No 2 TAF airfields, No 123
Wing was grounded by fog. Reports filtered through about the seaborne forces
encountering great resistance and being desperate for air support. George
Bell's recollection of this situation was that Group HQ telephoned Gp Capt
Scott to tell him air support ops were being called off and Scott replied that
he was 'not going to leave those poor bastards with no air support … and
123 Wing will be over Walcheren in the next hour or two'. And it was. Scott
and Dring constantly monitored the weather situation and when they walked

along their low-lying runway, the fog seemed thinner. They knew they could take off directly towards the destination and that the flight path to the target area would be at sea level, so Scott decided to risk it, hoping visibility would be good enough along the route. He called a full wing operation; everyone to fly! Desmond Scott briefed his wing to operate in two formations; he would lead the first formation of two squadrons and when airborne would decide whether or not to continue. If he did not call an abort, Walter Dring would take off leading the other two squadrons.

Scott's formation took off and within a few minutes found the cloud had lifted to 500ft and visibility improved. He was soon joined by Dring and when the four squadrons arrived in the target area they took up a patrol line off the coast between West Kapelle and Flushing. Scenes of devastation could be seen below, with broken vessels, bodies floating in the water and soldiers wandering around. German heavy guns were still keeping up a deadly bombardment and Desmond Scott recalled:

> It was a moment or two before the well-camouflaged heavy coastal batteries barked out their messages of death and we could pinpoint the seat of the trouble. But immediately we saw their flashes we answered them back and every time a gun fired, four Typhoons set upon it. As though stirred by the scene below, each pilot pressed home his attack almost into the gun barrels. Rockets exploded against the steel and concrete, sometimes in pairs, sometimes in salvoes. Flak flew in all directions, but we raked the flak guns with our cannon fire. We kept the pressure on and before long, the guns along the southern perimeter of the island ceased to fire.

The weather cleared even more during the day, allowing No 123 Wing and the others of No 84 Group to mount many more attacks on fortifications in other parts of the island. Walcheren was taken within days and the seaway into Antwerp was no longer under threat. No 123 Wing's contribution on that critical day was acknowledged in a signal from Admiral Ramsey, the Allied Naval Commander-in-Chief Europe: 'The timely and well-executed support by your rocket firing Typhoons when 80% of the landing craft were out of action, undoubtedly was a vital factor in turning the scales to our advantage.'

No 123 Wing was on the move again and on 25 November took up residence at B77 Gilze-Rijen, between Breda and Tilburg, Holland. This former Luftwaffe base had two long concrete runways with plenty of hard standings and well-built permanent domestic buildings, which must have been a welcome change from living under canvas. At that time, though, the airfield was only 12 miles from the front line and also under the flight path of V-1s being fired at Antwerp – someone counted as many as 148 of these noisy beasts flying over the airfield in a single day!

Apart from the usual 'cab rank' sorties in support of the Canadian army, Typhoon operations at this time were mainly directed against German mechanised units and supply depots across the River Maas, together with attacks on the V-1 launch sites themselves. On 28 November 1944 General Eisenhower visited the wing and personally thanked all the pilots for their efforts in the drive from Normandy. Winter was setting in hard; snow was falling and with temperatures plummeting, everyone hoped that No 123 Wing would see out the bad weather in the comparative comfort of Gilze-Rijen. Field Marshal von Rundstedt, however, had other ideas.

During a period of atrocious weather that, significantly, had already grounded Allied aircraft for many days – and would continue to do so – on 16 December the 5th, 6th and 7th German Panzer armies began a massive counter-offensive in the Ardennes region that would become known as the Battle of the Bulge. Walter himself did not fly for a month prior to 25 December, when he logged twenty minutes: 'Aerobatics (workout).'

General 'Ike' Eisenhower (centre) meets No 123 Wing CO, Gp Capt Desmond Scott (extreme right) and Wg Cdr Walter Dring (second from the right, with hands behind back) at B77 Gilze-Rijen, 28 November 1944. (John & Susan Rowe, Dring Collection)

Without air support, Allied forces were overrun or pushed back towards Brussels and in the direction of Antwerp. On 28 December, No 123 Wing was ordered to move 80 miles south immediately and take over airfield A84 at Chièvres from the Americans. Chièvres was 30 miles south-west of Brussels and from there, No 123 Wing was to give close air support to the American army. What with snow, ice and fog, it took until 31 December for the move to be completed. Not all the wing's Typhoons could move to the new base because, according to Desmond Scott, twenty-two had to be left at Gilze as unserviceable due to repairs or normal maintenance checks.

Poor weather favoured the German army initially, but with the prospect of it improving, and with it the return of the Allied ground attack fighters, the Luftwaffe was mobilised en masse to mount what became a last-ditch, pre-emptive strike. Due to mounting resistance and with its supply lines stretched to breaking point, German ground forces were about to grind to a halt. If the Allied air forces could take to the sky, the whole German offensive would be in serious danger.

The pre-emptive air strike, code-named Operation Bodenplatte, was a tactical operation to be carried out by fighters and fighter bombers of the Luftwaffe against Allied airfields. The objective was to cripple Allied air forces and facilities in Belgium, Holland and northern France at a time when the Battle of the Bulge was in danger of stagnating. Launched on 1 January 1945, it was planned originally to coincide with the start of the counter-offensive but was delayed by the unsuitable weather for ground attack operations.

Among seventeen airfield targets was Gilze-Rijen. Over 1,000 German aircraft, mainly Fw 190s and Bf 109s, were committed to the operation. Eighty-one enemy aircraft from JG 3 and KG 51 were tasked to attack the airfields of Eindhoven and Gilze-Rijen and they hit these at dawn on the 1st. Fortunately for No 123 Wing, most of its 'birds had flown' to Chièvres, but Eindhoven was brim-full, with around 300 aircraft and vast stores, and bore the brunt of the attack. The wings there lost twenty-six Typhoons destroyed and thirty damaged, plus five Spitfires destroyed. Gilze-Rijen escaped lightly, since the Typhoons left on the airfield were well dispersed, and although the attackers had the freedom to make several firing passes over the airfield, only two aircraft were destroyed, while the anti-aircraft defences claimed three of the enemy.

The outcome of the ground battle is now a matter of history and by 12 January the pressure on No 123 Wing was off, allowing Gp Capt Scott to consider returning to Gilze-Rijen. In the almost three weeks his wing was at Chièvres, only five days were fit for flying, but during that time it was business as usual for the RP Typhoons as they hit enemy tanks and motor transport hard. Snow conditions were so bad at Chièvres as to require bulldozers to clear the runway and this left huge banks of snow, 8ft high, stretching down each side of the runway, 'making it like a white-walled passageway'.

By January 1945 Walter Dring had been a pilot for three years, during which time he had accumulated 1,100 flying hours, of which almost 500 were operational. On 13 January, having been unable to get any aircraft into the air for some days, Walter sent up Flt Lt Prosser on a weather check to see if it was clear enough to send all four squadrons back to Gilze-Rijen. On his return Prosser reported that it was 'no joy' and the route was completely socked in by a wide front with cloud down to ground level. According to Desmond Scott this is what happened next:

> I accepted Prosser's report but Dring was not convinced and asked if he could go and take a look for himself. Perhaps there was a way round the weather. In front of his pilots I could not refuse his request, but I did not want to embarrass Prosser. Dring had been grounded for so long, I think he simply wanted to extend his wings. I said he could have a look if he so wished, but that I was satisfied with Prosser's report. It was the same story: we would have to wait until the weather cleared.
>
> Dring came back over the aerodrome and started a series of aerobatic loops, rolls and stall turns. It was Dring at his best, the master of the low attack, the smiling farmer who had taken to the skies. After completing a series of slow rolls he lowered his undercarriage and began the approach. There was no wind, but he seemed to have a slight starboard drift. Touching down, his aircraft ran along the runway for a few yards, swung sideways, hit the snow wall to the side of the runway, capsized and vanished in a great avalanche of snow.
>
> For a few moments the shock paralysed me. I knew there was no hope, for the whole canopy that covered his head had been torn from the aircraft and thrown high in the air. In stunned silence we lifted his broken remains into an ambulance. It was only after returning to my caravan that I felt the full impact of his death. On the chair where he sat in the evenings lay his old cherrywood pipe with its bent stem. He would suck away at it for hours and use countless matches which often burned his fingers. Wing Commander Walter Dring DSO, DFC, the 28-year-old Lincolnshire farmer had been my loyal companion since the blazing days of Normandy. I had never been to Woad Farm, but I knew every inch of it. His wife, Sheila, was expecting their first baby.

Medical officer Fg Off George Bell also witnessed the landing:

He was still quite high as he approached the runway and some way to the port side. He then manoeuvred the Typhoon so that it was still travelling slightly sideways as it touched down. The surface of the runway was still icy in parts and his 'plane continued its sideways movement towards the neat walls of snow at the side of the landing strip. As his starboard wheel hit the wall of snow, the Typhoon reared up and turned over on its back with a sickening bang. I rushed to the scene and with the assistance of the crash crew, took Walter Dring from the cockpit. There was nothing we could do … he had died instantly from a broken neck. We went through the motions, transferring him into an ambulance and then to the operating table but by that time the news was spreading rapidly throughout the wing, 'the Wingco's bought it'.

George Bell could feel the mood of disbelief tinged with anger pervading the mess for the remainder of the day, and in the evening it boiled over with the pilots giving vent to their feelings and emotions over this tragic loss, in the way that pilots usually did. He recalled:

I sensed this was a night for flying people only. They had to show their feelings. I left quietly … and returned to my room. As I undressed for bed I discovered that I had Walter Dring's wallet in my pocket. King's Regulations stated that you didn't carry identification with you when flying, so I had quietly removed the wallet sticking out of the Wing Commander's breast pocket, to return it quietly to the Adjutant.

Walter Dring's body was taken back to Gilze-Rijen when the wing began its return on the 15th, the move being completed by 26 January. He was buried in the military cemetery at Bergen-op-Zoom and is remembered on the memorial to Moulton Grammar School war dead in Moulton village church, and on a special panel in Weston church.

4

JUMPING THE WOODEN HORSE

Flight Lieutenant James Gordon Crampton

James Gordon Crampton, usually known as Jim, was the eldest son of Ruth and James Crampton, who ran the shop and post office in the village of Moulton, Lincolnshire, from 1914 to 1939. Educated first at the village primary and then at Moulton Grammar School, after leaving school he was apprenticed as a refrigeration engineer with a company in St Neots, Cambridgeshire. From an early age Jim wanted to fly aeroplanes and he made every effort to achieve his aim – eventually doing so with a little help from an innovative government scheme.

By the mid-1930s, the British government had become alarmed at the rapid rise in German military might and a scheme called the Civil Air Guard (CAG), which encouraged young civilian men and women to learn to fly, was introduced in July 1938. The scheme was conceived by Capt Harold Balfour MP, Undersecretary of State for Air, who opened negotiations with several flying clubs in the UK to identify those wishing to participate. The basis of this new organisation would be civilian in nature, operated by flying clubs around the country, who themselves would operate a separate Civil Air Guard section within the club. The Air Ministry paid a subsidy to participating clubs, with the aim of giving flying training to members of the public – both sexes – between the ages of 18 and 24. The annual membership fee for the individual was the sum of 2s 6d (12½p in modern currency; equivalent to about £6 in 2012), tuition thereafter was 7s 6d (37½p; equivalent to about £18 in 2012) per flying hour. This was a relatively low price when compared to the going rate of £3 per hour at a civil flying club at that time. It was expected that trainees would achieve an 'A' licence standard on the de Havilland Tiger Moth or Avro

Tutor trainer after about thirteen hours dual and four hours solo tuition. By September 1938 forty-eight flying clubs had signed up for this scheme and although the cost was relatively small, trainees were expected to buy all their own equipment, such as a helmet and goggles. With aptitude and applied diligence it was, however, still possible for a trainee to gain a flying licence for the princely sum of about £10 (equivalent to approximately £500 in 2012).

In 1938 Jim was working as an engineer with the East Anglian Electrical Company, based in Stowmarket, and lived a bachelor life in a caravan at Alconbury Hill in Huntingdonshire. It was while here that Jim joined the West Suffolk Aero Club at Bury St Edmunds airfield in June 1939 and learned to fly through the club's participation in the CAG training scheme.

The outbreak of the Second World War presented many a young man with the prospect of excitement coupled with a golden opportunity to learn to fly, and Jim was no exception. Volunteering for aircrew service in the RAF he was called up in June 1940 and received a rail warrant and instructions to report to No 1 Receiving Wing (1 RW) in Babbacombe, Devon. Seaside resorts all over the country were virtually taken over by the RAF as locations for initial training establishments, where the abundance of commandeered hotel accommodation allowed vast numbers of tyro airmen to be housed easily. Jim stayed at No 1 RW from 1 July to 14 July 1940. He now followed the path of a pilot u/t (under training) and on 14 July was posted just down the road to No 4 Initial Training Wing (4 ITW) in Paignton to undergo six weeks of pilot ground school. This type of study was just what appealed to Jim and he passed out satisfactorily, helped no doubt by his training with the CAG. Being in possession

Pilot under training Aircraftman Jim Crampton (right) at No 4 ITW Paignton, in July 1940. (Crampton Family Collection)

of a private pilot licence as a result of that training probably also enabled him to be graded at the ITW as pilot material without the need to go through the flying aptitude assessment stage at a 'grading' Elementary Flying Training School (EFTS). On 24 August Jim was posted to No 15 EFTS, a Class 'C' flying school located at Kingstown, Carlisle, and equipped with the single-engine Miles Magister tandem two-seat trainer aeroplane. Class 'C' was the smallest of the EFTS categories and Carlisle in August 1940 would at any one time be home to about sixty pupils, organised into two flights.

Flying – the RAF way – began for Jim on 26 August 1940 when he had thirty minutes in Magister N3780 under the critical eye of his instructor, Fg Off Ratcliffe. During that trip he carried out numbered flying exercises, which continued under dual instruction in a logical progression on subsequent days. Some exercises were repeated as necessary until the instructor felt Jim was competent enough to move on to the next exercise. Flying in a variety of Maggies, he was airborne twice a day. On 29 August he made two trips practising take-offs and landings with Fg Off Ratcliffe; he then went up with Flt Lt Townsend who checked him out for another twenty-five minutes. Upon landing, Townsend told him to stay in the aircraft, climbed out and sent Jim off on his own – a ten-minute solo circuit in T9735. Jim had done his RAF solo after just five hours and twenty minutes dual instruction.

For the next month Jim worked his way through all the required exercises, mainly flying solo but with occasional dual with Fg Off Ratcliffe and Flt Lt Townsend to assess his progress. Another instructor, Fg Off Hamilton, took him up for the dual instrument flying exercise (No 19). By 25 September he had accumulated a total of forty-five hours and at this milestone Fg Off Lash put him through a rigorous test of his flying ability. During his time at Carlisle, Jim flew in nine different Magisters: N3780, 3836 and 5407; R1850, 1853, 1854 and 1968; T9687 and 9735. By 27 September, with all his exercises completed to the satisfaction of his instructors, Jim had a grand total of forty-eight hours fifty-five minutes (twenty-three hours five minutes dual and twenty-five hours fifty minutes solo) in his logbook and it was time for him to move on.

By 28 September 1940 Jim Crampton was at his next flying training unit. It would seem he was destined for bombers since he was posted to No 3 Service Flying Training School (3 SFTS) at RAF South Cerney near Cirencester, Gloucestershire. This school, formerly designated No 3 Flying Training School (3 FTS), had at one time operated both single- (Hawker Hart) and twin-engine (Airspeed Oxford) aeroplanes, but in June 1940 it dropped its single-engine training role and, by the time Jim arrived, had become a Group II twin-engine school with an establishment of 108 Airspeed Oxford Mk I and Mk II aircraft.

Miles Magister R1853, one of several flown by Jim Crampton and the aircraft in which Arthur Edgley soloed when both airmen trained at No 15 EFTS Carlisle. (A.J. Jackson Collection)

There now began an intensive four-month period of flying the Oxford in all weathers in preparation for the heavy bombers he would fly on operations.

Jim's twin-engine training began on 30 September. His instructor, Plt Off Brown, took him up a couple of times in Oxford P6807 to show him the ropes; then after two more trips that day, Jim began carrying out a sequence of numbered exercises similar to those he had experienced at Carlisle. This pattern continued up to 25 October with between two and five flights a day, subject to weather conditions. During his three months at the SFTS, Jim flew in no fewer than thirty-five different Airspeed Oxford aircraft and did his first twin-engine solo in Oxford N6263 on 5 October, after only eleven dual flights totalling four hours and ten minutes. That was only the beginning, though, since the hard work to hone his flying skill continued, with many of the numbered exercises being repeated over and over, flying solo, then again under assessment by his team of instructors. By 1 November, having accumulated twenty-five hours dual and solo on the Oxford, he was about a third of the way through his course. As at Carlisle, the latter part of his flying course concentrated on air navigation, but this time it was at a more advanced level.

On 1 November Jim's first trip was a solo cross-country to Peterborough and back in P1952. With that hurdle over, he was teamed up with other trainees – LACs Job, Hanafy and Bruce – to plan and carry out different cross-country flights, of two or three hours' duration, with each of the pupils, in pairs, taking turns at flying and navigating the aircraft. In addition to these dual efforts, Jim had to continue flying many solo cross-country flights and also keep practising various numbered exercises. Meanwhile, for example on 15 November, he was checked out at the Relief Landing Ground (RLG) at Bibury by WO Knights, then taken up on his return to South Cerney for an interim flying test by the 'B' Flight commander, Flt Lt Ridge.

Towards the end of November 1940 Jim's logbook begins to show evidence of instrument flying cross-country and multiple-leg cross-country exercises. All through December he practised cross-country flights on instruments only, culminating on 27 December with a CFI test with Sqn Ldr Clarke in Oxford R6017. He completed that trip satisfactorily and was back 'beating the circuit' at Bibury RLG the same afternoon. It was here that Jim experienced his one and only mishap during training. He was flying Oxford N6378 with an instructor, WO Knights, at the time and recorded the incident in his logbook simply as 'crashed', but it could not have been too bad since he was back in the air a couple of days later. In later years, when retelling this story, Jim said the instructor was supposed to be in control but fell asleep! They were flying too low on approach and the undercart struck a low Cotswold stone wall. Neither of them was hurt but Jim and his wife returned to the scene many years later and found that same piece of wall – still bearing the scars of the passage of the aircraft's undercarriage through it.

Christmas and New Year 1941 went past in a blur with no let-up in the training schedule and on 2 January, reflecting the hard winter that year, Jim logged one trip with Flt Lt Ridge as 'air experience in snow!' He was now

Airspeed Oxford as flown by Jim Crampton at No 3 SFTS South Cerney in late 1940. (Author's Collection)

Newly commissioned Plt Off Jim Crampton in 1941. (Crampton Family Collection)

teamed up with three different fellow trainees – LACs Tubman, Symons and Bristow – and for the next ten days they and their instructors worked almost continuously. The course came to its final fever pitch on 16 January 1941 when Jim logged seven separate flying sessions during the day. Four of these were instrument flying practices lasting a total of about three hours, followed by two take-off and landing check flights with two instructors, followed finally by Jim doing four circuits and landings on his own. He had worked hard for three and a half months and now, having added a further seventy-one flying hours to his total – bringing him up to 120 hours – he was considered proficient enough to move on to the next step of becoming a bomber aircraft captain. Furthermore, Jim received his 'Wings' and a commission and was now off to his next posting as Pilot Officer Crampton.

After a spot of leave, Jim's next posting was to No 21 (Bomber) Operational Training Unit (21 OTU) based at RAF Moreton-in-Marsh in Gloucestershire. Established to train night bomber crews, this unit – one of several similar bomber OTUs – was formed in late January 1941 and began its task at the beginning of March. The main function of a bomber OTU was to take newly qualified pilots, navigators, wireless operators and air gunners from their respective training schools, to introduce them to the aircraft they would fly operationally and to train newly formed crews to work together as a team. They would spend six weeks at No 21 OTU during which time they would receive both ground and air training. Arriving at Moreton on 1 March, Jim was therefore one of the very first aircrew to arrive at the newly formed OTU. He was a member of No 1 Course, which had spent the preceding two weeks going through its 'crewing up' process at RAF Harwell. That was where a motley collection of aircrew from the various trades mentioned above were brought together in a large room or hangar and told to get on and form five-man crews amongst themselves. With the exception of No 1 Course, as explained above, this process for No 21 OTU would in future take place at Moreton itself.

On 3 March No 1 Course began flying at Moreton-in-Marsh as 'C' Flight and continued until 18 March, when No 2 Course was posted in and No 1 Course moved on to the operational flying training part of the programme with 'A' Flight. The aeroplane in use at Moreton at that time was the Vickers Wellington IC of which, by the end of March 1941, there were sixteen on charge, together with four Avro Ansons. The Anson Flight at a bomber OTU was generally responsible for training wireless operators, wireless operator/air gunners (WOp/AGs) and navigators in the work and procedures they would encounter on 'ops', while the pilots were receiving their own early initiation on flying the Wellington. Sometimes the Anson was used to give more instruction to pilots who, on arrival at the OTU, were deemed to require more day or night dual instruction before carrying on with the standard OTU programme. When each pilot was considered to be sufficiently capable of flying a Wellington, the navigators, wireless operators and gunners joined the crew captain and flew as a team until the end of the OTU course.

Having familiarised himself with the Wellington, both by day and night, when he moved to 'A' Flight Jim began making long cross-country flights as second pilot, which also enabled him to take over from his instructor for most of the time while airborne. One of the more adventurous of these was a four-hour formation exercise in T2853 on 31 March, with Flt Lt Williams in command and Jim and Plt Off Tweedie – another trainee captain who arrived at the OTU at the same time – taking turns at the controls. The formation left Moreton for Aberystwyth where practice bombs were dropped and the gunners were allowed to fire their weapons over the range; then on to Abergavenny where the formation dealt with a mock attack by practising defensive manoeuvres; on to Cirencester, then Cricklade before returning to base once more. Throughout the first half of April 1941, Jim frequently flew with Tweedie, each of them alternating as captain and second pilot, building up their hours on cross-country sorties the length and breadth of England. It was clear that the course was coming to an end when, on 10 April, all the trainees were sent off on what was really their 'proving' flights. In Jim's case this entailed a six-and-a-half-hour sortie in T2853 under the watchful eye of Flt Lt Williams. Jim and Plt Off Tweedie each spent half the flight – three hours and fifteen minutes – in command of the aircraft, two hours of which was flown at 10,000ft with everyone on oxygen. The course flown was: Moreton–Salisbury–Bassingbourn–York–Carlisle–Isle of Man–Bardsey Island (which was bombed) and back to Moreton; a long trip but of the type to which they would have to become accustomed on ops. After one more shared trip with Plt Off Tweedie and no instructor, during which they had to navigate to a given 'Point X', that was the end of the course and they were keen to know their operational postings. Jim had at last caught up with the war!

On 14 April students of No 1 Course at 21 OTU left RAF Moreton-in-Marsh to join their various squadrons. In Pilot Officer Jim Crampton's case, with a total of 203 hours in his logbook, he and his crew together with eleven other crews were posted to No 214 (Federated Malay States) Squadron at RAF Stradishall, Suffolk, which operated the Vickers Wellington in No 3 Group of Bomber Command.

Under the wing of one of the squadron's experienced 'A' Flight pilots, Sgt George McKeand (by end of war: Sqn Ldr, DSO, DFC), Jim and his crew familiarised themselves with their new squadron, their group locality and the aircraft itself. On five consecutive nights Sgt McKeand took Jim up to show him the ropes regarding what to look for during a pre-op air test and to put him through his paces on night take-offs and landings. Then finally the big day came.

Jim had his first taste of operational flying on the night of 20/21 April 1941. He was flying as second pilot in Sgt McKeand's crew in Wellington R1621, one of seventeen aircraft despatched by the squadron to attack an oil storage depot in Rotterdam. The other members of McKeand's crew were Sgts Shaw, Thomas, Turner and Page. Jim's logbook notes simply: 'bombed target'. At this stage of the air war the Wellington, though built with only a single pilot position, was generally operated with two pilots, while the navigator usually carried out the bomb-aiming task. The second pilot (not 'co'-pilot), who sat on a fold-down seat or stood by the side of the first pilot, was, more often than not, a new member of the squadron who was expected to make half a dozen or so operational sorties as second pilot in order to gain experience flying under battle conditions. There were no hard and fast rules about what the second pilot should do, but the main task was to get him used to coping with what the enemy could throw at you. In his first few sorties, a second pilot kept his eyes on the pilot's actions and in turn acted as a second pair of eyes for both the pilot and the navigator by trying to spot landmarks. He was allowed to slip into the pilot seat and take over the controls either on the way to the target or on the return leg, but gradually he worked up to being at the controls both to and over the target and for the return leg, while the captain stood by with words of advice. This was the usual way in which 'rookie' pilots were eased into operational flying before they were committed as captains of their own crew and aircraft – and with their very own rookie 'second dicky'.

A few nights later, on 25/26 April, Jim was on ops again, this time going to Kiel as second pilot with George McKeand and the same crew and aircraft. A force of sixty-two aircraft went out that night; thirty-eight were Wellingtons, with No 214 Squadron providing half that number. It was to be another 'maritime diversion' operation, which meant that because of the growing success of German surface raiders, U-boats and Fw 200 Condor aircraft, from the beginning of March 1941 Bomber Command was diverted from its main campaign and sent out time and again over the next four months against targets that supported the German maritime offensive.

Loaded with six 500-pounders, Jim took off in R1621 at 21.00. The crew reached Kiel and saw one large fire and several smaller ones scattered on both sides of the river. At 00.45 they attacked the port area in a glide from 11,000ft releasing the six bombs in a salvo, but none of the crew observed any result. The bombing height was a compromise between bombing accuracy and keeping above the effective range of light flak and searchlights, the latter combination being subject to continuous improvements that pushed bombing heights ever higher as the war went on. The tactic of bombing in a glide, with the engines throttled back to about a quarter power, was felt to be a way of trying to confuse any sound detection and locating equipment on the ground. The return trip was uneventful and they touched down at 04.20 after almost seven and a half hours in the air.

The next operation came on 28/29 April, when R1621 was one of twenty-four aircraft launched by the squadron that night. Airborne at 21.00, they set course for the port of Brest, in which the juicy targets of the German capital ships *Scharnhorst* and *Gneisenau* were docked. However, in common with most of the squadron that night, the ships were not located because of a smoke screen, an intense flak barrage and probing searchlight defences that were encountered. Reluctantly, McKeand ordered the bomb load to be jettisoned in the sea and the aircraft returned to base at 01.40 on the 24th.

When not on ops, Jim continued to fly training sorties with his crew as, for example on 3 May, when he carried out a dusk practice-bombing and air-firing sortie. Then it was back to second 'dicky' duty on the night of 4/5 May 1941 against the pair of German battlecruisers bottled up in Brest. Jim flew this sortie under the critical eye of Sqn Ldr Robert Sharp in T2709. The others on board were Plt Off Waite and Sgts R. Instone, H.E. Jones and Taylor who were actually Jim's own crew, so it was clear that the flight commander was checking him out in preparation to send him off on his own in the near future. The fact that Jim flew three sorties with Sqn Ldr Sharp is perhaps an indication of how relatively unhurried the process was of 'easing in' a new crew at this stage of the air war. Aircraft losses were not particularly high and there was an adequate supply of aircrew coming through the training system to feed the quantity of squadrons available at this time.

Ninety-seven bombers were sent to attack the capital ships in Brest harbour. No 214 Squadron supplied sixteen of the Wellington force of fifty-four aircraft and Sqn Ldr Sharp took off at 21.05. Reaching the target area around midnight they found the port already lit by several fires. They made their bomb run in level flight at 11,000ft, aiming the single 2,000lb and three 500lb bombs at the dry dock. Sqn Ldr Sharp believed the bombs fell on or near a ship in dry dock although no actual explosions could be seen. Once again the journey home was uneventful and they landed back at Stradishall at 03.10.

Port installations were again the primary target for Bomber Command on the night of 6/7 May 1941, when Jim Crampton and his crew were once more teamed up with Sqn Ldr Bob Sharp in T2709. Take-off was at 21.50 and they set course for Hamburg. They were unable to locate the main target so the skipper decided to drop his bombs among the flak and searchlights of Bremen from 14,000ft. The bomb load of three 250-pounders and 360 x 4lb incendiaries was released at 01.15 and Sgt Taylor in the rear turret claimed to have seen a fire start after the bombs went down. Sgt Taylor also had the chance to fire his guns in anger for the first time when he engaged two aircraft as the Wellington withdrew from the target area. He identified one as a Junkers Ju 88 and the other as a Heinkel He 111 and claimed to have damaged both aircraft.

Mannheim was the target for Jim's next operation on 9/10 May, flying again as second pilot to Sqn Ldr Sharp in Wellington T2709, one of 146 bombers despatched to the twin cities of Mannheim and Ludwigshafen. Although Mannheim was targeted mainly for its factories producing U-boat engines and accessories, there were indications of a subtle movement towards a strategy of area bombing when the Air Staff also declared it 'suitable as an area objective and its attack should have high morale value'. This target was a long haul and it was going to test Jim thoroughly before he was sent out as captain of his own aircraft. Take-off for T2709 was 22.15 and the primary target was reached at 01.00. The bomb load on this op was 2 x 500lb HE, 1 x 250lb HE and 360 x 4lb incendiaries, all of which were dropped in a shallow dive from 12,000ft. Afterwards, rear gunner Sgt Taylor reported that he saw the bombs bursting on the target and four fires were started, one very large. The 900-mile round trip from Stradishall was completed without incident and they landed back at 03.45.

Plt Off Jim Crampton did one more trip with Sqn Ldr Bob Sharp which took them back to Hamburg on 11/12 May in T2709. Visibility was good all the way in and out, and Jim took nominal command of the aircraft for this op. A force of ninety-one Wellingtons was despatched and it was the third time in four nights that the city had been bombed. It was around 01.45 when Jim ordered his bombs to be aimed at the dock area and released during a steady, throttled-back descent from 16,000ft down to 9,500ft. They were seen to burst on the target and start fires. Weaving his way out, he landed back at 05.00. Three Wellingtons were lost from the attacking force that night: one of which, R1462 from No 214 Squadron, was flown by 20-year-old Plt Off J. Toplis who died in the crash. John Toplis had trained with Jim at Moreton-in-Marsh and they had been posted to Stradishall together.

Plt Off Crampton had to wait three weeks for his first crack as aircraft captain entirely on his own. In the meantime, he and other pilots not on ops kept their hand in with regular training sorties. In Jim's case this included a cross-country navigation exercise on 24 May, a fighter affiliation sortie for RAF Coltishall on the 28th and a number of formation practice sorties.

When he was back on ops he would be taking along a 'rookie' pilot as 'second dicky' and giving him the benefit of his own, albeit rather brief, experience. Plt Off Lucian Ercolani was crewed as second pilot with Jim and their joint first experiences came on 2/3 June 1941 when, as one of twelve aircraft despatched by the squadron, they were part of a force of 150 aircraft – sixty-eight Wellingtons, forty-three Hampdens and thirty-nine Whitleys – sent to Düsseldorf. In addition to Plt Off Ercolani, Jim had his usual crew with him that night in Wellington R1613: Plt Off Waite, Sgt Instone, Sgt Jones and Flt Sgt Taylor. Taking off at 23.00 they reached the target area only to find it obscured by 10/10ths cloud and haze. Unable to identify the city with any great certainty, they made a timed run in and dropped 3 x 500lb HE, 1 x 250lb HE and three containers of 4lb incendiaries from 12,000ft, aimed at where they believed the city to be. It was reported later that only 107 of the bombers claimed to have attacked the city and only very light damage and casualties were recorded by the city council. Jim, however, was probably just happy to have his first trip as captain under his belt.

German ships were back on the menu and No 214 Squadron was one of two squadrons supplying a total of thirty Wellingtons to mount an attack on the battlecruiser *Prinz Eugen*. In company with the mighty *Bismarck*, *Prinz Eugen* had played an important part in the recent major encounter with HMS *Hood* and HMS *Prince of Wales*, but the two German ships separated and *Prinz Eugen* headed for Brest.

The squadron sent out ten aircraft and Plt Off Crampton, with his own crew and Plt Off Ercolani, set out for Brest in R1613 at 22.45 on the night of 7 June 1941. They dropped their five 500lb bombs although, in common with the rest of the force, no hits were scored on the battlecruiser. No aircraft were lost but, low on fuel, Jim landed at RAF Hinton-in-the-Hedges. That was the last time

Plt Off Lucian Ercolani, who flew
several operations as 'second dicky'
with Jim Crampton while on No 214
Squadron. (Via author)

that Plt Off Ercolani flew with Jim
Crampton. However, Ercolani was
not yet ready for his own aircraft
and flew as second pilot with other
crews a few more times before
he made aircraft captain. Lucian
Ercolani was destined to have a
distinguished career in the RAF.
The son of an Italian furniture
designer and manufacturer who
came to England in 1910, Lucian
was educated at Oundle, leaving in
1934 to join his father's company,
the well-known furniture maker
Ercol. He was decorated three
times for gallantry in bomber operations over Europe and in the Far East.
For one much-publicised incident, during which he was wounded and his
aircraft badly damaged in an operation with No 214 Squadron on the night of
7/8 November 1941, he was awarded an immediate DSO – a high honour for
someone of relatively junior rank.

On 11/12 June the target for thirteen Wellingtons from No 216 Squadron
was Düsseldorf (one other aircraft was sent to Boulogne). Part of an overall
force of ninety-two Wellingtons and six Short Stirlings sent to this city, Jim
Crampton made the trip in N2802 with his usual crew plus another Sgt Taylor
as his second pilot. Take-off was at 23.00 and the bomber approached the
target at 01.05 only to find haze obscuring the city below. Accurate bombing
was impossible but while Jim put the aircraft in a shallow dive from 16,000ft
to 13,000ft, Plt Off Waite released the bomb load of three 500lb, one 250lb and
360 4lb incendiaries. No one saw any detonations afterwards but rear gunner
Sgt Taylor reported seeing a large explosion as their aircraft was turning for
home. Stradishall was reached at 03.50 without further difficulty.

When Jim and his crew roused from their well-earned slumbers, they found
themselves on ops again that night, 12/13 June, and this time Hamm was 'on
the menu'. Bomber Command put railways firmly on the agenda and on this
night despatched a total of 318 Wellingtons, Hampdens and Whitleys to attack
marshalling yards in the Ruhr towns of Soest, Schwerte and Hamm just to the

east of Dortmund. Eighty-two Wellingtons were sent to Hamm and Jim, in N2802, was one of nine aircraft despatched by No 214 Squadron. Take-off was at 23.55 and he reached the target area around 01.50. Flying at 14,000ft, poor visibility and haze made definite identification of the aiming point impossible, so he ran in on an area that he thought was the city itself and Plt Off Waite let the six 500lb and one 250lb bombs go. Flashes were seen soon afterwards but no one could say for certain where their bombs ended up and a similar situation was also reported by the other crews. An uneventful return journey saw them land back at Stradishall at 04.15.

Jim's crew were stood down for a week and it was not until the night of 21/22 June that they were called for ops again. Up until now Jim had flown the Mk IC version of the Wellington, which was powered by two Bristol Pegasus XVIII engines. For the operation on 21/22 June he was allocated W5452, a Wellington Mk II powered by Rolls-Royce Merlin X engines, and this change of aircraft seems to have been related to the early in-service evaluation of the new 4,000lb High Capacity (HC) blast bomb that came to be known throughout the RAF as a 'Blockbuster' or 'Cookie'.

The Merlin engines gave the Mk II a superior performance to the IC and allowed a higher all-up weight to be achieved, which in turn gave it the ability to carry a greater bomb load or have an increased range by carrying more fuel. Coupled with a higher ceiling and cruising speed, the Mk II was considered a good platform to carry a 4,000lb bomb being proposed by the Air Ministry

A 4,000lb Cookie being loaded into a Vickers Wellington. (B. Parker Collection)

during 1940. The explosive, usually Amatol or RDX/TNT, comprised about 75 per cent of the total weight of this weapon, which measured 110in (279cm) in overall length, including a 27in (69cm) tail. The diameter was 30in (76cm). The Wellington bomb bay was stuffed pretty full by one of these beauties! The designer of the Wellington, Barnes Wallis, came up with the modifications required for the bomb bay area, including removal of the intermediate bomb doors; replacement of the normal bomb-carrying beams by special vertical supports inserted in the centre-section spar bracing; and the provision of additional fittings on the forward frame designed to assist the suspension of this new 4,000lb monster in the bay.

A 4,000lb Cookie was dropped operationally for the first time during a raid on Emden on 1 April 1941 by one Wellington from each of Nos 9 and 149 Squadrons. With the first production order for 1,000 bombs only being issued during April 1941, by mid-June just a small number of these had been dropped in anger. However, when suitably modified Wellington aircraft also began to roll off the line, both were gradually spread out among Bomber Command to give as many squadrons as possible a chance to try out this new weapon. It is recorded that 226 Cookies had been dropped by the end of August 1941 – and 93,000 by May 1945. By way of comparison, it is estimated that a Wellington carrying one 4,000lb HC Cookie carried over 2.5 times the amount of explosives as it would have done if the load had been 18 x 250lb or 9 x 500lb GP bombs.

Plt Off Jim Crampton was selected to do the honours for No 214 Squadron during an operation to Cologne on 21/22 June 1941. Having taken off at 23.45 with Plt Off Jenkins as second pilot for this trip, W5452 reached the city at 02.05 but cloud and haze made aiming difficult. Plt Off Jenkins was now to be the regular second pilot in Jim's crew and flew with him for the remainder of his operations.

The navigator saw two areas of fire in the northern part of the city and the 4,000-pounder was dropped in that area, its release being marked by the bomber taking a distinct surge upwards. Some of the crew thought they could see debris being thrown into the air from its detonation and Sgt Taylor in the rear turret reported a few scattered small fires as the aircraft left the target area. Thirteen other aircraft from No 214 Squadron claimed similar results, but in *Bomber Command War Diaries*, author Martin Middlebrook wrote: 'Cologne: 68 Wellingtons; cloud and haze encountered. Out of the 500 HE and nearly 5,000 incendiaries carried by the bombers, none are recorded as dropping inside Cologne's boundaries, only a few in villages to the west. No aircraft lost.'

After a couple of nights off, Jim and his crew were back on ops on 24/25 June, this time taking N2800, a Mk IC, to Düsseldorf along with eleven other aircraft,

Wellington Mk II, W5442, BU-V of No 214 Squadron, Stradishall. (Andrew Thomas)

while three more of the squadron's bombers attacked the port of Emden. One of the latter, R1609 captained by Sgt Godfrey Jones, failed to return and all but the second pilot, Plt Off Forrest, were posted as missing in action.

Düsseldorf was the objective for twenty-three Wellingtons and eight Manchesters and no aircraft were lost from this raid. Jim took off at 23.30 with a load consisting of one 1,000lb, four 500lb and one 250lb bombs. These were released over the southern part of the town from 15,000ft but no results were observed. The return leg was uneventful as usual and they landed back at 05.00. So far, the squadron ORB entries recorded no brushes with night-fighters and there was little or no comment recorded about flak or searchlight activity encountered.

This situation was unlikely to continue and indeed a sign that things were about to change became evident during Bomber Command's, and Jim Crampton's, next major operation, when seventy-three Wellingtons and thirty-five Whitleys were despatched to Bremen on 27/28 June 1941. Nineteen of these aircraft were from No 214 Squadron.

Lifting his aircraft off Stradishall runway at 23.15, Plt Off Jim Crampton took his regular crew in a IC, R1613, loaded with two 500lb bombs and six containers of 4lb incendiaries. Martin Middlebrook wrote of this raid:

They encountered storms, icing conditions and, reported for the first time in Bomber Command records, 'intense night-fighter attacks'. Eleven Whitleys

(33 per cent of the force sent) and three Wellingtons were lost, the heaviest night loss of the war so far. Many of the bombers must have found their way to Hamburg, 50 miles away. That city reported 76 bombing incidents and five bombers shot down over the city.

Fires were already visible in the town south of the river when Jim arrived to make his bomb run at 15,000ft at around 01.30. The crew believed they saw fires start from the explosions. There was no comment about enemy air activity and their aircraft touched down at 04.40.

Jim took R1613 to Bremen again on 2/3 July, dropping one 1,000lb, three 500lb and one 250lb bombs on the city. He reported afterwards that no definite results could be seen and no searchlights were operating at the time of his attack. Two nights later he set out in Mk II, W5452, with a Cookie on board, but had to abort the op and land – probably very delicately – at RAF Boscombe Down due to engine trouble. The squadron diary records that at least one other Mk II was in operation that night carrying a 4,000lb Cookie, so it seems several of these were filtering through to the squadron now.

At the beginning of July 1941 Bomber Command was allowed to move its operations away from maritime-related targets and return to its main task of attacking German transportation targets. A new directive ordered that during the moon period of each month, bombers should be despatched to attack a ring of land, rail and water-borne transport targets around the Ruhr. On nights with no moon a list of designated city targets close to the distinctive River Rhine was specified and when the weather was too bad for the Rhine targets, a list of other more distant cities would be attacked.

It was this new directive that saw twelve aircraft from No 214 Squadron among a total of 114 Wellingtons called upon to attack Cologne in near perfect weather conditions on the night of 7/8 July. Jim Crampton's crew in R1613 bombed the centre of the city at 01.30 with one 1,000lb and two 500lb bombs from 12,000ft. Out of the attacking force only three aircraft were lost – including T2992 flown by Plt Off Jenkyns from No 214 Squadron – and Jim's crew returned safely at 04.20. Two nights later, on 9/10 July, Jim went to Osnabrück in R1613 in company with sixteen other Wellingtons from the squadron. On this op, for reasons unknown, Sgt Greenaway was in the rear turret rather than Jim's regular gunner Sgt Taylor. Although all fifty-seven bombers despatched claimed to have bombed the target, reports from the town stated that no bombs fell in Osnabrück and only a few in a couple of nearby villages.

Things did not go well for No 214 Squadron from the start on the night of 14/15 July 1941, when the squadron despatched only four aircraft on ops to Bremen. The remainder of the attacking force was made up of seventy-four

Vickers Wellington IC, BU-Z of No 214 Squadron, airborne from RAF Stradishall. (Andrew Thomas)

Wellingtons and nineteen Whitleys and there were three aiming points allocated: the docks, the railway station and the city centre.

Wellingtons R1341 (Plt Off Guild), R1613 (Plt Off Crampton), R1614 (Plt Off Brown) and T2918 (Sgt Gwilliam) took off from Stradishall at three-minute intervals from 23.57. Just before midnight, over the North Sea, Plt Off Guild ran into some bad weather and icing conditions. Ice built up rapidly all over his aircraft and he could not get the bomber to climb, so reluctantly he decided to turn back, managing to land safely at 01.20. Sgt Gwilliam was also well out over the North Sea when he had to turn back, in his case due to engine trouble. He touched down behind Plt Off Guild at 01.20.

Plt Off Victor Brown was last away at 23.15 and he and his crew were never heard from again. It is believed he, too, may have become victim to the weather and severe icing over the North Sea. Plt Off Brown's body was washed ashore in Holland and is buried in Bergen op Zoom Commonwealth cemetery. The bodies of air gunner Flt Sgt William Lewis and wireless operator Sgt Ronald Hull came ashore on English beaches, but the rest of that crew (second pilot Sgt Max Collins, navigator Sgt Joseph Else and rear gunner Sgt Jack Taylor) were posted as missing in action and are commemorated on the Runnymede Memorial.

Jim Crampton had a new rear gunner in his crew that night instead of his regular Sgt Taylor. It was never clear what Sgt Taylor's initials and first names were and it is therefore possible that the Sgt Jack Taylor lost in R1614 might have been Jim's original rear gunner. Canadian air gunner Sgt Marshall ('Marsh') Johnson was new to the squadron, having arrived just a day or so before he was allocated as rear gunner in Jim Crampton's crew for this operation. Many years later, Marshall recalled: 'I threw my kit on the bunk, climbed into a Wellington for my first op and didn't come back!'

Wellington R1613, coded BU-G, reached Bremen and Jim settled at 10,000ft to begin manoeuvring ready for the bomb run. It was at this juncture that all hell broke loose. In later years Jim recalled that his rear gunner, Marshall, calmly announced over the intercom that 'we are under attack' as a night-fighter curved in towards the rear from above and to one side. At the same time Marsh met the attacker with a hail of gunfire from his turret. The German fighter's own fire raked the forward section of the bomber, killing second pilot John Jenkins and starting several fires in the fuselage. It was clear that the bomber was doomed so Jim gave the order to bale out. The remainder of the crew, with the exception of Sgt Robert Kent, managed to exit safely sustaining only minor injuries between them. Tragically, Sgt Kent's parachute deployed too quickly and the canopy became entangled with the tail of the burning bomber, dragging him to his death. His body was not discovered for two weeks, after which he was interred at Rheinberg cemetery near his friend John Jenkins. The four surviving members of Jim Crampton's crew were soon

Jim Crampton (standing, right) and his crew in front of Wellington R1613, BU-G, in which he was shot down. (Crampton Family Collection)

rounded up by the Germans, who sent two off to hospital and the other two to the aircrew interrogation and transit centre Dulag Luft in Frankfurt and thence to separate prison camps. When he was shot down, Jim was on his eighteenth operation.

Jim Crampton's parachute landing in a cornfield just outside Bremen signalled the start of almost four years of captivity, first in Oflag (*Offizier-lager*) VII-C at Laufen Castle in Austria and then in Stalag Luft (*Stammlager Luft*) III near Sagan in Lower Silesia (now Zagen in Poland), about 100 miles southeast of Berlin, to where he was moved in April 1942. This is the camp made famous by the 'Wooden Horse' and the 'Great Escape', and Jim was one of those who day after day, in the guise of a PT enthusiast, steadied or vaulted the famous gymnastic wooden horse while a tunneller worked inside it. He recalled: 'A German guard looked on placidly, smoking his pipe, little realising that just a few yards away someone was digging himself out of the camp.'

Often overshadowed by the later Great Escape, the Wooden Horse escape, which took place from inside the east compound, was the brainchild of Flt Lt Eric Williams and Lt Michael Codner who, when he helped with sand dispersal and the actual digging, invited Flt Lt Oliver Philpot to take part in the escape. Potential escapers in Stalag Luft III were faced with the problem of digging a very long tunnel because the accommodation huts, in which a tunnel entrance might be concealed, were not only raised off the ground but were a considerable distance from the perimeter fence. In addition, the subsoil was bright yellow sand, easy to detect and rendered tunnels liable to collapse. Williams and Codner came up with an ingenious way of digging their tunnel, whose entrance was located in the middle of an open area relatively close to the perimeter fence: they used a gymnastic vaulting horse to cover the opening. The horse was constructed from plywood used in Red Cross parcels.

Each day the horse, with one, and later two, diggers hidden inside, was carried out to the same spot and while a cohort of prisoners conducted gymnastic exercises above, a shaft and tunnel were dug beneath it. At the end of each digging session a wooden board was placed over the tunnel entrance about a foot below the surface and re-covered with the grey surface soil. Sand removed from the tunnel was stored in bags made from trouser legs hung inside the horse, which was then carried, complete with the digger, back to a hut by the gymnasts. This placed a great physical strain on those who carried the horse and they had to appear not to struggle with its weight. The gymnasts' activity also kept the sound of digging from being detected by seismic microphones which were known to have been planted around the perimeter.

For 114 days the three diggers, in shifts of one or two at a time, dug over 100ft of tunnel, 30in square at a depth of 5ft, using bowls as shovels and metal rods to poke through the surface to create air holes. Shoring was only used for the first few feet of its length to counteract the impact of the vaulters above and the fetid conditions inside the tunnel took their toll on the health of all three men. During the evening of 29 October 1943 the three men made their escape. Two reached Stettin and one Danzig (Gdansk), from which ports they all travelled by ship to neutral Sweden from where they were flown back to England, having made the first successful escapes ('home runs') from Stalag Luft III.

At this point it should be noted that Jim Crampton talked little of his experiences as a prisoner of war, nor is he known to have written any notes about it. However, it is believed Jim remained in Stalag Luft III until the camp was forcibly vacated by the Germans on 27 January 1945, when Soviet forces broke through German lines and advanced from Breslau and Posnan towards the River Oder, east of Sagan. Upon his return to Spalding after his repatriation, the *Lincolnshire Free Press* carried a short article:

> Flags and bunting were flying in Cley Hall Drive, Spalding throughout the weekend to welcome home Plt Off James Crampton after nearly four years as a prisoner of the Germans. Plt Off Crampton was in the camp where fifty servicemen who had escaped and had been recaptured were shot [a clear reference to Stalag Luft III]. He was also in a 100-mile [*sic*] march from Sagan to a camp near Berlin during which, but for Red Cross parcels, they would have had nothing to eat for five days. Released by the Russians, Plt Off Crampton was brought to this country by air.

From Jim's remark about 'doing gymnastics over the Wooden Horse', this places him inside the east compound of the main Stalag during 1943, since the Wooden Horse project took place there during the three months preceding the escape date of 29 October 1943. There are further factors to suggest that, at the time of the evacuation of Stalag Luft III, Jim Crampton was held in a compound known as Belaria, just a mile or so away on the north-east side of the town of Sagan. It was located on a barren hill with six barrack blocks built up on small brick plinths so that all activities under the buildings could be observed by the guards. More barracks were constructed as the population increased.

As the size of the main camp grew, Belaria compound was opened up in February 1944, with 500 British and Commonwealth officers and airmen being transferred from the east and centre compounds of the main camp. It should be noted that all the compounds, including Belaria, are generally referred to collectively as Stalag Luft III. Some American airmen prisoners were also transferred to Belaria later. Hot water and bathing facilities at Belaria were very limited and the prisoners were regularly marched to and from the main Stalag for showers and de-lousing, which would no doubt have led them to still regard themselves as being in Stalag Luft III. After his return to England, while Jim made specific reference to his involvement with the Wooden Horse episode, which took place in the east compound of the main camp, he did not make mention of the Great Escape in the same terms. This seems to confirm that, since the Great Escape took place in March 1944 from the north compound, being in the east compound he would probably have been unaware of it, and in February 1944 he was even further removed from it by being transferred to Belaria as part of the first batch of prisoners to be housed in that new compound.

Although for several days the prisoners had been aware of the possibility of a rapid evacuation and began to make whatever simple preparations they could, it was not until 19.00 on Saturday 27 January 1945, with the advancing Russians only 12 miles away, that the German commandant gave the order for the camp to be evacuated immediately; the destination was Spremberg in Germany. Gathering up whatever meagre rations and clothing they could, the first to leave were the Americans from the south compound at 21.00 and the west compound at 23.00. The British began to leave the north compound at 01.00 on Sunday 28 January, with the last of their column clearing by 03.00. The British in the east compound started out at 06.00 and it, too, was clear by 07.00. Prisoners in the compound at Belaria did not leave until the following day. For reasons that will become apparent later, Jim is believed to have been among that final column from Belaria.

Dawn broke on a bleak, starkly black-and-white scene. Snowing heavily, with 6in already on the ground and bitterly cold in the sub-zero temperature, Belaria compound became the last part of Sagan POW camp to be evacuated at 06.00 on Monday 29 January 1945. The delay had allowed time to prepare makeshift backpacks, build a few sleds, distribute any excess clothing and consume as much of the food that had been hoarded that could not be carried on the march. One inmate wrote that he wore three jerseys, one pair of long underpants, a set of pyjamas, a balaclava, a pair of long trousers, battledress, overcoat, shoes and mittens – and was still dreadfully cold!

Although this final group also had Spremberg as its objective, the Belaria column took a more northern and direct route towards the intermediate town of Bad Muskau, where all columns stayed on the second night. The earlier columns marched on from Muskau, eventually reaching Spremberg at 15.00 on Friday 2 February after about five days on the road. Here 3,000 men were herded into overcrowded, filthy railway cattle trucks and transported for two more days, with scant food and water, to a POW camp 10 miles north of Bremen, several hundred miles away in north-west Germany. After a short time many were then marched from Bremen to a prison camp at Lübeck where they were eventually liberated by British forces.

When the Belaria column reached Spremberg, the Americans among them were separated and sent away to join several thousand other American POWs already hived off from the British and making their way to various other POW camps throughout the German homeland. The remaining British and Commonwealth prisoners from Belaria were piled into railway cattle trucks and transported to Stalag III-A, located at Luckenwalde, a town just 18 miles south of Berlin, where they arrived on Sunday 4 February. Jim said he was sent to 'a camp near Berlin' and this is the factor that seems to firmly place him with the Belaria group.

Records show that the long-established camp at Luckenwalde – reputed to have an extremely harsh and brutal regime – was liberated by the Russian army, which also supports Jim's statement that (a) he was 'at a camp near Berlin' and (b) he was 'released by the Russians'. The German guards melted away from Luckenwalde on 21 April and the first Russians arrived on the 22nd, liberating the prisoners, but it took a week or two for the prisoners to be moved out and handed over for processing at reception and transit centres set up by American forces in that area. Repatriated to England by air in mid-1945, Jim was sent on a long-term-prisoner rehabilitation course at Rugby, after which he elected to stay in the RAF. He was eventually posted to RAF Manby, where, now a flight lieutenant, he flew Lancasters until he left the service in 1947.

This was by no means the end of Jim Crampton's flying career – in fact, quite the opposite. May 1947 saw the emergence of private aviation in the Spalding area when George Clifton, himself a former RAF pilot who flew Halifax bombers in the Second World War, established an air taxi company as part of his Spalding Travel Agency business, operating from a small grass field near Wykeham Abbey, 3 miles from Spalding. In January 1948 there was sufficient buoyancy in the air taxi market for George Clifton to invite Jim Crampton to join him in the business as a pilot. The sole aircraft owned by the company at that time was Auster J-1 Autocrat G-AJIU, which was flown on business and pleasure flights all over the UK and Europe; it was joined eventually by two more Autocrats, G-AJDZ and AIPU, Miles Messenger G-AJFF, Miles Gemini G-AKDK, Fairchild Argus G-AJPC and DH Dragon Rapide G-AEMH. It became necessary to employ more pilots and the operation moved to a larger, 60-acre field further down Spalding Marsh, where a blister hangar and a concrete-section office were erected. Jim became chief pilot and operations manager in 1949 and flew all these aircraft types at one

Spalding Airways air taxi business. The Auster Autocrat G-AJDZ is being flown by Jim Crampton (right), with George Bland as a passenger, in 1949. (Ted Crampton)

time or another; one of his most notable trips, for example, was to take a Spalding couple on holiday to Florence in Italy in Auster G-AIPU and collect them a week later. Although Jim was quite used to long sortie times, this represented a marathon for the small aeroplane and indeed for the two passengers, Mr and Mrs George Bland.

In 1950 what had become known as Spalding Airways grew so much that George Clifton decided to move to new premises on the former RAF airfield at Westwood, Peterborough. Around this time Jim Crampton left Spalding Airways and set up his own private and business air taxi company in a field in Costessey on the outskirts of Norwich, using a caravan as his office. This field later became the venue for the Norfolk Show. Trading as Norfolk Airways, in addition to air taxi work he took on a variety of flying jobs such as pleasure flights, aerial-banner towing and aerial photography on a commercial scale. During the British winter periods in the early 1950s Jim turned his hand to bush flying in Africa: crop spraying, locust spraying and undertaking aerial surveys over jungle regions. He said:

> We used to fly over the locust swarms in Kenya and spray them. I once got myself involved in a rebellion in the Sudan during one of the crop-spraying seasons. I had to fly over rebel strongholds with loud speakers fitted and a tape

recorder telling them in Sudanese to disperse and go back to their homes. I don't remember getting shot at and I don't know if they ever went home.

As part of his Norfolk Airways operations, Jim undertook pleasure flying from Clacton, Yarmouth and Cleethorpes beaches during the holiday seasons of the 1950s, and even flaunted regulations by landing at low tide on Scrooby sandbank off Great Yarmouth. He rented space at the former RAF airfield of Waltham (Grimsby), and between 1954 and 1958 offered summer pleasure flights from both the airfield and Cleethorpes beach, the latter using Austers, including G-AIBY, AJVT and AMSZ.

As Jim's own business grew it became necessary to find a more suitable base for the larger and greater quantity of aircraft needed. Norfolk Airways eventually moved to the former RAF airfield of Horsham St Faith on the outskirts of Norwich – later to become Norwich Airport. By 1969 his team of aircraft and pilots had notched up 1.5 million air miles, of which more than a third was flown on behalf of the Norwich Union Insurance Company, Jim's biggest customer since 1962. Another regular customer was Anglia Television, for whom he undertook aerial filming sorties and flew filmed stories from all over the eastern counties back to the Norwich studio so they could be included in TV news bulletins and other programmes.

Around 1965 Jim acquired a business partner – the well-known and colourful aero engineer Leslie 'Wilbur' Wright – who already owned his own air

Post-war civilian pilot Jim Crampton in the uniform of Rig Air, with a Fairchild Argus. (Crampton Family Collection)

business called Anglian Air Charter, operating out of Great Yarmouth (North Denes) airfield. Together they embarked on a series of steps that, over time, revolutionised the air travel industry in the east of England. Initially, recognising the growth potential of the North Sea gas industry for their businesses, the two companies launched a joint-venture operation called Rig Air which ferried rig workers between the various gas operator bases (but not to the rigs themselves). In addition to continuing their established charter work, a DC-3 aircraft was acquired to move gas personnel around the UK and the Continent from what was then Horsham St Faith airfield. This business was so successful that Jim and Wilbur decided to merge the three separate businesses under the name of Air Anglia. This airline grew to carry in excess of 400,000 passengers a year, serving eighteen airports in the UK and the Continent with twenty aircraft and 700 employees. The company also included an executive air charter division, an engineering services division that looked after its own and other operators' aircraft, and a separate inclusive holiday subsidiary called Anglia Holidays. In 1979 Jim and Wilbur sold 85 per cent of Air Anglia to British & Commonwealth Shipping and the airline was later renamed Air UK, with Jim and Wilbur remaining as non-executive directors for a time until they both retired. Later, British & Commonwealth sold Air UK to the Dutch airline KLM, who subsequently relaunched it as KLM UK.

Airline owners Jim Crampton (right) and Leslie 'Wilbur' Wright mark the addition of the first Fokker F28 jet to their Air Anglia fleet in 1979. (Crampton Family Collection)

Jim continued to fly in his spare time as he remained fascinated by the continuing challenge and excitement of flying, even learning to fly a helicopter in his sixties. Much of his remaining personal leisure time was spent in renovating Oxnead Mill, on the River Bure in Norfolk, and turning its associated buildings into a home for his family in a most picturesque setting. The huge interior of the mill allowed him to install several theatre organs, which helped to satisfy both his engineering and musical passions. Jim Crampton died in Norfolk on 26 September 1987.

Jim Crampton's Operational Flights in the Second World War

Date	Target	Role	Notes
20/21 April 1941	Rotterdam	2nd Pilot	
25/26 April	Kiel	"	
28/29 April	Brest	"	
4/5 May	Brest	"	
6/7 May	Hamburg	"	
9/10 May	Mannheim	"	
11/12 May	Hamburg	"	
2/3 June	Düsseldorf	Captain	
7/8 June	Brest	"	
11/12 June	Düsseldorf	"	
12/13 June	Hamm	"	
21/22 June	Cologne	"	
24/25 June	Düsseldorf	"	
27/28 June	Bremen	"	
2/3 July	Bremen	"	Aborted, engine failure
7/8 July	Cologne	"	
9/10 July	Osnabrück	"	
14/15 July	Bremen	"	Shot down over target

5

BLITZED, BURNED BUT UNBROKEN

Squadron Leader Alan Kenneth Summerson

When the German blitzkrieg rolled into France on 10 May 1940, a south Lincolnshire airman found himself in the midst of the chaotic air battle that followed. Pre-war Cranwell-trained apprentice LAC Alan Summerson's survival story is a minor epic in its own right, epitomising the resilience and strength of his own character, as well as that of the Fairey Battle and Bristol Blenheim aircrews thrown into the path of the blitzkrieg, like chaff in the wind. Not only did he survive that ordeal, but he went on to see post-war operational service in two more conflicts, moving from the interwar biplanes of the start of his career to flying jet V-bombers by the end.

Born in the Lincolnshire village of Donington in 1920, Alan Summerson was educated at Donington Grammar School where he took his matriculation exams. Then, in February 1936, aged 16 and 'mad keen on aeroplanes', he joined the RAF as an apprentice. As airman 568963, he was one of a total of 148 young hopefuls on courses 8M12E (wireless electrical) and 8J12 (instruments) making up the thirty-third entry at the Electrical & Wireless School (later No 1 E&WS) RAF Cranwell. A member of class 8M12E, Alan embarked on a three-year trade apprenticeship in what was essentially a ground-based trade, often referred to as 'Tech Sigs', but his abiding aim in life was to fly. From the names of interwar aircraft he wrote in his later flying logbooks, it seems certain that Alan indeed took every opportunity to get airborne during his training at Cranwell. We find such evocative names as Atlas, Gordon, Hart, Overstrand, Sidestrand, Seal, Tutor, Victoria, Vincent, Virginia, Wallace, Wapiti, Wellesley, and Wildebeest, which could reasonably only have been 'logged' up to the date he joined No 52 Squadron in January 1939.

Aircraftman Alan Summerson as a young Cranwell apprentice in 1936. (John Summerson)

During his time at Cranwell Alan acquired a nickname by which he became universally known in the RAF and beyond. Cranwell was not more than 20 miles from his home in Donington and as soon as the passage of time, regulations and money allowed him to do so, Alan, although 6ft 3in tall, bought an open-top MG sports car that became his pride and joy. This gave him the freedom to visit his home quite frequently. His notion of driving, however, seemed to be based entirely on two speeds: 'very fast' and 'stop'. This penchant for driving everywhere like a bat out of hell quickly earned him the nickname 'Zoom', which stuck with him for the rest of his days.

He was a bright lad and displayed undoubted aptitude and skill in his trade, having passed his apprenticeship course as an Aircraftman First Class (AC1) wireless electrical mechanic in January 1939. Thoroughly schooled in the intricacies of radio equipment and how to operate it (truly living up to the motto of No 1 E&WS: 'thorough'), with war clouds gathering he was able to seize yet another opportunity to fly by volunteering for aircrew training as a wireless operator/air gunner. In this he was successful and being highly qualified as a radio technician and operator already, Alan was posted to No 52 (B) Squadron based at RAF Upwood near Ramsey in Cambridgeshire to gain the other skills required by an air gunner.

As part of the rapid expansion of the RAF, Upwood had reopened with full station status in January 1937 and its two units, No 63 and No 52 (B) Squadrons, had also been reactivated, during the spring of that year, with Hawker Audaxes and Hinds respectively. By the beginning of 1938, No 52 (B) Squadron received the first of the RAF's Fairey Battle Mk Is into service, but the process of re-equipment was slow and still going on when Alan arrived a year later. Indeed, his logbook shows both the Hawker Hind and the Audax in the 'Types Flown In' list. At the beginning of 1939, No 52 changed its status to that of a training squadron – taking on a role similar to the later bomber OTUs – and it was at that point, February 1939, that Alan arrived at Upwood for his air gunnery training. His logbook records that he qualified as an air gunner with No 52 (B) Squadron on 5 May 1939, so he could now proudly wear the new air gunner half-wing flying brevet on his tunic, to go with his 'clenched-fist' wireless-trade arm badge. He had at last achieved his boyhood dream.

Alan remained with No 52 Squadron until early August 1939, getting to know his way round the Battle until – with the obviously deteriorating political situation – he was sent home on leave before the balloon went up. It is probable that, with his insatiable appetite for flying in anything he could get his hands on, it was during this period up to August 1939 that he 'logged' time in the turrets of a Boulton Paul Defiant and an Armstrong Whitworth Whitley, which are also recorded in his book. It was during this leave period that he and many like him received urgent telegrams, in his case recalling him to Upwood. Back at the station he was ordered to report to No 150 Squadron, an operational Fairey Battle unit based at RAF Benson. On 23 August 1939 the CO of No 150 Squadron, Sqn Ldr William MacDonald, was ordered to mobilise the squadron on a war footing as a unit of the Advanced Air Striking Force (AASF). One week later, on 3 September, war was declared and on that date the squadron had sixteen Fairey Battle aircraft on charge, organised into 'A' and 'B' Flights of eight aircraft each. Alan crewed up with Sgt George Barker, pilot, and Sgt James Williams, observer, in 'A' Flight and with just a few exceptions, Alan thereafter always flew with this crew. On Saturday 2 September 1939 AC1 Alan Summerson went to war.

Flying in the rear seat of K9380 Alan made a two-and-a-half-hour flight from Benson to Challerange in France as part of No 74 Wing of the AASF. With the arrival of the squadron's Miles Magister P2394, flown in by Fg Off R.A.Weeks on the 4th, the whole squadron had fully relocated to Challerange, a town located 25 miles east of Reims, where they set about preparing for operations. At 14.35 on 10 September, the squadron's first war operation was a three-hour reconnaissance by three aircraft from 'A' Flight led by Sqn Ldr MacDonald. On 12 September, having sorted themselves out and with all personnel and equipment having arrived, No 150 Squadron was ordered to move to an airfield at Écury-sur-Coole, near the River Marne south-west of Challons and 20 miles south of Reims. Alan Summerson made this short flight with Sgt Pay and Sgt Leitch in Battle L5225.

Alan's own first op came on 18 September. It was a reconnaissance of the Franco-German border with his usual crew, Barker and Williams, in K9380, but they were not airborne for very long before bad weather forced them to return to base. Next day the weather improved and Alan completed a two hour forty minute recco of the same area in K9379. He was on ops again on 25 September. This time it was a high-level photo reconnaissance along the

Franco-German border by six aircraft led by the CO of No 74 Wing, Wg Cdr Allan Hesketh. Alan Summerson flew on this operation with his regular crew of Barker and Williams in K9380. The formation was flying well inside German territory when they encountered some accurate enemy anti-aircraft fire in the vicinity of Zweibrücken, and, after the Wingco's aircraft L4948 was hit by shrapnel, they had to take a little evasive action, although the damage sustained was slight. A similar operation was carried out over a different sector by three more aircraft later that same morning.

Alan's next sortie came on Saturday the 30th; it was another photo-recco op and he flew again in K9380. Six aircraft, led by Sqn Ldr MacDonald, took off just before 11.00 and spent the next two and a half hours inspecting well over the German side of the border once again. Alan's aircraft was one of a separate section of three that took off shortly after the other six, to look at a different sector of the border. It turned out that Alan was very fortunate indeed to be in this smaller group because the first formation ran slap bang into eight Bf 109 fighters and was decimated.

No 150 Squadron's first encounter with enemy fighters came as a rude awakening indeed, but sadly it was a portent of what was to come. The vulnerability of the Fairey Battle, though tacitly accepted by pretty much everyone in command, had not yet been tested in combat and naturally the crews themselves just got on with the job. Today was the day it would all be tested. One of the six Battles developed engine trouble and returned to base – it was the lucky one – leaving the five remaining aircraft to carry on with the operation. When they crossed the border into the Saarland region to recco the area from Metzig to Saarbrücken, German flak batteries put up a barrage but no damage was sustained and the formation flew steadily on.

Irritated by these almost daily incursions into German territory, the Luftwaffe decided to challenge the RAF. At around 11.45 a formation of eight Messerschmitt Bf 109E fighters from the 2nd Staffel of I Gruppe, Jagdgeschwader 53 (2/JG 53) known as the *Pik-As* (Ace of Spades) Jagdgeschwader (fighter-wing), based at Wiesbaden-Erbenheim, arrived to patrol the same piece of sky and the two formations clashed. A short, sharp air battle took place and inside twenty minutes the 109s had torn into the unescorted Fairey Battles and shot down all bar one.

Flying Bf 109 'Red 1', the staffelkapitan, Spanish Civil War ace Oberleutnant (Oblt) Rolf Pingel, led his formation in a diving attack on the Fairey Battles and scored the first kill at 11.50 by sending K9484 down to crash to the west of Saarbrücken. The pilot, Plt Off John Saunders (aged 20), and WOp/AG AC1 Donald Thomas (19) died but the observer, Sgt G.J. Springett, baled out over German territory and was made a POW. Three minutes later Stabsfeldwebel

(Stfw) Ignaz Prestele shot down N2093 flown by Flt Lt Laurence Hyde-Parker, with his observer, Sgt William Cole (19), and WOp/AG AC1 D.E. Jones. This aircraft crash-landed near Metzig with the loss of Sgt Cole. Flt Lt Hyde-Parker escaped unhurt and his air gunner Jones was injured. By now the Fairey Battle formation had broken up in total confusion. It was every man for himself and survival seemed to lie in diving hard in the general direction of home. K9387, flown by Fg Off Fernald Corelli with Sgt L.B. Webber and AC Kenneth Gray, was cut off and badly shot up by Unteroffizier (Uffz) Franz Kaiser. It was this fighter pilot's first air victory and Corelli and Gray were killed in the hail of bullets. Observer Sgt Webber managed to bale out and descend safely into friendly hands. That was at 11.57. The fourth Battle, N2028, flown by Plt Off M.A. Poulton with Sgt T.A. Bates and AC1 H.E.A. Rose on board, was attacked by Uffz Hans Kornatz in 'Red 5' at about 12.05. This crew was fortunate to escape injury but their Battle was so badly damaged that there was no hope of reaching base and all three airmen baled out. This left the CO's aircraft, K9283, alone in the sky – but not for very long. After the shock of the first attack, Sqn Ldr MacDonald put the nose down and dived hard for the deck chased by several 109s, including that of Stfw Prestele. All the air gunners had found the fighters hard to hit but the CO's gunner, AC1 Alexander Murcar, managed to get a bead on Prestele's machine and 'draw blood'. Stfw Prestele's 109 was damaged, forcing him to break off the fight and return to base. Yet another 109 bore down on the CO's aircraft as he crossed the border. It was piloted by Uffz Josef Wurmheller, who was also seeking his first victory. Now twisting and turning at treetop height, Wurmheller pressed home his attacks and hit his target hard – later reports spoke of more than forty holes found in MacDonald's aircraft – slightly wounding the observer Sgt Fred Gardiner and AC1 Murcar. With his victim close to the ground and streaming smoke as he broke away, Wurmheller believed he had done enough to claim his first kill, but, despite all the damage, Sqn Ldr MacDonald was able to limp back to base. Lowering the undercarriage, he brought his battered Battle in to land but one of the wheels was shot up and the aircraft ground-looped, collapsed and burst into flames – so Wurmheller's claim indeed turned out to be valid.

Another outcome of this disastrous encounter can be found in the following citation from *The London Gazette*, dated 14 November 1939:

The Medal of the Military Division of the Most Excellent Order of the British Empire, For Meritorious Service. 517540 Sgt Frederick Gardiner RAF.

In September 1939, the aircraft in which Sgt Gardiner was air observer was attacked by enemy aircraft and severely damaged. Two petrol tanks were punctured and despite the fumes and bleeding from a slight gunshot wound over the right eye, this airman continued his duties and succeeded in setting an accurate course to the base. The aircraft caught fire on landing and although his clothes were alight, Sgt Gardiner commenced to extinguish the burning clothing of the wireless operator by rolling him on the ground and beating the flames with his hands. Not until his efforts were successful did he attend to his own clothing.

Sgt Gardiner and AC1 Murcar were whisked off to a hospital in Chalons to have their wounds and burns treated. Fred Gardiner's medal was presented to him on Plivot airfield by HM George VI in person, during his battlefield tour in December 1939. Even later, on 20 February 1940, *The London Gazette* announced awards of the DFC and DFM to Sqn Ldr William MacDonald and AC1 Alexander Murcar respectively, for their actions on that fateful day, 30 September 1939. In their cases no citations were published. Of the fifteen young airmen – many just 19 or 20 years old – in the five aircraft, eight made it back to Écury airfield by one means or another, six died and one was captured.

What is also interesting is that the two protagonists – No 150 Squadron and JG 53 – were destined to meet again in a far bigger battle before too long.

★ ★ ★

As a further consequence of the losses from the incident on 30 September and similar experiences in other squadrons, HQ AASF ordered that Fairey Battles were no longer to be used for daylight reconnaissance flights into enemy territory; this duty would be handed over to the Blenheim squadrons. It was not until March 1940 that No 150 Squadron recommenced operational flights over enemy territory, with some 'Nickel' (dropping propaganda leaflets) night raids, and Alan, now promoted to LAC, made his first of these leaflet-dropping ops on 25 March. He was with his usual crew in K9380 and they took off from Écury at 21.35 with a load of what many airmen regarded as 'free toilet paper' destined for Mannheim. However, they ran into bad weather quite soon and were forced to abandon the sortie, landing back at base at 22.10. Almost a month elapsed before Alan flew another Nickel raid, this time on the night of 21/22 April. Operational order 71/0/25/40 received from HQ 71 Wing required four aircraft from No 150 Squadron to drop Nickel on specified targets along the Rhine and to carry out reconnaissance along various parts of the river. Battle K9380, with Sgt Barker, Sgt Williams and LAC Summerson, was first up from Écury at 21.00 and flew to Worms via what was designated as Route No 3. Nickel was dropped over the town from a height of 10,000ft and the remainder of the op took in a recco of the River Rhine between Worms and Mannheim. This op was successful and Sgt Barker landed back at 23.30. The other three aircraft took off at intervals: K9369 with Fg Off Blom was airborne at 21.20, Nickelled Mannheim and recco'd the River Necker from Mannheim to Heidelberg, landing back at 00.10 hours. Next, K9379 was airborne at 22.00 with Fg Off Beale in command; he flew to Heidelberg, which was Nickelled from 10,000ft, and the Rhine was surveyed from 5,000ft between Mannheim and Speyer, before the return to base at 00.45 hours. The final aircraft, K9390, left at 22.30 with Flt Lt Parker at the controls, bound for Speyer. Nickel was dropped on the town from 10,000ft before descending to 3,000ft to carry out a recco of the Rhine between Speyer and Germersheim, then returning to base at 00.55. Similar operations were mounted by other crews on subsequent nights.

On 10 May 1940 the balloon went up. The German blitzkrieg advance into France began when enemy troops crossed the Dutch and Belgian frontiers. Their main thrust came in the south, through the Belgian Ardennes forest – which had been thought impassable to mechanised forces – and Luxembourg. General Heinz Guderian and his 19th Panzer Korps were heading for Sedan and the French moved their forces to confront this huge threat.

At noon on the 10th and acting on his own initiative, the British air commander, Air Marshal Barratt, ordered thirty-two Battles from Nos 12, 103, 105, 142, 150, 218 and 226 Squadrons to attack enemy troops advancing through Luxembourg. There would be no fighter escort and so the Battles were ordered to go in as low as 250ft and drop delayed-fuse bombs. Intense light flak and small arms fire accounted for the loss of thirteen of these aircraft and every one of the remainder sustained some degree of damage. It was while flying this operation that Flt Lt Bill Simpson from No 12 Squadron – of whom we shall hear more later – was shot down.

From No 150 Squadron four Battles were sent off at 15.30, in two sections of two aircraft each, to bomb a column of enemy troops on the Luxembourg to Echternach road. The first pair found the target but the second section led by Flt Lt Eric Parker could not and bombed a different column of troops – there was certainly no shortage of targets! Three of these aircraft were shot down. During the late afternoon, No 150 Squadron was again brought to thirty minutes' readiness but, no doubt with much relief, no further operations materialised that day.

At 06.10 the next morning the war reached Écury with a bang. The airfield came under heavy aerial attack by between eighteen and twenty-four enemy bombers dropping an estimated 150 bombs from 12,000ft altitude. By the end of the raid the airfield had eighteen craters across it and the armoury tent and

Fairey Battle JN-I, of No 150 Squadron, shot down near Sedan on 10 May 1940. (Andrew Thomas)

pyrotechnic store were set on fire and destroyed. Battle P2334 caught fire and was destroyed when its two 250lb bombs exploded. Battle P2335 sustained slight damage from flying fragments and five unexploded enemy bombs were littered around the northern edge of the field. That evening, in an effort to protect the aircraft, 'B' Flight's eight Battles were flown to a satellite airfield at Vatry, a few miles away.

'B' Flight returned at 09.00 on the 12th and at 14.45 a section of three aircraft from the flight, led by Flt Lt Weeks, with Sgt Andrews and Plt Off Campbell-Irons as the pilots of the other two, took off to attack a mechanised column between Neufchâteau and Bertrik. At 15.25 the formation ran into very intense flak a mile east of Neufchâteau. Ian Campbell-Irons' aircraft P2236 took a direct hit, exploded and crashed in flames just south of the town, killing him and his crew, Sgt Thomas Barker and LAC Reg Hinder. The two remaining aircraft found the target column a couple of miles west of Neufchâteau and dropping down to just 100ft, laid a stick of eight 250lb bombs with eleven-second delay fuses along its length. They both returned to base at 16.05 but one was badly damaged by gunfire and written off.

Just three days into the campaign, No 150 Squadron and indeed the whole AASF was taking heavy casualties in terms of men and machines. We should also remind ourselves that the French Air Force was heavily committed and suffering similarly badly. Early in the morning of the 13th the Germans reached Sedan, on the Meuse, and prepared to cross the river, which was perceived by the opposing French army as a strong defensive barrier – but they had never seen a strategy of the ferocity of blitzkrieg before! All through that day wave after wave of Stukas, Heinkels and Junkers Ju 88s of the Luftwaffe relentlessly pounded French positions across the river in one of the greatest air bombardments ever seen. Using pontoon bridges, by the middle of the afternoon Guderian's 19th Panzer Korps had launched its river crossing operations at three points in the Sedan sector and had soon established a bridgehead on the other side. Now it needed to be consolidated and expanded in the thrust for the Channel. During the 13th, rumours began to spread among French forces that tanks were already across the river and had penetrated their lines. This was not the case but it triggered a piecemeal, badly co-ordinated French retreat that, when German tanks did actually cross a specially strengthened pontoon bridge during the night of the 13/14th, caused a catastrophic gap to appear in the weakened French front that was exploited by the Germans. Now facing defeat at Sedan, with all its implications for the enemy's dash to the Channel, French Army Command urged the RAF to commit everything it had to stem the flow by destroying the bridges and pontoons on the River Meuse around the city. The RAF responded magnificently. It may have lacked effective aircraft but its aircrew were not found wanting. Alan Summerson was one of these men.

All that day and the next, enemy armour and infantry were seen massing in the area around Sedan – the sector in which No 150 Squadron operated – and (although figures for RAF losses on 14 May vary among historians) the situation was, in the words of aviation historian W.R. Chorley, 'beyond retrieval':

[14 May 1940] was a day calling for raw courage and those who flew into the cauldron at Sedan displayed a determination that won the respect of friend and foe alike. In the wake of what had happened in the fighting so far, no one now expected the Battles and Blenheims to turn the tide, but it would not be for want of trying.

The main weight of the Allied air attack [seventy-one bomber sorties] was pitched during the mid-afternoon and probably within the space of one hour, thirty-one Battles were shot down and the Blenheim squadrons were equally hard hit. By the end of that day at least forty-seven bombers were written off [and sixteen fighters were also lost]. Not surprisingly, a good percentage of the aircrew shot down were either killed or taken prisoner, but during the next few days, survivors of this desperate action arrived back with their units by various means and with miraculous tales to tell.

For No 150 Squadron, the 14th began at 04.00 when a half-section (two aircraft) was put on thirty minutes' readiness and the remainder at three hours' notice. Then at 05.45 a telephone message was received from Gp Capt Field at HQ requesting two half-sections to stand by for immediate take-off. 'B' Flight was alerted accordingly. At 06.30 Wing HQ rang through the target information: pontoon bridges over the Meuse, 1½ miles south of Sedan. At 07.35 the first pair took off: Plt Off Gulley and crew in L5524, and Plt Off Peacock-Edwards and crew in P2179. They encountered considerable light flak around Sedan and, despite taking hits, dive-bombed the pontoons from 4,000ft at 07.50 hours – the enemy was less than fifteen minutes away. Several explosions were seen but they did not hang about to assess the damage and landed back at 08.35. The second pair were airborne five minutes after the first. Sgt Beale in L5457 and Plt Off Long in K9483 attacked pontoon bridges west of Douzy but they, too, had to fly through an intense hail of flak, saw their bombs detonate on the target but could not assess the damage done. They landed back at 08.37.

Waiting around on the airfield must have been nerve-racking but Alan Summerson's time for action came when a second operation was ordered for the afternoon. On that fateful day he was the gunner in Fairey Battle P5232, one of four aircraft – again operating in two pairs – detailed for another low-level attack on the bridges near Sedan. Take-off was at 15.18 and 15.24. Alan's aircraft was first away and the other members of his crew were his usual pilot and observer, Flt Sgt George Barker and Sgt James Williams. The other aircraft in his section was that flown by Plt Off Posselt and the crews of the three were:

K9483   Plt Off Arthur Posselt; Sgt Donald Bowen; AC2 Norman Vano (18)
L4946   Fg Off John Ing; Sgt John Turner; AC1 William Nolan
P2182   Plt Off John Boon; Sgt Thomas Fortune; AC1 Sydney Martin

Not one of these four aircraft returned.

There was no time for recriminations or investigation. The German tide could not be held back and the next morning at 08.00, with the not-so-distant explosions ringing in their ears, those who remained at Écury-sur-Coole airfield were destroying any u/s aircraft and equipment while frantically packing lorries and trailers with stores and provisions for a rapid evacuation to Pouan airfield, No 150's new base about 30 miles south. The convoy drove off at 09.30 and the nine serviceable Fairey Battles remaining flew over it en route to Pouan.

Alan Summerson's pilot and observer were killed and he was the sole survivor among the crews of the four aircraft despatched. Although German light flak was deadly, he said later that his own Fairey Battle was brought down by gunfire from Bf 109 fighters. Due to its low altitude, the angle at which it crashed was fortunately quite shallow and it slithered along the ground before bursting into flames behind German lines, which were by now forming a huge salient to the west of the Meuse in front of Sedan.

This was the day that JG 53 wreaked havoc far and wide over the Sedan front. The whole Jagdgeschwader was committed and all those pilots who had crossed swords with No 150 Squadron back in September 1939 played a part in the carnage it suffered this day. In the heat of a battle on this sort of scale it is impossible to match losses accurately with claims, and this battle was particularly ferocious. JG 53 believed that – among forty-five claims made for all types (including eighteen French) – in the space of thirty-five minutes between 16.20 and 16.55, they shot down fourteen Fairey Battles near Sedan. Among the Luftwaffe claimants were Rolf Pingel, Franz Kaiser and Ignaz Prestele. It will be noted later that Alan said he had shot down two German fighters. Verifying that claim is impossible now, although it has to be said that there are two or three German losses on that date not fully accounted for. Interestingly, one of these relates to the renowned ace Werner Molders of JG 53, who is reported to have been shot down during the aerial melee around Sedan on 14 May. He was uninjured and back in action the next day. Who knows, maybe Alan bagged himself a 'big fish'?

LAC Summerson not only escaped from this crash but also survived the war and remained in the RAF until shortly before his death in 1976. During his lifetime he spoke very little, even to his family, about his horrific experiences in France in 1940, but with the help of his logbook and reminiscences in the graphic autobiography of Flt Lt William Simpson DFC, another brave airman from that ill-fated campaign, Alan's story emerged into the light.

Bill Simpson and Alan Summerson lay in adjacent beds for many months in a number of French hospitals, both suffering from severe burns sustained in their respective aeroplane crashes that left them in a very poor state of health. Indeed, it was said that when the Germans became aware of their existence they did not bother about the two men or consider placing them in a POW hospital, because they felt both would not survive their injuries. In retrospect a POW hospital might have resulted in better medical treatment and possibly repatriation on medical grounds.

Bill Simpson, a pilot with No 12 Squadron who had been shot down on 10 May, was terribly burned and recalled in his memoirs, *One of Our Pilots is Safe* (Hamish Hamilton, 1942):

> One day, while I was in a hospital in Bar-le-Duc [30 miles south of Verdun and ahead of the advancing Germans], the CO of 150 Squadron came in. He was paying a visit to one of his air gunners, LAC Summerson, who had his face, back, both hands and arms badly burned and a gunshot wound in one

leg. I saw Alan Summerson for the first time as we lay on stretchers in the ward, waiting to be taken by ambulance to the railway station. His dark hair was unkempt, his face black and red in patches – scab and mercurochrome – and his lower eyelids and his bottom lip were drawn down.

The squadron commander told Alan that things were getting 'dicey' and he had to move his squadron to a new airfield further south and would not be able to visit him again. When the hospital staff also told the two wounded airmen that they were to be 'evacuated' they realised there must be a large-scale retreat going on. Bill Simpson recalled they were put on to a hospital train and did not see each other again until they reached the Hôpital Militarie Carnot in Chalons-sur-Saône (60 miles north of Lyon). There they were taken on stretchers into a small room and were so weak that the doctors gave them an injection to stimulate the action of their hearts and put them both on plasma drips. Most of the time they lay still, too worn out to talk, and it was only at night, when sleep would not come, that they chatted at length. Alan described his home in Lincolnshire, and told Bill about swimming in the summer and skating on the Fens in winter; of rough shooting and hay-making, and particularly about his interest in ornithology.

Despite the hospital being full to overflowing and the severe shortage of many medical supplies, both Englishmen were fussed over by their nurse, Madame Gentille, who made sure they were well fed. There were also many visits from local people, including children, to whom the English airmen were something of a novelty. They brought gifts of fruit and flowers, and chatted to the men, completely ignoring the horrific nature and smell of their burns.

Dressings on their injuries were changed every three days but the doctor's methods in this process were somewhat crude and exceedingly painful. Bill Simpson said Alan's hands were particularly bad and waiting for his own turn, he could see that the pain from changing the dressings made Alan drip with sweat all over his body. His fingers were a mess of scarlet and because the bandages were not soaked off, blood ran freely from them all over the rubber sheet on the bed.

During those long days in hospital, with scraps of news bringing only tales of more retreat and the Germans about to enter Paris, Bill Simpson was able to draw out more of Alan's story.

Alan told him he was the gunner in one of four Fairey Battles carrying out a raid against a concentration of German troops halted in a valley near Sedan. While they were in the middle of their bombing run they were attacked by a swarm of Messerschmitt Bf 109 fighters. The pilots carried on with the bombing run while Alan and the three other gunners in the formation dealt with the fighters. The 109s came in very close, for they knew that the Battles were easy meat – slow and ill-defended in the rear. Alan was hit in the leg and the observer sitting between him and the pilot was killed, but Alan claimed to have shot down two Messerschmitts, which he said crashed in flames. His aircraft suddenly struck the ground behind the German lines and he was thrown out some distance clear of the aircraft. When he got up he found that, apart from the wound in his right leg, he was not badly hurt. Stumbling back to the Battle, which was now in flames, his one idea was to save the pilot trapped in the cockpit. Climbing on to the wing and standing in the middle of the flames, he dragged out the pilot, but Flt Sgt Barker was already dead and now he himself was severely burned. Determined not to fall into the hands of the Germans, Alan headed for some woods not far away. His leg was bleeding profusely and skin hung in loose shreds from his face and hands, but he reached the wood and lay in hiding until nightfall.

For two more days and nights Alan was on the run in territory already largely held by the enemy and he saw several German armoured car and tank units. He hid in houses and cafes that had been deserted by their owners in the face of the advancing army. Once, while he was upstairs in a bedroom, he heard German soldiers talking in the cafe below. He stumbled out of bed and hid beneath it for hours while, in the room below, German soldiers made merry with the cafe's stock of wine. Luckily the Germans never went upstairs or they could not have failed to see him. Eventually, however, they rolled out into the night and left him undisturbed.

All the time he was in great pain from the burns to his face, hands and back, and from his wounded leg. For food he managed to find in the houses bits of cereal and stale bread, which he soaked in wine to make it soft enough for his damaged lips. He was nearly blind, too, but in spite of his injuries Alan managed to walk almost 25 miles – fortunately in the right direction – and on the third night he stumbled across a French patrol. Challenged by a sentry whom he could barely see, he answered in French that he was an English airman. He was told to advance with his hands above his head, but this was awkward for him because, having lost his belt and with his braces broken, he could only support his trousers by pressing his arms to his sides. So, when he walked towards the astonished sentry, his trousers fell down around his ankles! The soldiers helped him to their patrol post where they laid him on a pile of coats and gave him brandy. It was only then that he became aware of his exhaustion and the greatness of his pain and he was eventually taken by ambulance to the hospital near Verdun.

LAC Summerson was hospitalised, albeit on the 'right' side of the lines now, but in what would shortly become an occupied country. Word came through that the Germans were in Rouen and next morning, with a quick change of bandages, the nursing staff dressed Alan and Bill in rough shirts and carried them outside on stretchers. They were on the move again. After a long wait at the local station, where Red Cross nurses satisfied their now ravenous appetites with ham rolls and coffee, what passed for a 'hospital train' drew in and they were loaded inside bare cattle trucks. Crammed to capacity with stretchers, baggage, nurses and wounded French soldiers lying, squatting or sitting in every vacant space, in the glorious sunshine their truck soon became hot and fetid. Even with the truck door open, flies plagued their skin and bandages but they had to just lay there, unable to move their limbs to swat the pests. As the train passed slowly through many stations they glimpsed hordes of people both on the move or in huge crowds just standing around.

It was pitch dark when the train reached Paray-le-Monial. For reasons not explained, doctors on the train decided that Alan and Bill should be taken off at this point while the train continued its journey south. The two men were left on their stretchers side by side on the platform as the train set off again. An ambulance crew came and drove them to another hospital near the town where the medical staff took one look at them and promptly put them on drips and fed them milk – they had had no food since the ham rolls nearly twenty-four hours earlier and were completely exhausted by the rough ride since. The Englishmen found this new hospital, run by Catholic nuns, a haven of peace, compassion and tranquillity, and here their soiled dressings were carefully soaked off and replaced with hardly any pain, with two doctors and three nurses taking two and a half hours to carry out this task on both men.

The haven was short-lived, though. A nearby bombing raid caused pandemonium and after just twelve hours the nuns put Alan and Bill back on to stretchers and packed them off to the station. Apparently it was a civilian hospital and all beds were needed for casualties from the air raid. A proper hospital train awaited them at the station but they were put on board into conditions made chaotic by bomb-blast damage from several near-misses during the air raid. But the up side was that at least they were fed on board, and at one of the stations en route they were given cakes, fruit and wine by a group of well-dressed French women.

In the early hours of 17 June 1940 Alan Summerson and Bill Simpson arrived in the town of Roanne, 40 miles west of Lyon. With the exception of some money and their medical notes, they had lost all their kit and personal possessions on the way, but they were now well inside what would soon become the 'unoccupied zone'. However, having thought they were also well away from the clutches of the Germans, they got a shock when German soldiers arrived in Roanne and occupied it until the formal signing of the French Armistice a few days later. Alan and Bill were naturally anxious that the French might hand them over to the Germans, who were believed to know that two Englishmen were in the hospital. But the airmen were still in such a bad state of health that the Germans left them alone. Now they would be guests of Vichy France.

During that summer of 1940, the benefits of staying in one hospital and having tender and attentive care steadily improved Alan's condition. The 'bullet' wound, which turned out years later to have been caused by a rivet from the aeroplane being driven into his leg, was almost healed. His hands were beginning to heal and he could now use some fingers on his right hand sufficiently to hold a spoon. Not only could he feed himself but he was able to get up and move around. Generally immobile, Bill Simpson was still dreadfully low, both physically and psychologically, but once Alan was back on his feet, there was no holding him. He scraped together some civilian clothes and after a few weeks went out on the first of many visits into the town of Roanne. He usually walked with his hands held up across his chest, as they were still in bandages and throbbed if he put them down by his side. Nothing deterred him, though, and he opened doors, for example, by gripping the handles with his forearms. With the only two fingers that were strong enough on his right hand, he managed to handle his money, smoke cigarettes and read a book.

It was early in September that Alan Summerson and Bill Simpson were separated into different wards. Alan visited Bill to talk and read to him most days but it was clear that Alan's thoughts were turning to how he could get back to England. Alan was now taking regular exercise and, being very tall and conspicuously battle-scarred, he soon became well known in the local town. Although German soldiers were around all the time, since he was clearly injured and dressed in rough French clothes, he was never stopped or questioned.

Just before the end of December 1940, after months of discomfort and suffering while undergoing treatment for his injuries, news came via the American Consul in Lyon that a medical board was sitting in Marseille for the purpose of assessing badly wounded British servicemen for repatriation to England. The hospital authorities decided he was fit enough to attend the board and he obtained the necessary papers – not without some difficulty – from the American Consul. On New Year's Day 1941, escorted by a French policeman, he travelled to Marseille and was passed by the Repatriation Board as permanently unfit to bear arms again and he prepared to leave France. It was not that easy, however. Hospital ships, which had been running between Marseille and England, were now held up permanently in Marseille harbour by the Germans. This problem did not deter Alan and he found what was vaguely stated as 'other means of getting back to England'.

The US Consulate document used as a passport by Alan Summerson in his escape from France. (Sybil Summerson)

The 'other means' turned out to be by train from Marseille, through Spain, then on to Gibraltar where he arrived on 26 February. He had been given a special visa by the US Consul in Marseille which allowed him to travel through Spain. In a letter to his parents dated 6 March 1941, written from King George V hospital in Gibraltar, Alan said:

We arrived here on Saturday after a very interesting ride through Spain and the south of France. We were travelling all the while from 11.50 Monday morning until about 08.00 on Saturday evening with stops at Port Bou, Barcelona, Madrid and Malaga. It's great to be in a place where you can hear English spoken again and buy English cigarettes. I hope to be back very soon, perhaps within the next few weeks. My hands are not fully useful yet but doctors say all hopes of recovery – for another smack at Jerry – four Messerschmitts [*sic*] aren't enough payment for all I've been through.

Alan Summerson left Gibraltar by ship on 11 March, arriving in Greenock on 17 March 1941, ten months after being shot down. In September 1941 *The London Gazette* announced that he was awarded a Mention in Despatches (MID) 'for distinguished services in France', and during his time in hospital in France the French authorities had also presented him with a *Médaille Militaire*, a *Croix de Guerre avec Palme* and a *Médaille des Blessés*.

Now promoted to sergeant, Alan Summerson did not, however, get his chance to 'have another smack at Jerry' or any other enemy – at least not in this war. Since he was classified as temporarily unfit for flying – and theoretically a non-combatant – he had to devote his energies to regaining his physical fitness. As part of this whole process he required treatment – in the event it was applied on and off over the next two years – at Queen Victoria hospital in East Grinstead in the form of plastic surgery on his burns. After many skin grafts at this wonderful facility, created by the renowned reconstructive surgeon Sir Archibald McIndoe – thus becoming one of his famous 'guinea pigs' – Alan did in time regain his fitness to return to flying duties category.

Following a period of leave, then initial surgery and convalescence between March and September 1941, his first new posting came in October 1941 as a signals instructor, teaching cadets of the Exeter University Air Squadron (UAS) the basics of radio as part of their ground tuition syllabus. This lasted until August 1943 when he was posted to a similar job with Southampton UAS. He remained in that post until October 1945, after which he was sent to carry out the same work with St Andrews UAS in Scotland until August 1949. While working at Southampton UAS Alan married Sybil Carter, daughter of Sqn Ldr and Mrs E. Carter of Donington, whom he had first met during 1941 while recuperating from his wounds at home in the same village. Sybil was a boarder at Donington Grammar School and they met at a school garden party to which Alan had been invited. Their wedding took place in Donington in 1944, after which Alan continued at Southampton while Sybil undertook assembly work at the Telecommunications Research Establishment (TRE) in Malvern, where she worked on the production of ASV radar sets until the end of the war.

In September 1949 Alan was promoted to warrant officer and having successfully pressed his superiors for a return to flying duties, he was posted as a wireless operator/signaller to No 88 Squadron, which was at that time based at Kai Tak in Hong Kong. The squadron was commanded by Sqn Ldr James Michael (Mike) Helme AFC (later DFC) and operated the Short Sunderland GR5 flying boat. Airmen fortunate enough to join these flying boat crews had to become adept at seamanship as well, and they are proud to be referred to as members of the RAF's 'Kipper Fleet'. Alan made the fifty-hour journey out to Kai Tak as a passenger in Avro York PE104 in six 'hops' as far as Tengah, completing the journey, after a few days' rest, by Dakota KN297 in two more hops from Changi via Saigon.

With the outbreak of war in Korea in June 1950, Alan – almost ten years after his last dose of active service – once again saw operational service during this UN campaign. From August 1950, Sunderland squadrons in the Far East were consolidated into the Far East Flying Boat Wing (FEFBW), comprised of Nos 88, 205 and 209 Squadrons, and as a result No 88 was moved back to Seletar, which had all the base facilities necessary to support the forthcoming Korea-oriented flying boat operations. The FEFBW was tasked to detach one Sunderland squadron on a roughly one-month rotation basis to Iwakuni air base in Japan, from where it flew operational patrols for the UN. Duties included assisting the enforcement of a maritime blockade of the Korean coast; carrying out weather reconnaissance; protecting the UN convoy routes between Japan and Korea; and general transport. At any one time there could be up to five Sunderlands on detachment, during which time the RAF flying boats came

Cartoon of a Christmas Eve 1949 Air-Sea Rescue operation in Hainan, China, involving Mosquitoes and Spitfires of No 81 Squadron and Alan Summerson's crew in Sunderland SZ577 'A'. (Sybil Summerson)

Sunderland SZ577 'A' of No 88 Squadron Kai Tak, in which Alan flew between October 1949 and May 1950, as well as on detachment to the RNZAF in the South Pacific in April and May 1950. (Sybil Summerson)

under the operational control of the US Navy's Fleet Air Wing 6, acting on behalf of the UN. With the exception of these Sunderlands of the FEFBW, no other purely RAF units made operational flights over Korea – although the army's Auster Air Observation unit's contribution should not be overlooked. It should also be pointed out that US Navy aircraft were heavily committed, contributing about four times the number of RAF sorties in the above roles and had two full squadrons of seaplanes and land planes based at Iwakuni.

Crewed with Flt Lts Hunter (captain) and Sims in Sunderland PP114 'B', on 9 July 1950 Alan left Kai Tak bound for Iwakuni, a former wartime seaplane base near Hiroshima, in Japan. For a few days they made several short familiarisation hops to and from Sasebo (near Nagasaki), Kure and Iwakuni to get the feel of the area, before the first of this new phase of operational flying began. Crews were usually briefed twenty-four hours before each sortie by US Navy Operations staff at Iwakuni base, allowing the flying boat crews time to bring their aircraft to readiness. The aircraft would be fully armed with ammunition for its ten machine guns (two .303in fixed each side of the forward fuselage, controlled by the pilot; two in the front turret; four in the rear; one .50in in each of two fuselage beam hatches) and would carry 250lb depth charges on the bomb racks. A crew could expect to fly an op every three or four days so with preparation, briefing, flying and debriefing, there was not a great deal of time for sightseeing on days off. Entering the patrol area, all guns would be manned and tested and the bomb racks run out. In the main the RAF Sunderlands were employed on ops known as air surveillance patrols (ASP) which usually followed one of two profiles: (a) ASP Tsushima Strait; or (b) Area Fox 'x' patrols. The roughly 400-mile Tsushima Strait links the Yellow Sea with the Sea of Japan, separating the Korean peninsula from the Japanese islands of Honshu and Kyushu. Except for regular position reports in Morse code to Iwakuni, ASPs were flown in radio silence. Having detected a ship, either by ASV radar or visually, it would be approached at about 100ft altitude, then circled while crew members took photographs with an F-24 hand-held camera, making detailed notes about its identity, construction features, cargo state and course. At the end of the patrol the aircraft would close on UN Task Force-77 (TF-77) and report shipping and weather data by VHF in a preset format, before running in the bomb racks, closing up all hatches and returning to base.

Sorties along the various predetermined Area Fox sectors took the flying boats all over the Yellow Sea and some of the tracks led well up towards Chinese territorial limits off Qingdao, the Shantung peninsula and towards Port Arthur. These predetermined patterns – usually designated by a letter, e.g. Fox Able, Baker (or, later, by colour: Fox Red, Blue and so on) – could go as close as 15 or 20 nautical miles to the Chinese mainland. ASPs were generally flown at heights of around 1,500ft – optimising ASV radar cover up to 35 miles range – decreasing to as low as a couple of hundred feet when closing Chinese territory in order to minimise exposure to 'enemy' radar and thus avoid possible interception by an unfriendly MiG-15! No RAF Sunderlands were engaged by Communist fighters, but for the Americans it was a different tale.

Another type of operation undertaken was that of night-time weather reconnaissance, mainly, judging by the entries in Alan's logbook, gathering 'met' data on the east side of Korea, which took some aircraft to within 50 miles of Vladivostok, but occasionally along the west side of Korea, over the Sea of Japan. Patrols were made both by day and night, with durations varying between eight and twelve hours or more, influenced by detours made to investigate shipping 'targets' and the weather conditions encountered. The roomy, on-board galley was a boon on these long-duration flights. During the intense cold of the winter, flying in the unheated Sunderland was extremely uncomfortable and hot food and drink, prepared by 'off-watch' crew members, became indispensable. The only problem was that the cold could be so bad that hot food and drink was best consumed in the galley out of the cooking utensils because it was liable to go stone cold if it was carried through the aircraft. In addition to his radio duties, Alan frequently manned the centimetric Mk 6C

ASV search radar, which was considered very effective (some said it could detect a floating sardine tin at 10 miles) and played a key role in the detection of surface vessels during these Korean patrols. When within 50–70 miles' range of a coastline this radar also became a useful navigation aid in poor weather or to assist the navigator in obtaining a pin-point 'fix'.

Take-off from Iwakuni on 16 July 1950 was at 06.20, with Alan flying in PP114 as WOp/AG and ASV radar operator, under the command of Flt Lt Hunter. This first patrol, a daylight reconnaissance in area Fox Able, lasted twelve hours thirty minutes, but was uneventful and the flying boat landed at Okinawa. A short ten-minute hop to White Beach, Okinawa, for refuelling allowed them to make the four-hour trip back to Iwakuni a couple of days later. On 27 July Alan's crew was rotated back to Kai Tak to be replaced by a different aircraft, but just half an hour into the flight, the radio packed up and they had to turn back to Iwakuni. Since these Sunderland crews were each made up of, and ran like, a close-knit independent 'family' of highly qualified tradesmen and technicians, they were able to carry out most of the routine maintenance and repair tasks. Based on experience, too, each boat carried a wide range of spares for just such occasions. This problem was sorted out and the next day they took off again, completing the twelve-hour flight non-stop, but this time with some VIPs aboard: the AOC Far East and AOC Hong Kong, no less! The remainder of August at Kai Tak was spent in practising photo recco, air gunnery and bombing in Kowloon Bay, mixed with general flying and air testing in the local area. On the 8th, however, Alan was in PP114 on a photo recco of some Chinese gun positions near Lemas, on the frontier with China, when the peace of the day was shattered by ugly black splodges of AA bursts. Alan noted in his logbook: '… fired on by the Reds, AA quite accurate.' Fortunately no damage was done.

A week later Alan was back at Iwakuni and his second and third ops, as WOp/AG, came on 10 and 16 September. They were both twelve-hour night reconnaissance flights over the Yellow Sea in Sunderland ML745 'B' – which was now the crew's regular aircraft – with Flt Lt Hunter in command. Both were equally uneventful, although on one of the days in between, three aircraft had to fly to Okinawa to dodge a typhoon. On the flight back to Iwakuni, Alan noted that ML745 'B' flew in formation with Sunderlands 'A' and 'C'. On reaching Iwakuni they did the second op, then on 18 September all three aircraft returned to Kai Tak. A week's rest then back they went to Iwakuni for a slightly longer spell of ops this time. On the 27th the crew of ML745 did an uneventful twelve-hour patrol over the Yellow Sea, then with Alan manning the radar set on the 29th they did a six-hour patrol searching for shipping from Pusan north to the 38th parallel and back. By the end of

September Alan had accumulated fifty-five Korean operational hours by day and night.

October 1950 was a varied month for the crew. Operation No 6, made in RN277 'D', was a ten-hour air surveillance patrol along the Korean coast and the Tsushima Strait. While the Sunderland crews were rotated on ops, the 'resting' crews picked up a number of odd jobs. For example, on the 6th, Flt Lt Hunter and crew in ML745 were ordered to do the one-hour transit to Sasebo (the US Navy Fleet's base) to collect some VIPs: C-in-C Far East Station Admiral Sir Patrick Brind and his staff. Alan's crew was briefed to fly Sir Patrick to Yokosuka then return to Iwakuni with twenty-seven US Navy ratings. After that interlude it was ML745's turn to go on ops again. With Alan on wireless and radar, op No 7 was an air surveillance patrol to the Wonsan area of Korea, during which the aircraft stood guard over the US Navy aircraft carrier USS *Leyte*, part of TF-77, circling it while it was being refuelled at sea. Op No 8 was a special transit trip in ML745 carrying a certain Captain Bauer of the US Navy from Iwakuni to Chinghai Bay in Korea and back.

Alan flew operation No 9 as WOp/Radar in ML745 'B' with Flt Lt Sims in command for the first time and Fg Off Boston as co-pilot. Take-off was at 06.10 on 15 October and involved a ten hour twenty minute recco from Iwakuni to Area Fox and back via Inchon and Taegu. Op No 10 came a couple of days later when Alan carried out air gunner and radar duty in ML745 flown by Flt Lts Sims and Laidlay. They flew to Area Fox again with a prowl down the west coast of Korea on the lookout for floating mines. On the 19th it was back to Kai Tak in PP155 'P', where Alan took some would-be flying boat air gunners up for a couple of hours' turret gunnery instruction and firing on splash targets out in the bay. By the end of October 1950, Alan had logged 101 hours on Korean ops and worked for a while at Kai Tak before he was sent back to Seletar on 21 November for a couple of weeks' leave; he made the ten-hour air trip via Saigon in a RNZAF Dakota, NZ3543, flown by Fg Off Innes. On 4 December he made the long trek back to Kai Tak in Sunderland NJ272 'A' and it was 22 January 1951 before he returned to Iwakuni for his next (eleventh) operational flight. This was on the 24th as signaller and air gunner in ML745 'B' once again. With Flt Lt Hunter in command they made an air surveillance patrol to the Wonsan area and also gave top cover to a US Navy refuelling operation. Four days later, on the night of the 28/29th, the crew, with Alan on ASV radar duty, carried out a mundane night weather and 'met' recco along the Korean east coast.

February and March 1951 were busy months for the flying boats and Flt Lt Hunter's crew completed op Nos 13 to 21 before being relieved. The Korean winter weather was pretty severe and during this mixture of day and night-time flying the Sunderland encountered icing conditions on several occasions. Alan carried out a combination of ASV radar, signaller and air gunner duties on these ops:

Number	Date	Aircraft	Purpose	Duration (hrs & mins)
Op 13	7 Feb	ML745	Weather recco, east coast, severe icing	8h 15m
Op 14	8 Feb	ML745	ASP, cover refuelling, radar u/s, bad icing	10h 0m
Op 15	10 Feb	ML882 'G'	ASP Tsushima Strait, turbulent conditions	11h 0m
Op 16	16 Feb	RN282 'C'	ASP Tsushima Strait, recalled, bad weather	8h 55m
Op 17	19 Feb	ML882	ASP west coast, top cover HMS *Theseus*	13h 10m
Op 18	24 Feb	ML882	Weather recco, east coast, radar homing, GCA	9h 15m
Op 19	3 Mar	PP155 'F'	ASP Tsushima Strait aborted in ML882	11h 40m
Op 20	6 Mar	ML882	ASP Tsushima Strait, recall, bad weather base	12h 25m
Op 21	8 Mar	ML882	Night weather recco, east coast Korea	8h 30m

Flt Lt Hunter's crew left for Kai Tak on 10 March 1951 in ML882 and spent the next three months at this base, honing the crew's skills in each of their trades during comparatively short sorties. In Alan's case, he manned the ASV radar, practised radio homings and fired on splash and towed targets with the beam .50in guns while the turret gunners did likewise. Flt Lt Hunter and the navigator practised bombing routines – all of this seemed to signify that their efforts might soon be directed towards Malayan operations.

Indeed, the next phase of Alan Summerson's flying career – it might even be regarded as only an 'interlude' in his Korean ops – came on 15 June 1951 when No 88 Squadron moved from Kai Tak to Seletar to begin air operations in support of the British Army fighting a counter-insurgency campaign in the Malayan jungle against communist terrorists (CT). This campaign was known as Operation Firedog, and since these sorties were classed as 'operations', Alan's number of combat 'ops' began to mount up once more. Sortie briefings were

Explosive bedfellows! Crates of 20lb bombs aboard a Sunderland, Operation Firedog, 1951. (V.M. Reeve via John Evans & Pembroke Dock Sunderland Trust)

given by an army liaison officer who, acting on intelligence material, allotted a specific target area of about 5 or 10 square miles in which the aim was to disrupt terrorist movements. The general idea was for the army to loosely encircle a suspected CT area with troops who would liaise by radio with the RAF. The area might be 'softened up' first by Avro Lincolns dropping 500-pounders or Bristol Brigands bombing or firing rocket projectiles (RPs). The Sunderland would transit to the designated area, with the signallers such as Alan in contact with the ground, then fly a pattern up and down dropping bombs from about 1,700ft, or a bit lower depending on the cloud base, and laying down gunfire until ground troops closed in to take up the fight. The flying boats carried up to 260 x 20lb HE fragmentation bombs fitted with proximity fuses. The bombing method was an 'interesting' procedure (to say the least!).

Before take-off, the moveable universal carriers on the four bomb rails – two each side – which could take sixteen of the 20lb bombs, were loaded. Once that first stick had been dropped conventionally by the navigator from the bomb-aimer's position, the process of reloading the racks in flight was found so awkward, time-consuming and fatiguing in the hot climate that the crews adopted a 'local method' of dropping the remainder of their lethal cargo by hand. The 'reloads' of 20-pounders were therefore stored in wooden crates, tucked into any spare space on the floor of the bomb room and the galley, and then dropped out of one side hatch of the bomb room or the galley hatch *by hand*, as instructed by the navigator. He stood on the flight deck with a stop-watch, target photo and bombing pattern and gave orders over the intercom when to start and stop bombing. Two or three of the crew would organise a human chain so that a bomb was picked up, its arming pin removed, handed to the 'dropper', who on the command 'start bombing' would let it go. The 'dropper' then continued to throw out a bomb every two or three seconds until ordered to 'stop bombing'. The pilot would bring the aircraft round on to a new bombing track and the process was repeated until all the designated area had been covered and all the bombs dispensed. The number of bombs to be carried and the drop interval required was carefully worked out by the navigator prior to the sortie. Primitive but effective! The bombing element of the sortie usually lasted about two hours and this was followed by an hour of low-level strafing by all the guns with the exception of the four fixed .303s – the angle was too flat for those – while flying at around 100ft above the dense jungle canopy.

For Flt Lt Hunter's crew, with Alan as signaller and air gunner, the first Firedog sortie began at 08.55 on the morning of 19 June 1951. Sunderland V, ML882 'A' took off from the sheltered waters of Seletar for a sortie last-ing seven hours ten minutes to an area east of Ipoh, 40 miles inland from the Malayan coast and about 700 miles north of base. Over the target area a total of 120 x 20lb HE bombs were dropped into the jungle canopy before the flying boat turned for home. Firedog (FD) ops 2 to 4 came at two-day intervals during the rest of the month, with Nos 2 and 3 being shorter, three-hour sorties during which 120 x 20lb HE bombs were dropped on targets in the Johore district. Alan also came into his own during these sorties with the opportunity to exercise his air to ground gunnery skills. The three air gunners on board managed to fire off a total of 6,000 rounds between them during the second sortie and 4,500 on the third. On 26 June the fourth sortie took ML882 back to Ipoh where the usual bomb load was dropped and 4,000 rounds fired.

The next day it was 'all change', and Alan's crew flew back to Kai Tak. While there, Alan had several opportunities to display his other skills at the ASV radar with some successful interceptions on RN surface vessels and a submarine. There was no time for complacency, though, and ML882 winged its way back to Seletar on 6 July. In the days between 10 July and 2 August ML882, cap-tained by Flt Lt Hunter, took Alan and the crew on Firedog op Nos 5 to 14.

Sunderland GR5, NJ272 'U' of No 88 Squadron over the Malayan jungle during Operation Firedog, 1951. (V.M. Reeve via John Evans & Pembroke Dock Sunderland Trust)

These sorties of between three and seven hours all had similar profiles and took them to targets in the Raub, Ipoh, Malacca, Perak, Rompin, Pahang and Johore Baeru areas. Bomb loads were usually 160, 232, 240 or 264 x 20lb HE – larger quantities being carried on shorter sorties – and in those ten sorties 2,140 x 20lb bombs were deposited on the jungle, while the turret air gunners, with Alan manning one of the beam .50s, had plenty of firing practice by loosing off a total of 45,000 rounds on to the heads of the insurgents.

No sooner had they returned to Seletar after op No 14 – with seventy-four hours on Firedog operations to Alan's name – than Flt Lt Hunter was ordered to transit ML882 to China Bay, Trincomalee, in Ceylon to participate in Fleet Exercises. The twelve-hour transit flight was made on 5 August and soon Alan was engrossed in two weeks of radar interceptions and shadowing exercises with surface vessels from the Royal Navy and Royal Indian Navy. On 18 August they were back in Seletar, bringing a 'new' Sunderland, RN303, up to top line ready for Korean ops. There was a small, pleasurable diversion for Alan and his colleagues when, on 1 September 1951, they were part of the splendid sight of no fewer than nine Sunderlands in a formation flypast over Kallang, Singapore. Next day, with Alan in the crew, Flt Lt Hunter made the two-day, eighteen-hour transit to Iwakuni via Manilla in the Philippines.

The crew's second phase of Korean ops began on 4 September 1951. On op No 22 Alan was signaller on the nine hour forty minute, dusk/night weather recco over the Yellow Sea. There was a little light relief when, nearing a US Navy carrier in the darkness, RN303 was intercepted and investigated by a jet night-fighter launched by the carrier. A few days later, while on op No 23 – an air surveillance patrol in the Tsushima Straits – they came across a suspected blockade runner. It was signalled visually to stop but seemed reluctant to oblige. Alan was told to man the front gun turret and fire across the bows of the vessel to encourage it to stop and, as he noted in his logbook: 'He did!' Op No 24 was a similar but uneventful eleven-hour patrol on the 9th, then it was another 'all change' and back to Seletar via Kai Tak for a spell of Firedog operations – no rest for the wicked!

Airborne at 09.00, Alan's Firedog op No 15 was a nine-hour shipping recco patrol on 19 September that took ML882 up the Malayan coast as far as the Thai border with Indochina, then back to Seletar. Two days later, Firedog No 16 deposited 240 bombs and 6,000 rounds into an area of Bahau, but a little light relief was provided – literally – during the following evening when Alan helped man the bomb room of ML882, as the squadron put on an airborne pyrotechnics display, tossing out 4in flares and firing off assorted other pyrotechnics while flying over Singapore to mark its City Day celebrations.

Alan was allowed to let his gunnery skills have free rein over the jungle during October when Firedog ops 16 to 25 were flown, including one on the 20th when they took the Senior Air Staff Officer (SASO) from HQ Far East along for the ride. During these ten ops a total of 1,974 x 20lb HE was dropped and 43,000 rounds of .303in and .50in calibre ammunition were sprayed on the CTs during repeat visits to the Cherok, Raub and Fraser's Hill areas – but it was rare indeed for the crew to detect any visual result of their efforts. In the middle of November 1951 it was back to Kai Tak, then a VIP ferry trip to Iwakuni, before going back on Korean ops with the joys of winter weather to look forward to.

Alan's Korean op Nos 25 and 26 were quiet, ten-hour ASPs in the Tsushima Strait; No 27 was a night-time combined weather recco and ASP up the east coast of Korea, but again there was nothing of note to report. As November drew to a close, No 28 was a long, eleven-and-a-half-hour ASP sortie but it included providing an escort to three 'chicks' – a group of Army Co-operation Austers – making the over-water leg of a transit flight from Ashiya, near Osaka, to Pusan, South Korea. Alan's final Korean op, No 29, came on 30 November 1951 as radar operator on an ASP and convoy escort which actually turned out to be his longest sortie to date: thirteen hours and ten minutes – perhaps accounted for by the terse comment 'wrong convoy' against his logbook entry.

On 2 December the crew returned to Seletar via Kai Tak with VIPs on board: Maj Gen K.F. Mackay-Lewis, Director of Royal Artillery at the War

Office, and his entourage, who were returning from a tour of British Army artillery units in action in Korea. The crew of ML882 managed three weeks' leave this month and also flew with a new skipper, Flt Lt Houtheuson, but there were only two Firedog ops – Nos 26 and 27 to Ipoh and Grik – completed on 29 and 31 December. Alan flew these as gunner and sigs/gunner respectively.

January 1952 opened with Flt Lt Hunter back in command of the crew of ML882, making its first night-time Firedog sortie with Wing Commander McKenzie going along for the ride. This was Alan's FD op No 28, with the usual bombing and gunnery profile over a designated area, but this time the tracks were made as timed runs from vertical searchlights operated by troops on the ground. For a change, Alan was one of the bomb-handling 'bods' on this sortie and he manned a .50in calibre on the next one: No 29 to Klawang on the 26th. In between these last sorties they had to make a seven-hour each way transport flight, carrying a football team from Seletar to Sandakan in Borneo – but he did not say how the match went! On 31 January Alan again helped to dispense bombs during Firedog No 30 to the Kuala Lipis area.

Whether there was a flap on is not clear but every day from 4 to 10 February, Flt Lt Hunter's crew flew a Firedog operation. Nos 31 to 37 had Alan back at his signals desk while ML882 covered Klawang, Butterworth, Bentong, Telok Anson and Pahang in sorties lasting between four and seven hours and depositing the usual load of ordnance upon the heads of the CT. And then it was all over – at least as far as Alan and the Far East was concerned. On 9 March he flew out of Seletar for the last time, arriving in England on 11 April, at which point he took some well-earned leave before starting his next posting.

'Zoom' Summerson returned to England in April 1952 with the rank of master signaller and a total of 2,645 flying hours to his name. In addition to his seven operational sorties with about twelve combat hours total during the Second World War, Alan had flown twenty-nine Korean and thirty-nine Malayan Firedog operational sorties, with 341 hours and 234 hours respectively – a total of seventy-five operational sorties and 587 operational hours. He had also received a second Mention in Despatches, gazetted on 29 August 1952, for distinguished service during the Malayan campaign, to add to that awarded for his exploits in France. The Korean War ended in July 1953, by which time the three FEFBW squadrons had between them flown 1,100 operational sorties and 12,500 operational hours. The final Malayan Firedog sortie by RAF flying boats was flown on 17 September 1954, by which time 400 sorties had been completed, with No 88 Squadron having contributed 165 of these.

★ ★ ★

In the period between June 1952 and November 1953 Alan was posted to No 1
Air Signallers School, based at RAF Swanton Morley, as a Radio and Radar
Instructor. During this time he still had plenty of opportunity to increase his
time in the air by accompanying signals students in the back of Avro Anson
Mks XIX and XXII aircraft. Then, in February 1954 he was sent on a one-
month course at No 1 Maritime Reconnaissance School at RAF St Mawgan.
Here he studied the theory and practice of air–sea warfare related to his role
as a signals and radar operator. The course included flights in Lancaster GR3s
while practising sono-buoy attacks against a submarine in co-operation with
surface escort vessels. At the end of this course Alan found himself back on
Sunderlands with a posting to the Flying Boat Training Squadron in Pembroke
Dock, where he was the signals leader. Three months later Alan was posted to
No 201 Squadron – still on the Sunderland at Pembroke Dock – and for the
next two years flew mainly navigation exercises and anti-sub exercises of all
shapes, sizes and durations from Rockall to Malta and all points in between!

In May 1956 Alan Summerson's rise through the RAF took another significant change of direction when he was selected for training as an officer cadet
at RAF Jurby on the Isle of Man. He was 36 years old upon completion of
his course in August of that year and commissioned as a pilot officer in the
Air Signals Branch. Alan was now to begin a long association with jet bombers and his first posting was to No 232 Operational Conversion Unit (OCU)

Officer Cadet Alan Summerson stands ramrod-straight in the foreground on the end of
the row, while inspected by HRH Duchess of Kent, RAF Jurby, Isle of Man, 1956. (John
Summerson)

Vickers Valiant B1, XD826 of No 7 Squadron Honington, in which Fg Off Alan Summerson flew many sorties as AEO in Sqn Ldr Fallas's crew during 1957. (Tony Clark Collection)

at RAF Gaydon, Warwickshire, to fly in the Vickers Valiant B1, the first of the RAF's jet-engine V-bombers. At this unit he would acquire new skills in the field of air electronic systems that would become common with the advent of the new V-bomber force. It was here in October 1956 that 'Zoom' Summerson teamed up with Sqn Ldr Fallas and became a regular member of his crew. After completion of the conversion course Alan was posted, with Sqn Ldr Fallas, to No 7 Squadron at RAF Honington, where he flew regularly as an air electronics officer (AEO) in the latter's crew, often in XD826, until June 1959.

In August 1958 Alan was sent off to RAF Hullavington to attend an advanced signals course at No 1 Air Electronics School and upon completion was promoted to flying officer and confirmed as an AEO in the General Duties Branch of the RAF. He returned to No 7 Squadron at RAF Honington until posted in June 1959 to No 232 OCU at RAF Gaydon to convert to the Handley Page Victor. At the end of this course Alan joined No 57 Squadron, which operated the Victor B1 from RAF Honington, before moving to RAF Cottesmore in September 1959. It was with the Victor aircraft that Alan would be associated for the remainder of his RAF career and he became widely known in the RAF as the man who trained many of the AEOs that served in the Victor fleet.

In October 1960, now a flight lieutenant with No 57 Squadron, Alan became involved with the aftermath of the 350th anniversary of the founding of Jamestown, Virginia, as the AEO in Flt Lt E. Matthews' crew; celebrations had taken place during 1957 on both sides of the Atlantic. On 4 October 1960

Flt Lt Matthews and his crew were on a routine training detachment, with an overnight stop at Goose Bay in Labrador, Canada, to Offutt US Air Force Base in Nebraska. Upon arrival they were asked to carry back to England three plaques commemorating John Smith (the colony's founder) from the Jamestown Foundation, for distribution to places in Lincolnshire (he was born in Willoughby in the county) and London. The London-bound plaque was to be inset in a new statue of Smith, in Cheapside, due to be unveiled by the Queen Mother on Monday 31 October 1960. For the return flight on the 7th and 8th, Victor B1, XH645 was routed via Goose Bay to RAF Mildenhall, where it landed in a violent rainstorm, having completed the final leg of 2,200 miles in four and three-quarter hours. Others in the crew were Flt Lts A.G. Farlam, co-pilot; S.G. Templeman, navigator; and P.R. Bentley, radar operator.

Another event that caught the eye of the media occurred while Alan was with No 543 Squadron at RAF Wyton, to which he had been posted in August 1966. The Victor SR2 as operated by No 543 Squadron was a formidable reconnaissance aeroplane that could carry an impressive array of cameras, photo-flares/flashes and fuel in its modified bomb bay. Its superior performance brought a photographic coverage capability twice that of the PR Vickers Valiant. It was able to photograph, by conventional camera or radar, some 400,000 square miles in eight hours. In two hours it could cover an area the size of the UK and four SR2s could cover the whole of the North Atlantic in six hours. Radar reconnaissance equipment allowed it to operate by day or night and the services of the squadron were called for all over the world.

Flying as AEO in Victor SR Mk2 XM715, Alan Summerson was part of the crew, captained by Sqn Ldr 'Red' Harrington, with ACM Sir Wallace Kyle AOC-in-C Bomber Command on board as co-pilot, that made a non-stop flight from Piarco in Trinidad to Wyton on 20 February 1967. The flight of 3,896 miles, made in seven hours and thirty minutes at an average speed of 592mph, was an unofficial speed record. This was the culmination of a short association with ACM Sir Wallace Kyle that began when his hand-picked crew from No 543 Squadron – with Sqn Ldr 'Red' Harrington in command and Alan as AEO – were airborne from Wyton on 19 September 1966 in XL193 to give the AOC-in-C his first taste of handling a Victor bomber. It was in preparation for the AOC's whistle-stop visits first to Offutt USAF base in Nebraska and then to Malta. This trip set off on 4 October in XH672 with the same crew taking ACM Kyle via Goose Bay to Offutt Air Force Base, Nebraska, returning on the 9th direct to the UK, where bad weather caused a diversion to Lossiemouth, finally recovering to Wyton on the 10th. On the 13th the AOC and his crew were off again, this time out to Luqa in Malta and returning the next day to Wyton. It was February 1967 before the AOC-in-C used the same crew for another short tour of US bases. ACM Kyle brushed up on the Victor with a flight to Leuchars in XM715 on 7 February; they then set off on 13 February via Goose Bay to Maxwell AFB, Alabama, then Carswell AFB, Texas, and thence to Piarco in Trinidad, where they arrived on 17 February. It was from here that they departed on 20 February for the record flight back to Wyton.

Now flying regularly in Sqn Ldr Harrington's crew, Alan began another overseas trip on 5 May 1967 in XH674 out to RAF Muharraq in Bahrain and spent a couple of days on an aerial photo detail before returning to Wyton via Luqa on 10 May. June 1967 was spent flying training sorties over the UK in preparation for carrying out an aerial survey of Denmark for mapping purposes. For some unknown reason Denmark had not been mapped accurately and its government financed the RAF to carry out on its behalf a comprehensive aerial photo survey in July 1967. Under an RAF code name of Fair Focus, Sqn Ldr 'Red' Harrington's crew made three six-hour sorties in Victor SR2, XL165, over Denmark on 13, 17 and 23 July, and made a further fourteen sorties, lasting between four and six hours each, under the banner of Fair Focus up to the end of that September.

During June 1968 ACM Sir Wallace Kyle called once more for 'his' crew to carry him out to inspect some of his Middle East 'patch' and to visit Australia. The routine was slightly different from before: Sqn Ldr Harrington, Alan and

Flt Lt Alan Summerson (third from left) with No 543 Squadron. He was AEO in ACM Sir Wallace Kyle's (right) crew after the record flight in Victor XM718 from Trinidad to Wyton in September 1967. Sqn Ldr Harrington is second from the right. (Sybil Summerson)

Alan Summerson's logbook entries relating to ACM Sir Wallace Kyle's tour of South East Asia and Australia in June 1968. (Sybil Summerson)

Handley Page Victor K2, XL188 of No 55 Squadron Marham. Alan Summerson flew as AEO in this aircraft when, as a B2R version, it was used by ACM Sir Wallace Kyle on his Far East and Australia tour in June 1968. (Author's Collection) the usual crew accompanied ACM Kyle to Leuchars and back on 6 June in SR2 XL718 while he re-familiarised himself with the handling of the Victor. The AOC-in-C then made his way out to the Middle East independently before meeting up with Red Harrington and the crew at Tengah, Singapore. Harrington captained a B2R, XL188, from RAF Wittering on 11 June via Akrotiri, Muharraq and Gan to Tengah. On the 19th, ACM Kyle took the co-pilot's seat and off they went to visit Pearce RAAF air base just north of Perth, returning to Tengah with the AOC on the 25th.

Alan was involved in more aerial surveying later in 1968 when No 543 photographed Libya that November. His last major long-distance flight came in February 1969 when Sqn Ldr Harrington and crew took SR2, XH674, three-quarters of the way round the world then back again. The Victor left Wyton on 18 February 1969 and routed: Goose Bay; McClellan AFB, near Sacramento, California; Hickam AFB, Honolulu; Wake Island; Anderson AFB on Guam (crossing the International Date Line); and finally reaching Tengah, Singapore, on the 25th. Then, after a few days' rest, the crew of XH674 turned round and went back the same way, re-crossing the date line and landing at RAF Wyton on 6 March.

In 1973, now with the rank of squadron leader, Alan's last posting was to No 55, the Victor air-refuelling squadron at RAF Marham in Norfolk, where he spent the last two years of his service as senior operations officer; essentially a ground-based post, it was one that also made him available to fly and instruct if required. He and his wife Sybil had made their home near Stamford and he commuted daily to Marham – a long drive but he still loved driving and it allowed him to observe the wildlife of the countryside through which he motored. From his youth he had had a keen interest in wildlife, and birds in particular, and it was his ambition to pursue a career in wildlife conservation when he retired from the RAF.

Highly regarded as an expert in his air electronics field, Sqn Ldr Alan Summerson MID★ retired in January 1975 after an RAF career spanning almost forty years, during which he had logged 7,768 flying hours from biplanes to V-bombers. Sadly his retirement was short-lived, as he died suddenly of natural causes in 1976, just a few days before his fifty-seventh birthday. Memories of Alan's gallant service in the RAF were revived with pride when, in 2009, Cllr Bryan Robinson made an eloquent plea to members of Donington Parish Council during a debate about naming streets in a new housing development in Alan's home town. So persuasive was Cllr Robinson's case that it was unanimously decided to name one of the new streets Summerson Close. The street name sign was unveiled in April 2012, a fitting tribute indeed to Alan 'Zoom' Summerson's memory and to his extraordinary flying career.

6

GUEST OF THE GESTAPO

Warrant Officer Arthur 'Joe' Edgley

What was it like to go on 'ops' to the maelstrom that RAF bomber crews euphemistically called 'Happy Valley'? Lincolnshire man Arthur Edgley had more reason than most to remember his last op there. It will be recalled that earlier we heard of Alan Summerson's evasion experiences at the beginning of hostilities, but now we will hear how it was done at the height of the air war over Germany itself.

Arthur, who preferred to be called 'Joe' during his RAF service, was born in the village of Gedney Dawsmere in south Lincolnshire, where he grew up within sight and sound of the Holbeach Marsh bombing and gunnery range and the former RAF station at Sutton Bridge. Born in 1921, from childhood he was fascinated by anything to do with aeroplanes and was always among the first to go and see those that came to grief for one reason or another while operating over and around the range. He left school in 1935 and found employment on Dennis Clifton's farm at Gedney Marsh, where he remained until he volunteered for the RAF in 1940. Like thousands of young men of his time, the outbreak of the Second World War presented him with the opportunity to fulfil a boyhood dream and fly – and as he was quick to point out: 'at His Majesty's expense, too!' He applied for training as a pilot but because he was a farm worker and thus in a reserved category of employment, his application was turned down. The Air Ministry did not reckon with Arthur's determination, however, and after making five separate attempts officialdom finally relented and he was selected for pilot training. After the usual induction process Arthur was posted in late 1941 to No 12 Initial Training Wing (12 ITW) located in St Andrews in Scotland. It was here in May 1941 that the

RAF had set up one of its many ground schools for would-be pilots. Arthur spent six months absorbing the theory of subjects such as airmanship, flying and navigation, together with brushing up his maths and learning the customs and regulations that ruled life in the RAF, before graduating successfully. He was posted to No 15 Elementary Flying Training School (15 EFTS) at RAF Carlisle, where his flying capability was assessed and he received basic flying training to solo standard in the Miles Magister aeroplane. Arthur soloed in Magister R1853 on 21 April 1942 and after a few more flights on his own found himself selected to train overseas under the British Commonwealth Air Training Programme (BCATP). This programme was the outcome of an agreement, originally made between the UK, Canada, Australia and New Zealand in December 1939. It was strategically important because it made available airfields for flying training that were beyond the practical reach of enemy aircraft; the training programmes were run to a common system and the scheme formed the basis for a pooling of Commonwealth air resources.

Arthur was sent by ship to Canada where his group went to No 31 Personnel Depot in Moncton, New Brunswick. There followed a five-day train journey via Montreal, Winnipeg, Brandon and Regina before he and seventy-nine fellow airmen arrived in Moose Jaw, Saskatchewan, home to No 32 Service Flying Training School (SFTS), in the middle of June 1942. Here Arthur was assigned to No 34 EFTS for flying training at Assiniboia, a new airfield located 65 miles south of Moose Jaw. He was delighted when he discovered he was to be flown there in a Tiger Moth by one of the instructors, who let Arthur pilot the aircraft for the whole of the trip.

Assiniboia was one of seven BCATP schools in the Canadian province of Saskatchewan and it was staffed and administered jointly by the RAF and Canadian civilians. It opened officially when No 34 (RAF) EFTS was formed on 11 February 1942 and was joined on 6 July 1942 by No 25 (RCAF) EFTS, a unit that was run by a civilian organisation called the Central Manitoba Flying Training School Ltd. Airfield facilities such as runways were not fully operational when Arthur arrived in mid-July 1942, so his training flights were made from strips mown out of the wheat fields in the prairies that surrounded the airfield. Having gone solo, Arthur looked forward eagerly to building up his hours on the DH Tiger Moth but, having put in some solo trips, he and the rest of his course were called together one day to be given stunning news out of the blue that, due to an oversupply of pilots, only the top thirty out of the eighty airmen would be retained to complete their pilot training to 'Wings' standard. To his great disappointment, Arthur was not in that top thirty and found himself posted out to Trenton, Ontario – another three-day train journey with a stopover in Toronto.

De Havilland Tiger Moth with full canopy, as used by BCATP flying schools in Canada to cope with severe winter weather. (Author's Collection)

At Trenton the authorities offered Arthur a choice: he could be discharged from the service and return home as a civilian or he could re-muster for training from scratch in another trade. Making the best of his misfortune, still very keen to fly and quite liking the idea of handling weapons too, Arthur re-mustered as an air gunner – and harboured no regrets about doing so. As a keen game- and wildfowl-shooter back on the farm, he had been used to handling guns and felt going for air gunner was a good move. It took about a month for the new paperwork to be sorted out and then – sometime around September 1942 – he was posted with eight others to No 9 Bombing & Gunnery School at the RCAF station Mont-Joli close to the bank of the St Lawrence Seaway in eastern Quebec. Mont-Joli was one of eleven bombing and gunnery schools in Canada that operated the Fairey Battle IT, a variation of the Mks I, II and V with its glasshouse cockpit reduced in length and a rotating Bristol gun turret mounted in the vacant space. Of the 739 Battles used by the RCAF, 212 were converted in this way for aerial-gunnery training because the original open gunner position was unsuited to the severe Canadian winter climate. The course lasted about six weeks and divided into two phases: theory and practice. Ground tuition concentrated on the maintenance and operation of Browning machine guns and Bristol turrets, as well as aircraft recognition. Gun turret handling was practised both on the ground and in the air. The budding air gunner

Trainee air gunners of Class 12, Course 38A, No 9 Bombing & Gunnery School, Mont-Joli, Canada, in April 1942, in front of a Fairey Battle IT. Arthur Edgley is in the back row, third from the right. (Arthur Edgley)

Newly qualified, LAC Arthur Edgley proudly wears his air gunner flying badge in 1942. (Arthur Edgley via John Reid, Stirling Bomber Research Society)

spent between fifteen and twenty hours in the air, shooting at towed targets and taking part in other exercises, such as firing at targets along the river shore.

Promoted to sergeant on completion of his gunnery training – he passed out second in his course – Arthur was sent back to Moncton in preparation for a return to England. Two or three weeks later he was in Halifax, Nova Scotia, for embarkation on the *Queen Elizabeth*, and four and a half days later he docked in the Clyde. Arthur was sent immediately to Harrogate RAF receiving centre where he was given leave. Ever since he had joined up, he had been corresponding with Joan Lawson, his childhood sweetheart from his own locality, and he spent his leave with Joan and her family. As always, his father let him borrow his car for the duration of his leave and this was a happy time for both Arthur and Joan. It was December 1942; the war soon beckoned once more and all too soon he was summoned to report to No 12 Operational Training Unit (12 OTU) at Chipping Warden in Oxfordshire.

Chipping Warden was a Wellington OTU; a place where embryo bomber crews were formed and received flying training that would prepare them for operations with front-line squadrons. Arthur recalled that 'crewing up' was a pretty informal process:

> They put bomb aimers, air gunners, navigators, wireless operators and pilots – about eighty of us – all in one hut, closed the doors and said 'sort yourselves out'. I, not being backward in coming forward, mated up pretty quickly with a bomb aimer from Holt in Norfolk. Then I shouted: 'does anyone want a bomb aimer and a rear gunner?' This good-looking Aussie pilot walked over and said: 'You two look OK to me.' We all shook hands and that was three of the five sorted. We then picked out a wireless operator from London and finally the pilot said: 'I'm going off to the officer's mess to get a navigator.' He came back after a little while and said we were all complete now.

That crew was:

Pilot:	Sgt Jack Oliphant Wilson from Sydney, Australia.
Navigator:	Plt Off Brian Cooper from Chile.
Bomb aimer:	Sgt Patrick Arnott, from Holt, Norfolk.
Wireless operator:	Sgt Sidney J. ('Maxie') Maxted from London.
Rear gunner:	Sgt Arthur Edgley from Gedney Drove End, Lincolnshire.

The new crew left Chipping Warden for its satellite airfield at Turweston in Northamptonshire where they were introduced to the Vickers Wellington Mk III, the version powered by two 1,675hp Bristol Hercules radial engines:

'Tail End Charlie', a Stirling rear gunner. (Author's Collection)

Dressed for action. Arthur Edgley, on the right, with his crew (from left to right): Maxted, Arnott, Wilson (pilot) and Cooper, of No 12 OTU, Turweston, February 1943. (Arthur Edgley)

'They never let us down,' recalled Arthur. Initially their training consisted of daylight 'circuits and bumps' with an instructor pilot alongside Sgt Wilson to show him the ropes. Then Jack went solo and the process was repeated in darkness until again, in quick time, Jack Wilson was adjudged competent enough to go solo at night with his crew. In Arthur's opinion, 20-year-old Wilson was 'a wonderful pilot'. Arthur, at the grand age of 22, was the oldest among the crew:

> We then flew many training sorties, some up to six and a half hours in duration such as from base to the coast of Ireland, up by the Isle of Man, on to Scotland, then down to Liverpool and back to base. Imagine, six and a half hours cramped up in the rear turret – although it was at least warm being wrapped up in an electrically-heated 'Teddy Bear' flying suit. But I was not the only one doing it …!

He chuckled when he recalled the old rear gunner's tale: 'Did you know that us rear gunners were the only chaps that went to war backwards? And another thing that we could claim was because the tail lifted off first, we got more flying time in than the rest of the crew!'

Christmas 1942 was spent with his sweetheart Joan at her home: 'Her parents were so kind to me they treated me like their own.' Back at RAF Turweston, after numerous training sorties lasting many hours and flown over the length and breadth of the country, Arthur's crew passed out successfully in March 1943. During their time at OTU, he recalled there was only one occasion when his crew was put on standby for operations – a raid on Dortmund – but it was called off.

They were due to join No 115 Squadron which was in the process of re-equipping with the Avro Lancaster, but instead they were given three weeks' leave and never actually joined No 115. Arthur said:

> I spent that leave with Joan and her family, and of course Dad had let me have the car again so we visited my Mum and Dad often, too. While I was on leave I received a telegram ordering me to report for duty at RAF Stradishall, Suffolk, when my leave was over.

It came as quite a shock to the system to arrive at No 1657 Heavy Conversion Unit (HCU) at Stradishall that April day and be confronted with the four-engine Short Stirling, which made it necessary to acquire a flight engineer and a mid-upper gunner to bring the crew up to the required complement of seven. Arthur's crew was allocated Sgt Ron Pittard, a Londoner, as flight engineer and Sgt Eddie ('Bud') Seabolt, a Canadian from British Columbia, as mid-upper gunner:

We all hit it off well and we were then taken out to one of the Stirlings to have a closer look. Oh dear! What a sight. This four-engine monster was 22 feet tall, 84 feet long and had a wingspan of 100 feet. The instructors had all done a tour of operations – some more than one. Over the next month we did daylight cross-country sorties and once or twice we had one engine pack up on us. However, Jack Wilson soon soloed on this monster and then we began instruction on night flying which culminated in a final check flight for Jack under the watchful eye of an Air Commodore no less. Then we were declared to be an operational crew and on 1 May 1943 were posted to No 15 Squadron at RAF Mildenhall.

No 15 Squadron operated the Short Stirling bomber within No 3 Group and when Arthur arrived, it was committed to what became known as the Battle of the Ruhr. This phase of Bomber Command operations would come to be perceived as covering the period between 5 March and 24 July 1943, when thirty-one major night raids were mounted against towns and cities in the Ruhr valley and adjacent industrial conurbations, for the loss of 981 RAF aircraft. Not for nothing did the crews euphemistically refer to the Ruhr as Happy Valley! The Stirling bomber's poor altitude performance under full load, struggling to reach operational heights of around 14,000ft, put it very much at the mercy of the awesome concentrations of flak and searchlights in the Ruhr valley. It was during this phase that its performance was finally recognised as being inadequate to take on the ever-improving ground and air defences that would be encountered all over Germany. Rear gunner Sgt Arthur Edgley was about to find out just how deadly that barrage was.

Pilot Sgt Jack Wilson did three operations with an experienced crew, flying as 'second dicky' to get to know what it was like under 'shooting war' conditions. Arthur was also 'commandeered' to fly an op as rear gunner with a different crew because its own gunner was ill, but he didn't complete that trip because the operation was cancelled and the gunner returned to duty. During early May, main force operations were not laid on during the moon period, although the first op for Arthur's crew came on the night of 13/14 May 1943 when, by way of 'getting their hand in', they laid five magnetic mines off the Frisian Islands. They flew out as far as Terschelling, turned over its shoreline, then headed out to sea, dropping the parachute mines crossways to the coast from 600ft altitude at intervals of a few seconds each. Arthur said:

> I was the only one to see the splash as they hit the water, which I had to watch out for and report they had all gone. We then flew back over Norwich and were fired on by some machine guns. We were only at 1,500 feet when

tracer rounds shot past my turret but fortunately they were some distance from us. Later we heard that there had been an enemy air raid on the city a little earlier.

A few days after our first operation my pilot asked me where my sweetheart lived. I told him Sutton Bridge [only 30 miles north-east of Mildenhall]. 'Right,' he said, 'we'll give her a visit.' We took off and flew to Sutton Bridge, passing over her parents' house at 600 feet. Four times we flew over from different directions. On the last pass, my fiancée and her mother were outside, waving a tablecloth. I, being in the rear turret, saw it all. I let my handkerchief go but they told me they hadn't seen it. About two minutes later one of our engines stopped and we had to fly back on just three. That was the last time I saw Joan for two years.

After a break in main force operations that lasted about ten days, during the morning of Sunday 23 May Arthur's crew were told that operations were 'on' for that night (23/24 May) and they should get their aircraft air-tested: 'We took off from Mildenhall and flew up to Lincoln. On the way there our route took us right over my parents' house at Gedney Drove End. I saw our bungalow from 17,000 feet up and it looked like a little matchbox.' The air test went fine and they were briefed to take off again at 23.20. The target was Dortmund and Bomber Command despatched 826 aircraft – the biggest raid of the war so far (with the exception of the 'Thousand Bomber' raids). Arthur recalled the operation:

I tested my guns with a three-second burst into the North Sea just before we crossed the Dutch coast at 14,000 feet. I remember thinking: 'so this is what it's like.' We couldn't get any higher in our Stirling, BF533, although the Lancaster and Halifax bombers were above 20,000 feet. Fifty miles from the target the crew could see it was well alight but I couldn't see much because I was facing backwards of course. We reached the target, dropped our bombs and turned for home, then I could see what was going on. What a sight below; it was one massive great fire. I could still see the red glow in the sky maybe fifty to a hundred miles away from the target. It all went off well and we had no trouble. At the end of our four hour and five minutes trip we were debriefed, had the usual post-op meal and then off to bed.

Command adjudged the raid to be highly successful. Pathfinder Force had done its job well, marking the target accurately in the clear night sky, and large tracts of the city were destroyed. Over 2,000 tons of HE and incendiary bombs were dropped within one hour and under this onslaught most of the ground defences

Short Stirling BK611 of No 15 Squadron, with its ground crew. Named Te Kooti by its first crew, the Maori emblem can be seen below the open cockpit window. (Arthur Edgley via John Reid, Stirling Bomber Research Society)

in the target area were crushed. The clear conditions also worked in favour of the flak and searchlight defences, which were intense at the beginning but as the attack developed, both these elements were suppressed. On the return leg, though, night-fighters were still active well out over the North Sea and a total of thirty-eight aircraft were lost that night, including six Stirlings.

Two days later, on the night of 25/26 May 1943, No 15 Squadron was among those ordered to bomb Düsseldorf in a raid, involving 759 aircraft, that Bomber Command later considered a failure. Arthur's crew was on the squadron roster in Stirling I, BK611, coded LS-U. This aircraft was named Te Kooti by a previous crew whose pilot, Plt Off I.W. Renner, came from New Zealand. Painted on the port-side fuselage just below the cockpit window was a fearsome-looking symbol depicting Te Kooti, a Maori warrior chief. Take-off was at 23.56 and Arthur recalled the events that followed:

As before, I tested my guns over the sea then settled down to begin the long, lonely vigil, constantly turning the turret back and forth, straining my eyes in search of enemy night-fighters.

Somewhere around 01:30 we were on the last leg in to the target, flying at just over 12,000 feet altitude when I saw three or four flak shells burst close to us. Before anything could be done by way of evasive action another salvo of flak hit our starboard engines putting them both out of action, and the loss of the hydraulic pump in the starboard inner stopped my turret from working. As the Stirling began to shake violently, the skipper ordered the bombs to be jettisoned, then struggling to keep it level, told us to prepare to bale out. From his mid-upper vantage point, Bud Seabolt reported that the starboard outer was on fire with the prop missing and the inner engine was minus the cowling and its prop had gone, too. A few minutes later Bud's voice came on the intercom again, asking the pilot if he could bale out. The skipper said 'Yes' and out he went, about five miles south-west of Düsseldorf. Although we had jettisoned the bombs the moment we were hit, Jack Wilson was still having great difficulty holding the aircraft level, so he gave the order for everyone to bale out.

When I found my turret wouldn't work – it was powered by a hydraulic pump in the now-defunct starboard inner engine – I unplugged my oxygen pipe, intercom and electric wires to my heated suit; turned the turret by its emergency handle to centralise it, locked it, opened the turret doors and clambered back into the fuselage. I found my parachute pack in its stowage rack, clipped it on and pushed out the gunners' rear escape hatch on the starboard side. The hatch cover was whipped away by the roaring slipstream and I sat down and began to edge myself out into its force. As I hung there swinging sideways I could see we were flying pretty level so, with the thought in my mind that we might yet be able to press on and maybe ditch somewhere, I made an almighty effort and pulled myself back into the aircraft.

Having hauled himself back into the aircraft, Arthur crawled back into his turret to use the intercom to tell his skipper that he had been out and struggled back in again. 'He said "well done; with a bit of luck we might make it."' With his own gun turret out of action, he manned the empty mid-upper position. It was still in working order as it ran off a different engine and he rotated it to have a look at the damage. He said:

The starboard wing was a sorry sight but the port engines were running fine, although that wing was a bit low and the rudder was pushed hard over to one side to counteract the swing. The pilot was showing great skill in keeping the aircraft flying and I asked him what altitude we were at. He replied '9,000 feet' and I began to think we might make the coast. A little later, though, I asked him about the altitude and he said we were down to 5,000 feet and told the wireless op and me to get rid of any excess equipment.

Arthur and Maxie began to throw out anything that could be lifted but still the aircraft sank lower. Now it was at 3,500ft. The navigator reported passing the Dutch border. The skipper said he could not keep her airborne much longer and told them to go to the forward hatch and bale out while he and Sgt Arnott, the bomb aimer, wrestled with the controls. It was time to get out! First to the hatch, Arthur turned the handle. To his dismay it broke away in his hand! Frantically waving the handle at the others, he shouted at them to go back to the rear hatch. Up the steps past the pilot, Arthur showed him the broken handle, pointed to the rear with it and Jack raised his hand in acknowledgement. The altimeter registered just 1,500ft. Arthur crouched by the rear hatch:

> I beckoned the navigator to go and he slid off into the night. Then I bent down to go next but saw Sgt Pittard our flight engineer and I let him go out first. Then I sat down on the lip of the hatch ready to jump when there was a sudden renting, tearing, crash. I covered my head with my arms for protection as the bomber smashed into the ground.

That was around 01.45 on 26 May. From then, events developed rapidly:

> The aircraft turned over and sideways a number of times before coming to rest. When my world stopped tumbling, I found myself still in the rear of the aircraft but miraculously I was unhurt. Wreckage was burning fiercely and there was the sound of ammo exploding all around. Picking myself up, I was able to scramble out and shouted to see if anyone else had survived. To my delight, Maxie the wireless operator shouted back, saying his leg hurt but he could walk. The pair of us removed our parachute, harness and flying clothes, tossed them into the flames then started looking for the pilot and bomb aimer but it was in vain as wreckage was strewn over a wide area and there was no sign of them. So we decided to make our escape.

Jack Wilson and Patrick Arnott died in the crash. Ron Pittard – who Arthur had allowed to go out in front of him – baled out too low for his parachute to deploy and he died as a result. Bud Seabolt, who baled out first, landed heavily and was badly injured, then captured and confined in hospital for some time. Plt Off Brian Cooper, the navigator, landed safely and he managed to evade capture until he was picked up in Brussels on 30 June. After spending two weeks in St Gilles Prison, Brussels, he was sent to Stalag Luft III.

Arthur and Maxie later found out that their bomber had come down near the village of Grubbenvorst, 300 yards south of the Horst-Venlo/Sevenum–Grubbenvorst crossroad, roughly 5 miles north-west of Venlo in Holland. After fifteen minutes weighing up their prospects, these two survivors of the crash decided to try to evade capture and using their escape kit compass, strode out westwards. An hour of walking brought them to the Venlo-

Helmond railway line across which they could see a farmhouse. Knocking on a window woke up the farmer who, after an interchange of sign language, refused to let them into his house but gave them food and indicated firmly that they should go away.

Another hour or so of walking and they came to a second farm. Here they found some sacks in the yard and took them into a cornfield to make a bed of sorts. Arthur found sleep did not come, though, because the ordeal of the night weighed heavily on his mind. At 07.15 he and Maxie decided to press on. There was a village in the distance so, heading for it, they took a chance and knocked on another door. Their luck was in and they were given coffee and some hot food. Moving on they approached two men working in a field nearby who took them back to a house in the same village, believed to be near Someren. Resting here for a while, they received a note written in English telling them that the Germans were searching the area and they should move on towards Belgium. The man, Menheer Bomen, who had sheltered them gave them coffee, eighteen hard-boiled eggs, butter, cheese, bacon, two loaves of bread and a knife – a veritable feast and enough to keep the fugitives going for a few days. Arthur continued his tale:

> When we were well clear of the village on a cart track, we hid in a ditch until about 20.30, then set off again. We stopped an elderly Dutchman on a bike and he told us to go to the next farmhouse. Here we were given cigarettes, a drink and some food and directions to the Dutch-Belgian border. Darkness was falling now so we walked as far as the village of Meijel which was reached just after 06.00 on the 27th. Thinking we should keep out of sight in daylight, we knocked on one door but were turned away, while another old woman and her son whom we approached said they could not help us either. You couldn't blame them because it was dangerous for all so on we walked, until we came across a farmhouse on the edge of some heathland [Aan 't Elfde] and here we were given refuge until the evening.
>
> Later that night the man we had met in Meijel, Menheer Smets, came to the farm. It transpired that he was a schoolmaster who spoke English and he brought us some civilian clothes. The people at the farmhouse added a few more items and wearing the civilian clothes over our uniforms, we left the farmhouse to walk across the marshy heathland. Shortly afterwards the schoolmaster caught up with us on his bike and gave us a map and directions on how to reach the Belgian frontier.
>
> We walked all that night; hiding up in some straw in a farmyard at daybreak on 28 May, where we slept for a while. When we woke up and took a cautious look around we spotted a farmer milking cows in a nearby field.

Eventually he came into our yard and had quite a fright when we emerged from the straw and approached him. Explaining to him who we were, he gave us coffee and food and later that day he and his son took us to another farm. Here we remained in a shed for the rest of the day, then as it grew dark we set off again for the frontier.

Our nocturnal path brought us into contact with a group of Belgian corn-smugglers who took us to a point about half a mile north of the town of Budel, close to the frontier. Parting company with the smugglers, we crossed the Weert-Eindhoven railway line, found ourselves another hay rick and went to sleep. At 05.30 on the 29th, wet with morning dew, we awoke and began walking again, keeping Budel church spire on our left so that we could keep clear of the town. Just before we expected to see the frontier we were stopped by a Dutch policeman who wanted to see our passports. I thought the game was up but we were able to make him understand who we were and he let us pass. At the frontier itself we approached a lone Dutch guard in a black uniform [Marechaussee?] and asked him for help. He, too, was sympathetic and helped us across the border by going ahead on his bike and signalling the way was clear. We had been lucky indeed – so far.

Over a period of several days Arthur and Maxie had been fed, hidden and guided by a variety of very brave Dutch folk. They had now reached Belgium where equally brave Belgians kept them moving. Indeed, it turned out to be a time of constant movement; to-ing and fro-ing between people and houses, not knowing where they were going from one day to the next; always living in fear of discovery. Much of the time sequence of the period that follows is derived from the contents of the MI9 debriefing that Arthur went through in 1945, with supplementary information from Belgian escape line histories and not least from Arthur's own unpublished memoir written around 1986:

Just north of Achel we knocked on the door of yet another farmhouse. While the family gave us food a man who spoke English was brought to the house to talk to us. He instructed us to follow another man and this we did until we reached the outskirts of Neerpelt. This man, who also spoke English, arrived on a bike and guided us through Neerpelt and on to the outskirts of Overpelt. Here he stopped, told us we were now on the main road to Antwerp and biked off, leaving us on our own again.

We walked to a farm south of Lommel where we spent the night and next morning the farmer bought us rail tickets to Antwerp; he told us not to speak at all during the journey as many Germans were travelling to and fro on this line. It was Sunday morning – 30 May – when we arrived in the city.

We tried to find a bridge over the river without success and at about 14.00, frustrated and really hot from all the clothes we were wearing, we sat down on a park bench, pondering what to do next. There was an old man nearby so we decided to tell him who we were and ask for his help. Our luck held and he took us to a pub where the inn-keeper spoke English. Here they gave us cigarettes and beer, while some of the customers hugged us and told us they feared for our safety.

Someone led us to a shop owned by a Belgian woman, Madame Filke Cleaver-Bayer. Madame was married to an Englishman and she ran a sec-ond-hand clothes shop so was able to kit us out with some decent clothes and arranged for one of her sons to cut our hair. Looking much less scruffy, we were taken back to the pub where a man arrived and took us to his house in Chaussée de Merxem in the Antwerp suburb of Duerne, where we hid in the care of Marcelle Cornelis (known as 'Jim') and his wife, Séraphin Tange [Arthur met both after the war], until 8 June. This couple took an enormous risk to hide us for so long and they generously even gave up their own bedroom for us. Jim ran a laundry, so during this period we were able to get ourselves spruced up somewhat, while another chap took down our personal details so that our identities could be checked out with London.

In the evening of 8 June, at around six o'clock, a woman, Mariette Merjay and a youth arrived at the house from Brussels and escorted Maxie and me by train to that city. On arrival in Brussels this youth led us to a man – who I think was in the Salvation Army – standing outside the station, handed us over to him and he then took us to the house of Paul Calame-Rosset [said to be a Swiss national] in the southern suburb of Uccle. During supper his wife, who was supposed to be Irish, questioned us closely but seemed satis-fied with our replies since I remained at the house until 23 June – although we had the feeling the Irish lady occasionally listened outside our bedroom door. Calame-Rosset took both of us to the cellar of his house and showed us a secret tunnel that ran for several yards before coming up among some bushes on a bank. He said it was the means of escape if the Germans came and urged us to try it out. We both got into it and emerged the other end – but on reflection we were pretty foolish to try it out because it could so easily have become our grave! On the 22nd for some unaccountable reason, Maxie was taken away to another house but we met up again a day or so later when I was moved to the Salvation Army man's house.

Reunited, Maxie and I had breakfast before being moved into the centre of Brussels, to a flat in the main square occupied by a young nurse named Louise. She moved out to allow us to stay there until 26 June. Meals were brought to us by the Salvation Army man and the nurse. During the afternoon of 26 June two ladies, Caroline Maes [née Gouilly], a school teacher, and her aunt appeared and took us by train to their house in Rue des Héllènes, Ixelles, Brussels.

From Caroline's flat we were taken on 1 July by a woman and a stout man in a car, to a place known as 'The Captain's' house, somewhere in Brussels and it was here we met up with several other airmen who had been shot down. 'The Captain' – one of the aliases of a man named Dezitter – didn't live there but visited us every day and different airmen kept to-ing and fro-ing every day. Visits were arranged to see a photographer [possibly Jean-Marcel Nootens] for pictures to be used in forged documents such as passports with false names – but I have forgotten what my own *nom de plume* was.

We stayed with 'The Captain' until about 8 July, when our 'host' issued us each with identity card, passport and railway ticket and said: 'You are leaving now; you boys will soon be back in England.' Under the watchful eye of a couple of 'escorts' – a Belgian lady doctor and an unknown man – six of us: me, Maxie, Sgts Cole, Hugo, Mullaney and Smith, were driven to the Gare du Midi, Brussels' main railway station, bound for Paris. There was a very nervy moment when the train was brought to a halt at the Belgian/French border near Mons and searched by German soldiers. Everyone was ordered off the train for a search and passport check. Feeling decidedly on edge, we remained in our carriage and when a German soldier entered our compart-ment we thought the game was up. However, our guide had a conversation with him and he gave us just a cursory look then went away – we were the only ones who did not leave the train – all of which on reflection did seem very odd and it certainly set us thinking. It seemed very funny that they didn't search us. However, the train arrived in Paris at 14.30, without any more trouble and we were taken by Metro to a hotel in the south of the city. Sgts Cole and Hugo were separated and taken to another hotel but rejoined us later without comment. As meals were not available in the hotel we were taken out by the guides and treated to a really good meal before returning to the hotel for the night.

Next morning, 9 July, I woke at 07.00 feeling quite confident that before too long I would be in dear old England again. Our hopes were raised because a man arrived at 08.00 to take us, he said, to a railway station to begin our journey southwards to Bordeaux and Spain. But this is where it all started to go wrong.

Walking through the streets of Paris, after half an hour he handed us over to another man. Our new guide shook hands with all of us and wished us 'good morning' then we set off. After about ten minutes our little group was straggling somewhat and the new chap became agitated, all the time urging us to keep together. We had just closed ranks and were walking down a long tree-lined avenue when all of a sudden eight men in plain-clothes, brandishing pistols, rushed at us from the side streets. They surrounded us, shouting 'Hands up! You are British airmen!' Our 'guide' was last seen disappearing in the distance and that was the last we ever saw of him. We were all searched, handcuffed and marched to board a bus that was conveniently waiting just around the corner. Our destination was the notorious Fresnes prison and we were to be guests of the dreaded Gestapo.

The airmen were betrayed by pro-German collaborators who had infiltrated the 'Jackson' escape line and caused havoc. There were several such groups of collaborators working in Holland, Belgium and France during the war but it was alleged that the ringleader of the particular operation that snared Arthur and Maxie was Prosper Dezitter, sometimes known as 'the man with the missing finger', a Belgian with a highly chequered background who spoke fluent English. He used many aliases and carried out his deceptions in conjunction with his mistress Florentine Dings, who also used many different identities, and with several other male and female collaborators. He often passed himself off as a British officer, calling himself 'Captain Jackson' or simply 'The Captain'. Having operated since the beginning of the war, he managed to infiltrate several groups of Belgian people who were genuinely assisting Allied soldiers and airmen, and was responsible for the arrest of many and the death of many patriots. The timing around when Arthur and Maxie were put into the Captain's supposedly safe house in Brussels coincides with information alleging that it was Dezitter who was running this 'safe' house and fake escape line in Brussels at that time, and Arthur was indeed quite certain it was Prosper Dezitter whom he met.

After a life spent living by his wits, on the wrong side of the law on both sides of the Atlantic, Dezitter could be extremely plausible. Belgians he worked with were often fooled into thinking they were aiding a genuine British agent and a real escape line. Allied airmen were only too ready to trust any escape route on offer because it was the only hope they had. In this way over seventy RAF airmen were led into Gestapo traps from the 'safe' houses in Brussels – and among these unfortunates were Arthur and Maxie. In addition to them, it appears there were many USAAF airmen, together with RAF airmen from Antwerp and Bruges and a number of British soldiers, entrapped by Dezitter's operation. The past, however, eventually caught up with both Dezitter and Dings and they were executed by firing squad in 1947.

Captured on 9 July along with Arthur and Maxie were: WO Frank Hugo, a bomb aimer, and Sgt William 'Bill' Cole, a flight engineer, both in the same

No 7 Squadron crew; Sgt John (Jack) Smith from No 218 Squadron; and air gunner Sgt Walter Mullaney from No 429 RCAF Squadron – actually an American who had joined the RCAF. On arrival at Fresnes, the prisoners were separated and Arthur was first put into a tiny box measuring just 6ft high and 2ft wide, with a little shelf to sit on. There was a row of these boxes and he managed to communicate with the occupant of the next cubicle:

> I asked, in a low voice, who was there and he said he was a Group Captain. Later on I found out he was Group Captain D.E.L. Wilson RAAF. He was station commander of RAF Holme-on-Spalding Moor, an elderly chap who had gone on a raid as a passenger just to see what it was like but his aircraft was shot down and he ended up as a POW. Eventually he became the SBO [Senior British Officer] in Stalag Luft III.

Group Captain Wilson was appointed station commander at Holme-on-Spalding Moor on 1 April 1943. Aged 44, he went on a bomber operation on 22 June and was shot down. He evaded capture for some time, during which period he is also believed to have passed through Prosper Dezitter's hands – which may have contributed to some unusual allegations about this officer's own evasion experiences.

It was getting quite late in the day when Arthur was moved to a larger cell which – even in July – was cold and damp. All his possessions were taken from him and laid outside the cell door. He was given one blanket and left alone again for the night. Around six o'clock next morning he was given something hot to drink:

> I still don't know what it was – it was like nothing I ever tasted before. I never saw my possessions again. Later that day I was interrogated by a Gestapo officer. He told me a few things about me – who the rest of my crew were and that I was trained in Canada and so on. It was all true but I never let on.

After interrogation Arthur was taken to the top floor of the five-storey prison and locked in cell No 484:

> It was at least a bit larger cell, being about twelve feet by nine feet and I was put in with Frank Hugo, Bill Cole and Walter [Arthur referred to him as 'Larry'] Mullaney. We were kept in that place for six weeks during which time we were very hungry, slept on the floor, sharing it with fleas and other assorted bugs.

Arthur Edgley, POW No 222506, July 1943. (Arthur Edgley)

It was rumoured that Fresnes — the headquarters of the Gestapo in Paris — held several thousand inmates at this time, among them political prisoners, saboteurs, members of the French Resistance and spies — Arthur believed the legendary Odette Sansom was there at the same time as him — many of whom were shot: a daily occurrence. Although some airmen were beaten, Arthur said he was not and after being robustly questioned again by the Gestapo, despite many threats of punishment and even death, he stuck to giving just his rank, name and number, 'which did not please them', he said. From time to time his six-week incarceration did have a few lighter moments, as Arthur recalled:

All the cell doors in Fresnes had a small glass-covered hole, so the guards could keep an eye on us. One day we heard a guard tramping along the corridor and could hear him sliding the eyehole covers. Larry Mullaney said: 'watch this'. A second or two before the guard got to our door Walter put his eye right up to the glass. When the guard looked in the two eyes met about an eighth of an inch apart, then all hell broke loose with the guard running round bawling his head off.

The walls of our cell had scores of names scratched on them, nearly all French, with dates going back many years. The cell had two windows, joined in the centre and opening inwards. They were locked and had frosted glass so we could not see outside. There was also a small ventilator just below the ceiling and one day, coming from it we heard an English voice asking if anyone could hear him. Because the vent was so high up, one of us bent down while the other two lifted the fourth on to his back so that we could converse. The unseen man said he was an RAF airman who had been told he would be leaving the prison in a few days and had been given some tobacco — but did not smoke. If we could contact him somehow he would give us the tobacco. His cell was on the fourth floor, one below ours.

We undid the binding on one of our blankets and when they brought our bread (just a tiny piece of crust) we tied a piece on the end of the blanket cotton and lowered it down the ventilator. Luck was on our side. Our unknown benefactor got it, tied a little bundle of tobacco and cigarette papers to it and we gently hauled the line back up. We rolled two or three cigarettes and now the next problem was how to get a light! This was resolved when our soup was brought in by a Frenchman under the guard of an elderly German soldier. We asked the German for a light, which he gave while telling us he had been a prisoner of war in England during the First World War.

Another time we broke off a small piece of metal from the fold-up bed and used it to prise open the window. At last we could see outside. It was August, beautiful, but a guard, peering through the eye hole in the door caught us in the act and ten minutes later the cell door flew open and three or four German soldiers stormed in shouting their heads off. It was impossible to hide anything in that bare cell and they soon found the piece of metal and took it away.

At about eight o'clock one evening, somewhere around the fifth week of being in prison, the door opened and a food parcel was brought in; sent it seems by some French people. We shared it out and had a few fig rolls each – lovely, as we were desperately hungry.

Things turned a bit ugly when, at nine o'clock one evening in the sixth week, a German *unteroffizier* [corporal] came into the cell and with a stern face announced that as we had all been caught in civilian clothes we were classed as spies and were to be shot. One of us replied: 'Oh well, we expected it,' at which the German laughed loudly, saying: 'but you don't understand me, it is just a joke' – followed then by the best words I ever heard – he said: 'tomorrow you are going to a prison camp in Germany.'

Next morning, 21 August, some Luftwaffe guards came and took all of us, except Walter Mullaney, by rail to Oberursel, near Frankfurt, which was where *Dulag Luft* [*Durchgangslager Luftwaffe* – lit. transit camp of the Luftwaffe], the German Air Force main interrogation centre, was located. Walter, poor chap, was not released from Fresnes until early December 1943 and was in pretty bad shape by then. We were nearly lynched while we waited on Frankfurt railway station and a howling mob had to be pushed back by our guards wielding their rifles. We reached *Dulag Luft* on 23 July and a few days later, on 29 July, we left Oberursel bound for Stalag IVB, between Berlin and Dresden and which, as POW No 222506, would be my home until April 1945.

It was almost three months since Arthur had crashed into Holland when he and about 100 airmen left Dulag Luft on board cattle rail trucks en route to Stalag IVB, Mühlburg in Saxony, 30 miles north-west of Dresden.

It was a miserable morning in early September 1943 when I first saddened my eyes and heart with the depressing sight of Stalag IVB. Its barbed wire fencing greeted us coldly as we marched up the road from Neaburdorf, near Mühlburg to the camp near the River Elbe.

One of the largest POW camps in Germany, Stalag IVB was located in the Saxony plain, an agricultural and woodland area about halfway between Dresden and Leipzig. Wheat fields could be seen surrounding the camp while not far to the west was a large area of fir trees. Three miles to the west flowed the River Elbe. A pleasant enough area for a home!

Arthur described how the tall sentry boxes stood dripping and shadowless in the morning mist and a group of German soldiers regarded the latest batch of prisoners with a mixture of scorn and dislike, for this was the time of the *Terrorflieger* (Terror Flyers) propaganda. The new arrivals soon found that guards here did not call them 'sergeant' or bid them 'good morning' as they had done at Dulag Luft. No, here the camp's 75 acres were guarded by men with rifles who would, as later events proved, use them if necessary.

It was not so pleasant inside the wire. Essentially a camp for soldiers, it was divided into numerous compounds that originally separated the various nationalities. One of the compounds housed RAF prisoners, of whom there were about 2,500 in total. The compounds were divided by a double row of barbed wire and the main road. After Italy capitulated, many more prisoners arrived; so many that the compounds were allowed to mix since the majority were now British airmen and soldiers. The barracks were large wooden huts housing, in most cases, about 400 to 500 men each, and Arthur was housed in hut 36B. Invariably the huts were dirty because the Germans did not supply any brushes or cleaning material. The prisoners made their own brushes from bunches of twigs tied together.

Each barrack had a room for washing but water was never turned on until late evening. A single tap provided water for everyday use. Arthur described the sanitary conditions in the wash rooms and in the outside latrines as 'medieval'. The latrines were designed to seat forty persons in four rows of ten about 2ft apart, with no privacy whatsoever. The single bath house – which was for the whole camp – was, however, a fairly modern building with hot and cold showers and an effective de-lousing unit – but these conveniences could only be used about once every three weeks.

Arthur also noted:

Discipline is not as strict as I expected it to be. Our day starts at 06.30 with a roll-call, from then until 20.00 when the second and last roll-call is made, the day is ours. Occasionally we have inspections but they are too rare to be classed as discipline. Most of the Camp work is done by other nationalities and the British are, outwardly at least, the most favoured and I came to realise there were far worse places to be.

Time was always the other enemy but prisoners had much scope to create ways of occupying themselves. There was no lack of space for sport in the Stalag. This suited Arthur and he recalled there was some form of sport, competitive or otherwise, played pretty well every day, with football, rugby and volleyball being the most popular. The British and French constructed theatres and during the winter several concert parties toured the huts and were considered good entertainment. British POWs could occupy themselves with a wide choice of lectures on all manner of educational subjects, too – ranging from big game hunting to the cost of dry cleaning and everything in between. Lectures would keep a hut quiet for an hour or so and as an alternative, there was imitation horse racing and indoor and outdoor concerts by the several good bands that were formed.

Arthur's favourite card game was bridge and he and his playing partner, another Stirling rear gunner named Frank Elliot (twenty-eight ops with No 214 Squadron), won lots of cigarettes that way. His hut also ran a bridge league. Occasionally there were parcels from home and even some from No 15 Squadron which had formed a POW Fund and sent such things as a book and an LP record (Arthur could not recall what the title of the record was), but cigarettes remained popular gifts that could also be turned into a form of currency.

Sometimes a new contingent of prisoners would shuffle through the main gate and a crowd would always gather, eagerly searching for faces from the past. Arthur remembered one of those days:

In late 1944 a party of new arrivals turned up and I was among those peering at their faces. I spotted Taff Davies, a bomb aimer from 'Pop' Regus's crew in 15 Squadron. He looked real downcast. I shouted to him: 'cheer up, Taff' and as he looked over at me his face lit up. I told him Maxie and I had been here for fifteen months. When he settled in we met and mulled over the old days and he brought us up to date on what had happened in England since May '43.

Things were enlivened a little by attempts to escape. In Stalag IVB the recreation hut was located in the RAF compound and it fulfilled many uses: the barber shop, sports store and table tennis were all housed in the building. At one point the Germans closed it down when a tunnel was discovered running from the hut to about 6ft outside the wire. It only needed the escapers to break the surface and the way would be clear, but it was discovered before that could happen. The guards filled the tunnel with human refuse then reopened the hut. Not a particularly hygienic way to discourage tunnel diggers – but very effective. Arthur recalled another attempt:

> One very cold night in the winter of 1944 my 'mucker' Les Ellingham informed me he was going through the wire with several others. I said I hoped he would make it. They went out at about seven o'clock at night. About nine o'clock he staggered back into the barracks saying it was so bloody cold that they would not survive out there. A brave attempt.

In December 1944 Arthur received a letter notifying him that he had been promoted to flight sergeant, backdated for several months. By March 1945 the biggest issue was that everyone in the camp was so very, very hungry. One of its effects was to make a person liable to black out if they rose off their bed too quickly and other movements had to be made slowly otherwise you might fall down.

Nevertheless, towards the end of March 1945 there were many signs that the war was almost over. Arthur recalled hearing bombers go over the camp and seeing the night sky lit up in the direction of Dresden. There were lots of aircraft about during daylight, too. On 21 March three P-51 Mustangs machine-gunned the camp, putting several holes through huts 47A, 47B and 49B and knocking the searchlights off one of the German guard towers. From the beginning of April, American fighters came over the camp daily, machine-gunning anything that moved outside the wire and one day they hit a woodcutting party, killing and wounding eleven Russians, British and Germans. Six American P-47 Thunderbolts pounced on an ammunition train about three-quarters of a mile from the camp and left it blazing merrily until it disappeared in a string of thirty to forty violent explosions. USAAF P-38 Lightnings with long-range tanks strafed enemy positions and formations of B-17 Flying Fortresses attacked nearby rail centres. The end seemed to be close.

Each POW nationality in Stalag IVB – and there were believed to be soldiers and airmen of thirty-three different nationalities in the camp – had its own head person, known as the 'man of confidence':

> On Sunday 22 April 1945, these men were called to a meeting with the German Commandant. He asked if any of them wished to take their

contingent over to the west side of the River Elbe via the bridge at Mühlburg. Only the Poles went.

The Germans also left the camp that same night. Most of the camp just turned in and went to bed, although not many slept as heavy guns seemed to be firing all round us. At 07.00 next morning we paraded for roll-call and while the count was taking place, to our great delight we saw hundreds of Russian Cossacks on the south side of the camp. We were free at last!

An estimated 30,000 prisoners were in the camp by this time, of which 7,250 were British. Orders were given that prisoners must remain in camp and there was to be no looting, but within two hours hunger got the better of everyone and most of the camp inmates – Arthur and his mates among them – were wandering outside searching for food. Potatoes, onions, wheat, pigs, cows, bullocks – almost everything edible was brought into the camp. Arthur and two pals returned with a huge hulk of beef that the Russians had given them:

What a feed we had, but having been starved for over three months, the rich food gave many of the POWs diarrhoea and some became quite ill. Next day we went into the local village, which was almost deserted, and discovered such luxuries as porridge, tinned and powdered milk, bottled fruit, white flour, sugar, all of which were liberated in a frenzy of eating.

This spree continued until 30 April when the Russians moved all the British prisoners to the town of Riesa but our liberators were clearly in no hurry to repatriate the British and Americans to their homelands. We crossed the Elbe and were herded into large brick houses that had been occupied by the German army. Life seemed much brighter now particularly when other luxuries such as wireless sets, sheets, pillows and so on, began arriving having been commandeered from deserted German homes.

We listened to the VE-day broadcasts on the radio. How much longer must we wait to go home? A few more days passed and we became restless, so five of us went for a look around for food. We found some pigs and since I had worked on a farm it fell to me to lead the process of turning the pig into food! One of them was man-handled to a deserted house; a fire lit under the washing copper, water brought to the boil and we did what was necessary to make the beast edible. That pig was killed, cooked and eaten within five hours!

Nothing seemed to be happening in Riesa so three of us decided to try to reach the American lines. Percy Brett, a Stirling pilot from RAF Witchford; Eric Weare, a navigator on Lancasters with No 156 Squadron at Warboys; and myself gave the Russians the slip one morning about 07.30. We waited until the guards couldn't see us and made a bolt for it, heading west towards Leipzig, which was about 60 km from Riesa. Nightfall found us tired out and wondering where to sleep. An elderly German approached us and took us to his home where we spent the night in real beds. Next morning he asked us to write our names down on a piece of paper and each to sign it. This enabled him to obtain for us bread, butter and meat from the village *burgermeister* [mayor]. General Eisenhower had made a radio broadcast in which he promised that any German citizen who helped POWs would be rewarded for their efforts, so the 'chitty' was very valuable to this particular German, too.

Setting out after a hearty meal, by midday we reached the town of Wurzen. More Russian soldiers were guarding the bridge over the smallest of two rivers that ran near the town but we told them we were Americans, so they let us pass. Crossing the main river, the Mulde, was far more difficult as the bridge was completely down. The railway bridge, however, was only half collapsed and on nearing it we spotted several American soldiers. They helped us climb on to the bridge then we inched our way over very slowly until we reached the other side – which was American-held territory.

Now in high spirits, walking the next seven kilometres didn't seem quite so bad. Then an American lorry pulled up. It was full of soldiers and equipment and the driver said he was sorry but there was no room for us, but not to miss out on this chance to relieve our weary legs, my two pals squeezed in and I rode outside on the front wing, holding on to the small side light for all I was worth. The driver by-passed Leipzig and took us on a marvellous autobahn to Halle. At a prisoner reception centre in Halle the Americans took down our particulars, gave us cigarettes, chocolate and a good meal and we were given a bed for the night. Next morning we found we were not alone and several hundred ex-POWs were taken to Halle airfield to await transport – HOME. Two hours passed then the wondrous sight of thirty-three C-47s [Skytrain] landed, we embarked and were flown to Belgium.

Landing at Nivelles airfield, south of Brussels, we were met by RAF trucks and plied with cigarettes and sandwiches before being driven to Brussels for the night. Next day, I and many others were interrogated and even <u>paid</u> and that afternoon I boarded an RAF Dakota which flew to RAF Ford in dear old England. Stepping down from that aeroplane on to the tarmac, we must have looked a pretty sorry sight. A row of huge marquees was set up on the airfield to process us and it was straight into de-lousing, a thorough wash, and my tattered uniform and other rags of clothing were taken away and burned. In another marquee I was issued with a new uniform and other new items of clothing and in yet another tent one of an army of WAAFs sewed

Dulag-Luft. Kriegsgefangenenkartei.

Erkennungsmarke
(Gefangenen Nummer)

Nr. *222506 IVB*

Dulag-Luft
Eingeliefert
am: 22.8.43

NAME: E D G L E Y

Dienstgrad: Sgt   Funktion: A/G

Vornamen: Arthur William

Command	Group	Squadron	Flight	Station

Matrikel-No.: 1104451   Religion: C of E

Geburtstag: 27.3.21   Ort: Gedney, Dawsmere Lincolnshire

Verheiratet mit: nein

Staatsangehörigkeit: G.B.

Anzahl der Kinder:

Zivilberuf: *BEAMTER*

Heimatanschrift: Mr.Charles W.Edgley
Gedney Drove End
Spalding, Lincolnshire

Vornamen des Vaters: *CHARLES W.*

Familienname der Mutter: *WATSON*

Abschuß am: 25.5.43 bei: Venlo   Flugzeugtyp:

Gefangennahme am: 9.7.43   bei: Paris

Nähere Personalbeschreibung

Lichtbilder	Figur	Größe	Schädelform	Haare	Gewicht
	schlank	D. 5.6½ E.	oval	schwarz	72
	Form Gesichts-	Farbe	Augen	Nase	
	oval	rund	braun	gerade	

Fingerabdruck des rechten Zeigefingers	Bart	Gebiß
		gut

Besondere Kennzeichen:

Arthur Edgley's POW record card, which he 'liberated' from Stalag Luft IVB in 1945.
(Arthur Edgley)

on my rank badges – at which point I learned I had been promoted to the exalted rank of Warrant Officer. I was then issued with a rail warrant to RAF Cosford.

On my way through London lots of people flocked to the train and I was asked if I wanted any telephone messages sending to relatives. There was not much time to spare so I asked one of these ladies if she would phone my family and tell them I was back in England and I gave her some money to make the call. I wondered if this was all just a 'con' but it turned out to be absolutely genuine – my mother received a phone call that same day to say I was safe, well and back in England.

Arriving at Cosford, I was issued with more equipment, yet more back pay, a rail warrant and – the best bit of all – nine whole weeks' leave. I left Cosford at 4pm and arrived at long last at my fiancée's home in Sutton Bridge on Sunday 19 May 1945. What a home-coming that was! It was not long before I 'popped the question' and having asked her father's permission, Joan and I married on 15 June 1945 in Sutton Bridge. I returned to RAF Cosford at the end of my leave and was posted to RAF Wittering but I had lots more leave thereafter – I was at home more than with the RAF – and was finally 'de-mobbed' in March 1946.

After the war Arthur returned to farming and, under a government scheme, was able to take up a smallholding consisting of 40 acres of arable land and a house where he has been content to remain ever since.

BIBLIOGRAPHY

Bell, George Armour (2001), *To Live Among Heroes* (Grub Street)

Chorley, W.R., *RAF Bomber Command Losses of the Second World War*, Volumes 1–9 (Midland Publishing)

Davis, Jim (1995), *Winged Victory* (R.J. Leach)

Dundas, Hugh (1988), *Flying Star: A Fighter Pilot's War Years* (Stanley Paul/Penguin)

Empson, Gp Capt Derek K. (2010), *Sunderland Over Far-Eastern Seas* (Pen & Sword)

Evans, John (1993), *The Sunderland: Flying Boat Queen*, Volume 2 (Paterchurch Publications)

Falconer, Jonathan (1995), *Stirling Wings* (Sutton Publishing)

Goodrum, Alastair (2005), *No Place for Chivalry* (Grub Street)

Goss, Christopher (1997), *Bloody Biscay: The History of V Gruppe/Kampfgeschwader 40* (Crécy)

Halley, James J. (1980), *The Squadrons of the Royal Air Force* (Air Britain)

Hastings, Max (1981), *Bomber Command* (Pan)

Mason, Francis K. (1961), *Hawker Aircraft since 1920* (Putnam)

Middlebrook, Martin & Everitt, Chris (1985), *The Bomber Command War Diaries* (Viking)

Pitt, Barrie (1980), *The Crucible of War: Western Desert 1941* (Jonathan Cape)

Rolfe, Mel (1998), *To Hell and Back: True Life Experiences of Bomber Command at War* (Grub Street)

Saunders, Hilary St G. (1954), *Royal Air Force 1939–1945*, Volume 3 (HMSO)

Sawyer, Gp Capt Tom (1985), *Only Owls and Bloody Fools Fly at Night* (Goodall)

Scott, Desmond (1982), *Typhoon Pilot* (Leo Cooper/Secker & Warburg)

Searby, Air Cdre John (1991), *The Bomber Battle for Berlin* (Airlife)

Simpson, Flt Lt William (1942), *One of Our Pilots is Safe* (Hamish Hamilton)
Stewart, Adrian (1982), *Hurricane: The War Exploits of the Fighter Aircraft* (William Kimber)
Terraine, John (1998), *The Right of the Line* (Wordsworth Editions)
Thetford, Owen (1957), *Aircraft of the Royal Air Force since 1918* (Putnam)
Thomas, Graham A. (2006), *Firestorm: Typhoons Over Caen, 1944* (Spellmount)

Other publications:
Air Link, Magazine of Lincolnshire Aviation Society
Flight (magazine) digital archive
Lincolnshire Free Press and *Spalding Guardian*
The London Gazette
The Times digital archive

A selection of records in The National Archives has been consulted:
RAF Form 540s for the following: AIR 26 Wings; AIR 27 Squadrons; AIR 50 Squadron Combat Reports
AIR 76 First World War Personnel Records
Extracts from IS9 post-war debrief interview documents dated 29/8/1945

Internet sources consulted:
www.tactical-airpower.tripod.com – No 2 TAF and the Normandy Campaign by Paul Johnson
www.tangmerepilots.co.uk – on the Normandy Campaign
www.pprune.org – for facilitating contact with Peter Brett
www.luftwaffe.cz – for information on aces of the Luftwaffe
www.cwgc.org – for information about airmen casualties
home.clara.net.clinchy/neeball.htm (www.belgiumww2.info) – for information from *Escape and Evasion in Wartime Belgium* (© John Clinch, 2004)

INDEX